PARIS ON FOOT

John Baxter's
INSIDER GUIDE

PARIS ON FOOT

by JOHN BAXTER

MUSEYON, NEW YORK

Published in the United States and Canada by:
Museyon Inc.
2322 30th Rd.
LIC, NY 11102

Museyon is a registered trademark.
Visit us online at www.museyon.com

Library of Congress Cataloging-in-Publication Data available.

ISBN 978-1-940842-75-2

Printed in China

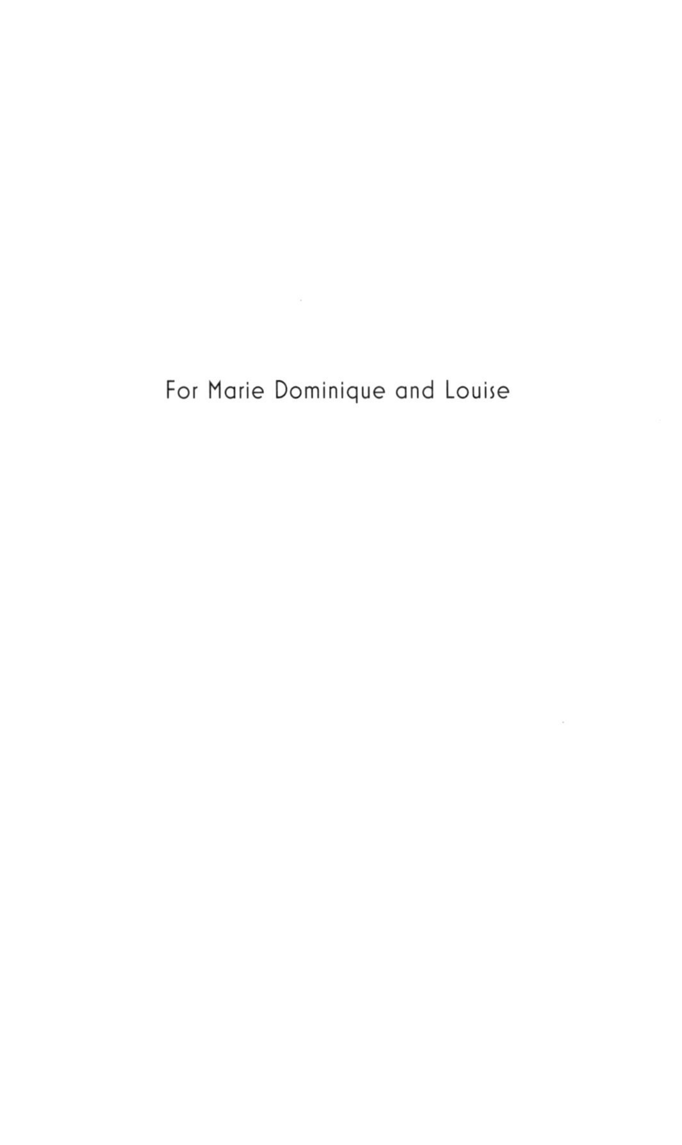

For Marie Dominique and Louise

TABLE OF CONTENTS

INTRODUCTION

Paris may be, as one writer famously observed, "a moveable feast," but it is also a city best appreciated on the move. Not, however, from the upper deck of those buses that cruise the most familiar sites while a recorded voice tells you which way to look and what to think. It's on foot, at a relaxed pace, and sometimes even better yet alone, that one discovers the tastes, smells, sights and sounds of Paris, and the voices of its people.

The French have a word for such thoughtful strolls. They call them *flanerie* and those who enjoy them *flaneurs*. The walks in this book have been formulated with *flanerie* in mind. Some cover the neighborhoods that visitors come here to see—Montmartre, Montparnasse, St. Germain—but do so in unexpected ways. Other promenades are aimed at those interested in food, fashion, in Paris at war, in the importance to the city of women, and in things of the spirit.

Paris has been my home for more than thirty years. During that time, I have taken thousands of visitors on walks around the city and, via my books, many hundreds of thousands more. There are few questions I haven't answered, few corners I've not explored. Scattered among these itineraries are my personal observations, anecdotes, references to other books where you can continue your exploration. Let me show you the Paris visitors seldom see.

Since the walks are organized by theme, you may find some places appear more than once. Feel free to mix, match, or connect the tours to suit your preferences—and enjoy your stroll!

Absinthe Robette, 1896, Henri Privat-Livemont

PARIS BRIEF TIMELINE

52 BC Roman conquest of Lutetia by Julius Caesar.

200s Lutetia renamed "Paris" after the Parisii tribe.

508 Clovis I makes Paris the Frankish capital.

1163 Construction of Notre-Dame Cathedral begins.

1257 The Sorbonne is founded.

1572 St. Bartholomew's Day Massacre.

1624 Molière's theatre career takes root in Paris.

1648 Académie Royale de Peinture et de Sculpture founded.

1682 Palace of Versailles becomes the royal residence.

1765 The first restaurant opens in Paris.

1785 The Comédie-Française moves into its permanent home.

1789 Storming of the Bastille sparks the French Revolution.

1793 King Louis XVI executed; Louvre opens as a public museum.

1806 Arc de Triomphe commissioned by Napoleon.

1830 The July Revolution leads to King Charles X's abdication.

1831 Victor Hugo's *The Hunchback of Notre-Dame* published.

1835 Balzac's *La Comédie Humaine* series begins.

1848 Second Republic declared in Paris.

1855 The Exposition Universelle debuts in Paris.

1858 Charles Frederick Worth opens Paris's first haute couture house.

1859 Georges-Eugène Haussmann begins transforming Paris with wide boulevards.

1862 Maxim's opens, a Belle Époque dining institution.

1863 Manet's *Le Déjeuner sur l'herbe* shocks at the Salon des Refusés.

1871 The Paris Commune uprising.

1874 First Impressionist exhibition.

1875 Opéra Garnier opens.

1880 Émile Zola publishes *Nana.*

1881 The Moulin Rouge opens in Montmartre.

1889 Eiffel Tower opens for the Exposition Universelle.

1895 Lumière brothers debut their first film.

1899 The Olympia concert hall opens.

1900 Paris hosts the second modern Olympics and the Paris Métro opens.

1902 Georges Méliès releases *A Trip to the Moon.*

1907 Picasso paints *Les Demoiselles d'Avignon,* launching Cubism.

1909 Colette publishes *The Vagabond.*

1910 The Great Flood of Paris devastates the city.

1913 Marie Curie establishes the Radium Institute.

1920s Les Deux Magots becomes a literary hotspot.

1922 James Joyce's *Ulysses* published in Paris by Shakespeare and Company.

1923 The Théâtre des Champs-Élysées becomes a hub for modernist performances.

1924 Paris hosts the Summer Olympics and André Breton publishes *Surrealist Manifesto.*

1929 *Un Chien Andalou,* a surrealist film, premieres.

1930 Café de Flore becomes a literary hotspot.

1930s Le Monocle becomes a hub for lesbian nightlife.

1942 Jean-Paul Sartre publishes *Being and Nothingness.*

1944 Liberation of Paris during WWII.

1947 Dior unveils the New Look; Albert Camus releases *The Plague.*

1951 Samuel Beckett's *Waiting for Godot* debuts.

1953 Jean Cocteau releases *Orpheus* and Simone de Beauvoir publishes *The Second Sex.*

1954 Coco Chanel reopens her salon post-WWII.

1956 Édith Piaf debuts *Non, je ne regrette rien.*

1959 François Truffaut's *The 400 Blows* defines French New Wave cinema.

1961 Paul Bocuse revolutionizes French gastronomy.

1966 Yves Saint Laurent introduces prêt-à-porter fashion.

1968 May student protests reshape French society.

1981 The Left Bank's Latin Quarter declared a protected heritage site.

1986 Musée d'Orsay opens.

1989 The Louvre Pyramid unveiled.

1991 The Banks of the Seine gain UNESCO World Heritage status.

2013 Same-sex marriage legalized in France.

2014 Fondation Louis Vuitton opens.

2015 Paris hosts the COP21 Climate Agreement.

2019 Notre-Dame suffers a catastrophic fire.

2024 Paris hosts the Summer Olympics.

LE PLAN DE LA VILLE, CITE, VNIV
La place Royalle
Ceste ville est un autre monde
Dedans un monde florissant,
En peuples et en biens puissant
Qui de toutes choses abonde
Matheus Merian Basiliensis Fecit 1615

ET FAVXBOVRGS DE PARIS AVEC LA DESCRIPTION DE SON ANTIQVITE
LA RIVIERE DE SEINE

PARIS WALKING TOURS

WALK 1 — PARIS À LA CARTE: A WALK FOR FOODIES

WALK 2 — MONTMARTRE I: THE BUTTE

WALK 3 — MONTMARTRE II: THE BOULEVARDS

WALK 4 — PARIS ON PARADE: ART, FILM AND FASHION

WALK 5 — THE LUXEMBOURG GARDENS: THE PEOPLE'S PARK

WALK 6 — FROM THE OPERA TO THE LOUVRE: THE BELLE ÉPOQUE

WALK 7 — THE LEFT BANK: A STROLL BY THE SEINE

WALK 8 — MONTPARNASSE: A WALK ON THE WILD SIDE

WALK 9 — PARIS AT WAR: THE NAZI OCCUPATION

WALK 10 — PILGRIMAGE: A PARIS OF BELIEF

WALK 11 — PARIS IN REVOLT: ST. GERMAIN AND ITS ABBEY

WALK 12 — SISTERS WHO DID IT FOR THEMSELVES: THE PARIS OF SINGLE WOMEN

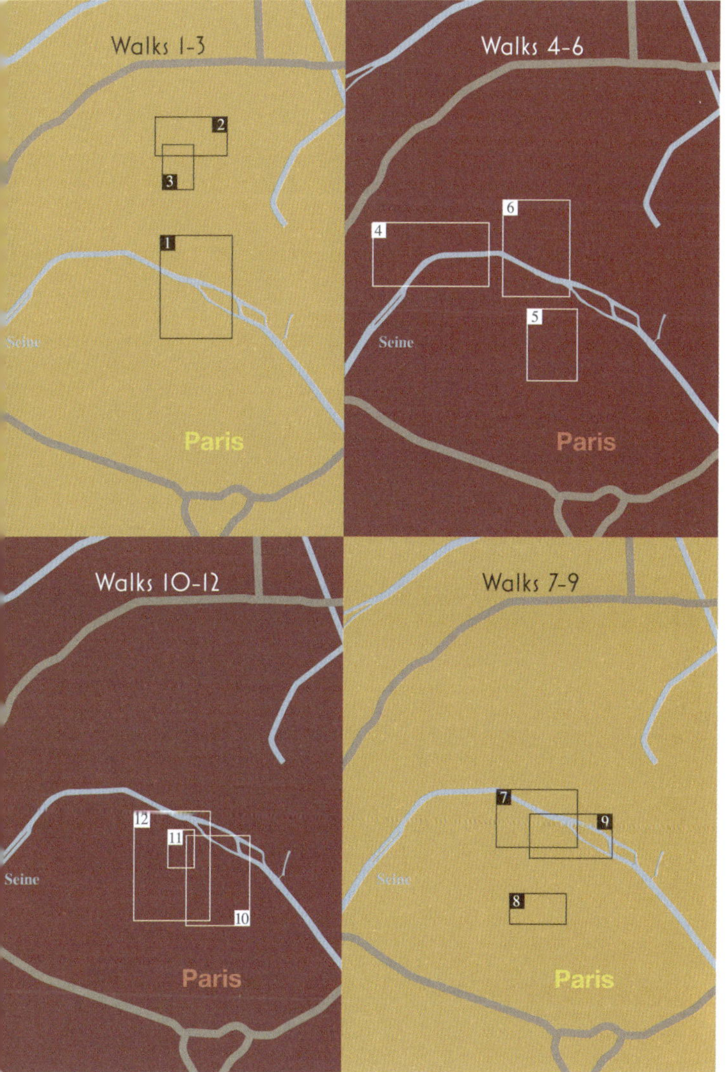
Walks 1-3
2
3
1
Seine
Paris
Walks 4-6
6
4
5
Seine
Paris
Walks 10-12
12
11
10
Seine
Paris
Walks 7-9
7
9
Seine
8
Paris

July 14th Ball 1909

WALK 1

PARIS À LA CARTE: A WALK FOR FOODIES

START: Metro Les Halles (Line 4)

FINISH: Metro Odéon (Line 4)

PARIS À LA CARTE: A WALK FOR FOODIES

❶ **Church of St. Eustache**
❷ **Site of Les Halles**
❸ **Ecoute (Listening)**
❹ **Bourse de Commerce of Pinault collection:** 2 rue de Viarmes
❺ **E. Dehillerin:** 18-20 rue Coquillière
❻ **Palais Royale**
❼ **Le Grand Véfour:** 17 rue de Beaujolais
❽ **Carrousel du Louvre:** 99 rue de Rivoli
❾ **Monnaie (Restaurant Guy Savoy):** 11 quai de Conti
❿ **Statue of Henry IV**
⓫ **Place Dauphine**
⓬ **Papeteries Gaubert:** 41 place Dauphine
⓭ **Lapérouse:** 51 quai des Grands Augustins
⓮ **Pablo Picasso's Studio (1936-1955):** 7 rue des Grands-Augustins
⓯ **Relais de Louis XIII:** 8 rue des Grands-Augustins
⓰ **Place Saint-Michel**
⓱ **Roger la Grenouille:** 28 rue des Grands Augustins
⓲ **Passage du Commerce-St. Andre**
⓳ **Site of Shakespeare and Company:** 12 rue de l'Odéon
⓴ **Site of La Maison des Amis des Livres:** 7 rue de l'Odéon
㉑ **Beach and Monnier's Apartment:** 15 rue de l'Odéon
㉒ **Odéon Theatre**
㉓ **Café Voltaire (plaque):** 1 place de l'Odéon
㉔ **La Méditerranée:** 2 place de L'Odeon
㉕ **Café Tournon:** 18 rue de Tournon
㉖ **Crèmerie Polidor:** 41 rue Monsieur le Prince

Previous page: *The Vegetable Market*, 1878, Victor Gabriel Gilbert

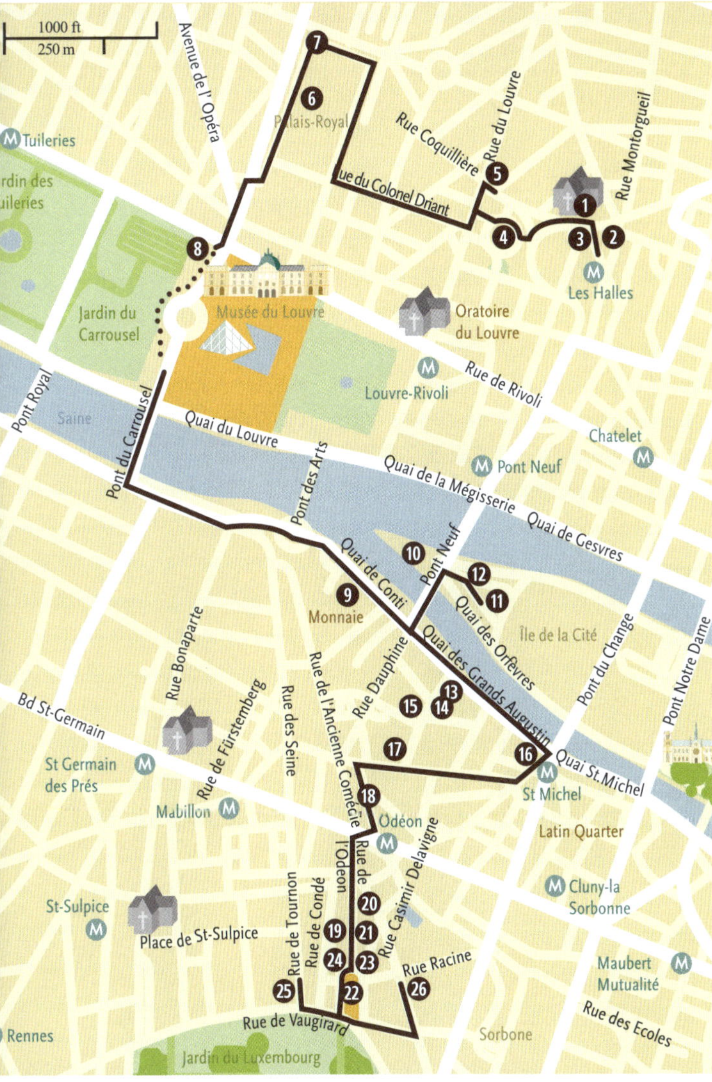
1000 ft
250 m
Avenue de l' Opéra
Palais-Royal
Rue Coquillière
Rue du Louvre
Rue Montorgueil
Tuileries
Jardin des Tuileries
Rue du Colonel Driant
Les Halles
Jardin du Carrousel
Musée du Louvre
Oratoire du Louvre
Rue de Rivoli
Louvre-Rivoli
Pont Royal
Saine
Pont du Carrousel
Quai du Louvre
Chatelet
Pont des Arts
Pont Neuf
Quai de la Mégisserie
Quai de Gesvres
Quai de Conti
Monnaie
Quai des Orfèvres
Île de la Cité
Pont du Change
Pont Notre Dame
Quai des Grands Augustin
Rue Bonaparte
Rue Dauphine
Rue de l'Ancienne Comédie
Rue des Seine
Rue de Fürstemberg
Bd St-Germain
St Germain des Prés
Mabillon
Quai St. Michel
St Michel
Odéon
Latin Quarter
Rue de l'Odeon
Rue Casimir Delavigne
Cluny-la Sorbonne
St-Sulpice
Place de St-Sulpice
Rue de Tournon
Rue de Condé
Rue Racine
Maubert Mutualité
Rue de Vaugirard
Rue des Ecoles
Rennes
Sorbone
Jardin du Luxembourg
1
2
3
4
5
6
7
8
9
10
11
12
13
14
15
16
17
18
19
20
21
22
23
24
25
26

Since Roman times, the French have excelled in the preparation, presentation and appreciation of food. The vocabulary of cooking and eating is overwhelmingly French, from *bouquet, bouillon, banquet, canapé, crouton, consommé, carafe, chef, entrée and gourmet* to *menu, paté, purée, sauce, sauté* and *terrine.*

This walk takes us through two centuries of eating. It mirrors the *menu de dégustation* or tasting menu with which the best restaurants demonstrate the skill of their chefs. Made up of many dishes, but small servings of each, these remove hunger from the equation. One doesn't eat just to satisfy but also to appreciate. (A failure to do so can, occasionally, bring chef and client into conflict. A cartoon pinned up in the kitchen of a Michelin-starred restaurant showed a furious chef ejecting a client into the street. A waiter explains to a colleague, "He tried to add salt.")

Today's visitors are less adventurous than those of earlier eras, who had little choice in what they ate. With hamburgers, pizza and barbecue unknown in France, they learned to like *foie gras, croissants* and *escargots,* as well as inky coffee, crusty bread, salted butter and drinks without ice. American journalist Waverley Root, newly arrived in the 1920s, had read of local drinking habits, and ordered a carafe of Bordeaux with his first meal on French soil. The waiter didn't feel it was his place to explain that even the French didn't drink wine with breakfast.

New arrivals grappled with the concept of the café. Accustomed to such bright, busy places for dining as New York's Tony Pastor's and London's Café Royal, they were baffled by what expatriate writer Richard Wright called "cafés for frowsy housewives who play the horses,

Les Halles, 1898–1924 by Eugène Atget

students, greying bank clerks, government workers, artists, writers, the *demi-monde,* lesbians, homosexuals, and, lastly, that queer grey cloud of foreigners who, despite fierce French chauvinism, live in Paris the year round."

We begin our food tour next to the 17th-century ❶ **church of St. Eustache**, at the edge of ❷ **the former site of Les Halles** (the Halls), for more than a century the city's meat and produce market. The nearest Metro stop is **Les Halles (Line 4.)** Our starting point is ❸ ***Ecoute*** (Listening), a massive sculpture of a human head and hand, carved by Henri de Miller in 1986 from 70 tons of Burgundy sandstone. *Les Halles,* called by Émile Zola *le ventre de Paris* (the belly of Paris), collected and distributed produce from farms ringing the city. In 1780, 1600 varieties

of fruit, flower and plant grew within a hundred miles of Paris. Individual villages, now suburbs, were noted for a single product: Argenteuil for asparagus, Montreuil for peaches, Montmorency for cherries, Vaugirard for strawberries, St. Germain for peas, Clamart for artichokes. Supplies of all these arrived daily in season, making it possible to prepare dishes with a distinctive local character.

Beginning in the early hours, farmers piled fruit or vegetables into carts, put their son on top of the load, and sent him off into the dark. The boy went to sleep but the horse knew the way, and took the road into the city, joined by other carts until whole caravans plodded through the night, headed for *Les Halles,* where wholesalers distributed their contents to shopkeepers and restaurateurs. As trading ceased, signaled by the ringing of a *cloche* (bell), the homeless, loitering in surrounding streets, surged in to scavenge bruised or squashed produce. A vagrant or tramp is still called a *clochard* (bell person).

At its busiest, *Les Halles* seethed with activity. Loaded handcarts maneuvered through the crowds, dodging the porters, known as *forts* (strong men), who balanced sheep and pig carcasses on their shoulders and baskets

of vegetables on their heads. The role of *fort* was a distinction. One had to be a French citizen with a clean police record, have completed his two-year military service, be able to read, write and calculate, and also carry a 200-kilo load on his back for 200 feet. Each first of May, a deputation of *forts* in their distinctive blue tunics, wide-brimmed hats and silver badges of office visited the Presidential Palace with a bunch of *muguet*, the small white, highly scented flower, known in English as Lily of the Valley, which traditionally announces the arrival of spring.

To keep up their strength, *forts* relied on onion soup. A bowl of this beef *bouillon*, topped with toasted bread, caramelized onions and melted gruyere cheese, constituted an entire meal. Pop-up kitchens in the market provided it in giant steaming *marmites*. It first appeared in France around 1750 when the Duke of Lorraine, father-in-law of Louis

Morning soup at Les Halles, 1897

XV, brought the recipe to Versailles. Its royal pedigree gave *soupe à l'oignon* a special status. Party-goers, before going home to bed, would drop by *Les Halles* to enjoy a bowl at *Le Chat qui Fume* or *Àu Pied de Cochon,* particularly since the smell of onions and cheese disguised any hint of alcohol on the breath.

When Georges-Eugène Haussmann began modernizing Paris in the 1850s, he saw that buyers and sellers needed to get in and out of the market quickly, an impossibility with the existing stone buildings. The walls had to go. "It is vast umbrellas that I need; nothing more," he told his architect, Victor Baltard, urging him to forget stone and instead use "iron, iron, nothing but iron!" Baltard's twelve open-sided pavilions of iron and glass multiplied the number of buyers and sellers using the market.

As Paris expanded, produce was sourced from farther afield, and the inner city location became inconvenient. The markets moved to Rungis, south of Paris. Between 1969 and 1973, *Les Halles* was demolished, replaced by a subterranean mall, with cinemas, stores, a swimming pool and a Metro interchange. More recently, the street-level *Forum des Halles* shopping precinct was added. Scandalously, Baltard's pavilions were sold as scrap iron. (One survives as a concert hall in the town of Nogent-sur-Marne.) An inscription on the base of *Ecoute*, a kind of obituary for the lost community of *Les Halles*, reads, "Listening to underground murmurings, this sculpture is like a pebble randomly cast by an imaginary tide onto the shores of time."

At the western end of the *Halles* site is the sole building surviving from the original market, ❹ the former **Bourse de Commerce** or Corn Exchange, now housing the Pinault collection of contemporary art. Built between 1763 and 1767, this Roman-style rotunda, admired by Thomas Jefferson, existed for the sale of grain and other dry goods. Twenty-five concentric galleries enclosed an atrium which admitted natural light, essential for traders who needed to assess quality at a glance. One 19th century traveler called the dome "as light as if it had been suspended by the hand of fairies. In the arena, what peas, beans and lentils are sold! In the surrounding divi-

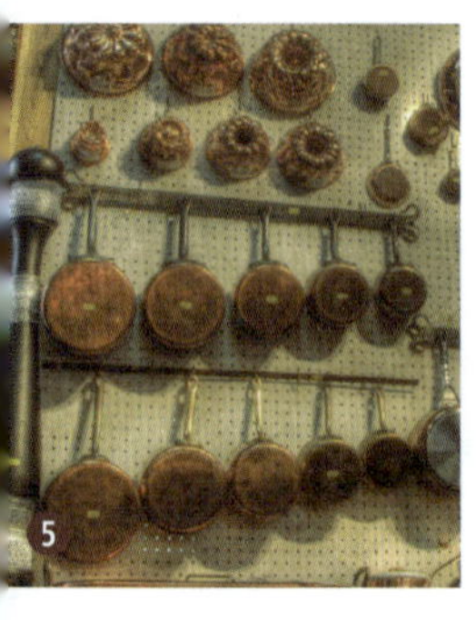

sions there is flour on the benches. We pass by double staircases, turning one on the other, in spacious apartments to put rye, barley, oats, all so well planned and so well executed that I do not know any public building in France or England which surpasses it." After the markets moved to Rungis, the Bourse became a center for trading in sugar, cocoa, coffee and other commodities. Computers took over the futures markets in 1998, and it was repurposed for the display of art.

Exit onto rue du Louvre and turn right to rue Coquillière. ❺ **Nos. 18/20** house **E. Dehillerin**, one of Paris's premier stores for luxury cooking equipment. Eugène de Hillerin established his business here in the 1880s, close to where chefs and restaurateurs came to find their ingredients. His gleaming copper utensils soon became famous, and remain a feature of most fashionable kitchens.

Return to rue du Louvre and continue to rue du Colonel-Driant, which ends at ❻ the **Palais Royale.** Built by Cardinal Richelieu in

1628, the palace and its grounds were given to Louis XIII in 1636. Anne of Austria lived there with her son, the future Louis XIV. In 1682, when Louis moved the court to Versailles, the palace passed to the liberal Louis Philippe Joseph, Duc d'Orléans, who preferred to be called *Philippe l'Egalité* (Philip the Equal.) He opened the gardens to everyone except "drunkards, women in excessively indecent

From left: Cardinal Richelieu, Anne of Austria, Philip the Equal

dress, and those in tatters," and commissioned Victor Louis to enclose the park with shops and a covered colonnade. Gaming rooms moved in, attracting petty criminals, political plotters, and prostitutes, but the Parisian police were helpless, having no authority to enter the Duke's private property,

If the restaurant as we know it has a birthplace, it is the Palais Royale. In June 1786, the Provost of Paris, despite resistance from butchers and other vendors of ingredients for home cooking, issued a decree making restaurants legal, and authorizing them to serve meals until eleven in the evening in winter and midnight in summer. Until then, travelers went to inns or *auberges*, where they sat at communal tables and ate whatever the host's wife had prepared: the *table d'hote* (the host's table). At a restaurant, however, ordinary people—at least those with money—could eat *à la carte* (from a menu). Seated at individual tables with

Speech made at the Palais Royal by Camille Desmoulins: July 12, 1789

linen tablecloths, they were served by waiters. Among the first to take advantage of the new law was Antoine Beauvilliers, former chef to the Comte de Provençe, who opened the *Grande Taverne de Londres* in 1786. Then, as now, nothing counted so much for a restaurant as location, so Beauvilliers shrewdly chose the Palais Royale.

On July 12, 1789, news spread through the gardens that the king had dismissed his Minister of Finance, Jacques Necker, who had tried to give more power to tax-paying farmers and land-owners and less to the free-loading aristocracy. A young lawyer, Camille Desmoulins, leaped onto a table, grabbed a pistol from a military officer and fired into the air. "Monsieur Necker is dismissed!" he shouted. "We only have one resource left, and that is to take up arms and wear a cockade to recognize one another." Snatching a leaf from one of the plane trees that fringed the gardens, he tucked it into his hat band. After a second's hesitation, hundreds did the same. Led by Desmoulins, they marched through the city, sweeping up pedestrians, emptying theaters. Two days later, on July 14, the same crowd, multiplied a hundred-fold, with every member now wearing a cockade of red, white and blue, stormed the Bastille prison, a symbol of royal power, and launched the Revolution.

These days, the Palais Royale is almost sleepy, with art galleries, antique dealers and boutiques replacing casinos and houses of prostitution. In 1870, restaurateur Jean Véfour purchased the Café de Chartres, opened in 1784, and renamed it, modestly, ❼ **Le Grand Véfour**. It's the oldest restaurant still trading in the Palais. Brass plates set into its tables record the celebrities who ate there, including author Victor Hugo, gastronome Jean Anthèlme Brillat-Savarin, Napoléon Bonaparte and his empress Joséphine. Novelist George Sand was such a regular customer that the restaurant used a cast of her hand to create its ashtrays. The elderly Colette, who lived nearby (9 rue de Beaujolais), was regularly carried down from her apartment to dine there, often with her neighbor Jean Cocteau, who designed its menus.

Colette, 1932

Jean Cocteau, 1923

At the outbreak of World War I in 1914, the French suspended all foreign currency transactions. Expatriates living on money from home had nothing to eat. Chinese students invaded their embassy and, to the aston-

ishment of the ambassador, emptied his larder, while stranded Americans welcomed news of a Volunteer Corps, members of which would be paid and, more important, fed. Recruitment began in a shopfront at the Palais Royale. Candidates, told to present themselves at 8 a.m. every morning for drill, didn't wait long before demanding "When is the grub going to begin on this deal?"

Exit onto Place Colette and cross rue de Rivoli to ❽ the **Carrousel du Louvre**. This underground shopping center, featuring a smaller inverted version of I.M. Pei's glass pyramid, offers a number of cafés and *patissiers,* as well as branches of Maxim's and McDonald's. You can enter the main Louvre galleries from here through its book and gift shop, but of more interest is what lies beneath: a medieval museum and the mighty piers on which the weight of the palace rests.

Ascend into the gardens of the former Tuileries Palace, torched in 1871 during the anarchist uprising of the Commune, and cross the

Seine by the Pont du Carrousel. A candle-lit supper on a *bateau mouche*, as shared by Audrey Hepburn and Cary Grant in *Charade* (1963), is integral to any romantic visit to Paris. A crew member in Stanley Donen's film adds spice by turning a spotlight on couples enjoying the darkness along the *quais*.

On the Left Bank, turn left and follow the river. ❾ **The Monnaie** or Mint at **11 Quai de Conti** houses the Medals and Decorations section of the service that prints France's currency. Also within the building is the **restaurant of chef Guy Savoy**, one of the most honored (and expensive) in Paris.

Restaurant Guy Savoy

At Pont Neuf, cross as far as ❿ the equestrian **statue of Henry IV** (1553-1610.) Henry belongs in the annals of gastronomy for his frequently misquoted promise to his subjects of "a chicken in every pot" on Sunday. What he actually said was, "If God gives me life, I will make sure that no peasant in my realm will lack the means to have a fowl in his pot on Sunday." Listeners would have understood, when he spoke of a pot rather than an oven or spit, and a *poule* (fowl), not a *poulet* (chicken), that he wasn't thinking of a tender young bird that the rich might eat, but rather a tough old hen which, having laid its last egg, could be

View of Paris and the Seine, taken from the middle of the Pont-Neuf, 1665–1666, Hendrick Mommers, Louvre Museum

boiled until it dissolved into a rich stock: a dish which all but the poorest household could afford. Augmented with vegetables and grains, this would feed the family for a week. It was a plea to use ingredients with intelligence and economy; advice as relevant today as five centuries ago.

Henry's statue faces the narrow entrance to ⓫ **Place Dauphine**, a triangular 17th century park. At one time a *potager* or vegetable garden for the nearby palace, its shape and position in relation to the two central islands, which, seen from above, can suggest a female body, inspired André Breton to call it *"le sexe de Paris,"*—the city's pubic triangle— and to set part of his only novel *Nadja* here, a story of obsessive love. The Palais de Justice, France's high court, fills one end. Next door is the police headquarters at Quai des Orfevres, where Georges

Simenon's fictional Commissioner Maigret has his office. Among the shops on the *place* is the stationers ⓬ **Papeteries Gaubert**. Colette wrote exclusively on an ice-blue paper available only from them. As Gaubert's main customers were lawyers, who used lots of paper, they sold it by the kilo, as they still do today.

(**JB**: When I moved to Paris in 1989, my first home was a tiny studio apartment on Place Dauphine, just above a restaurant, the *Caveau de Palais*. Each day, suppliers left the restaurant's order by our shared front door. The small heap of boxes and cartons was my window into a different way of looking at food. I learned that Camembert cheeses came wrapped in waxed paper, in individual round boxes made from paper-thin sheets of white wood stapled together; the same wood used in oyster baskets from Ile d'Oléron, on the Atlantic coast. A wind-dried ham from the Auvergne was wrapped in muslin stiff with salt, and fat *morteau* sausages still bore the traditional strings, tightened by a tiny twig, by which they'd once dangled from the rafters of some Lyonnaise farm. As I peered at these puzzling objects, a baker's boy came by on a bike and deposited a large paper bag from the open top of which poked twenty *baguettes,* so fresh I could feel heat radiating from them and smell that distinctive fresh-bread odor. No cans? No famous brands?

Paper instead of shrink wrap? Warm bread in a paper sack? What kind of cooking was this?)

Return to Pont Neuf and the Left Bank, and follow quai des Grands-Augustins to the corner of rue des Grands-Augustins, site of famous restaurant ⓭ **Lapérouse**. Among the pet projects of Louis XVI was an expedition led by Jean François de Galaup, Comte de Lapérouse, to take two ships around the world. He left in 1785 but when Louis faced his execution in January 1793, nothing had been heard of him for years. Mounting the scaffold, the king asked hopefully, "Any news of Lapérouse?" He died unaware that the count and his crews had all perished in the Solomon Islands five years before.

After the Revolution, a M. Lefebre, Louis XVI's personal beverage maker, set up business in this building as a wine merchant. The painted glass panels at street level date from that time when shops were open to the street. His best clients had offices on the first floor—which

From left: Georges Auguste Escoffier; La Belle Otero; Liane de Pougy

doubled as places for clandestine assignations. By 1850, the building was, as one historian put it, "the rendezvous of all Paris—literary, political and romantic." In 1878, a new owner, Jules Lapérouse, further enhanced its reputation by opening it as a restaurant. No relation of the Comte, he nevertheless named it *Lapérouse,* called its larger dining rooms *Boussole* and *Astrolabe,* after the unlucky explorer's ships, and decorated the walls with south sea motifs.

Lapérouse won a reputation for its food, particularly when Georges Auguste Escoffier—"king of chefs," in the words of the German Kaiser, "and chef to kings"—ran the kitchens, but its private dining rooms or *salons privées* remained its most popular attraction. Behind their doors, on red velvet banquettes, courtesans exercised their skills and virgins surrendered their virtue, often in return for some piece of jewelry. To test that it was a real diamond they'd been given, they tried it on one of the mirrors, which soon became so scratched it was impossible to see their faces in them. The mirrors are preserved as part of the décor in the rooms, now named for such famous courtesans as La Belle Otero and Liane de Pougy.

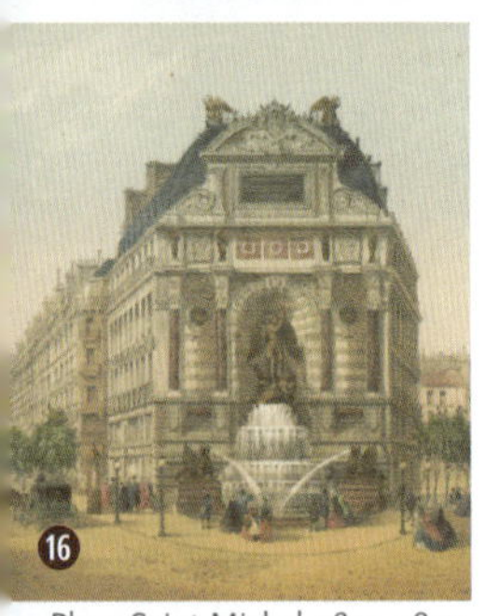

Place Saint-Michel, 1870–1879

In 1931, food critic Julian Street praised the menu and cellar of *Lapérouse,* but acknowledged its racy reputation. "Almost every earnest and discerning eater who has known Paris in the last 75 years has at one time or another lunched or dined there. Tradition marks it as a favorite eating place of British novelist William Makepeace Thackeray and of Robert Louis Stevenson, and when, a few months after the death of King Ferdinand of Romania, Prime Minister Bratiano also died and Crown Prince Carol was reported on his way to Romania where a *coup d'etat* in his favor was expected, the prince was in fact ensconced in a private dining room at *Lapérouse.*" More recently, Serge Gainsbourg courted young British actress Jane Birkin here, and Kim Kardashian and Kanye West partied in a *salon privé* at a soirée organized by couturiers Balmain.

Take rue des Grands-Augustins to ⓮ **No. 7**, where a plaque identifies the building in which **Pablo Picasso** had his attic studio from 1936 until 1955. Notoriously stingy, Picasso, presented with the *addition* after a meal, just turned it over and drew a bullfighter or a fish, knowing this made it worth far more than anything he'd eaten. It was in this building that he painted *Guernica,* inspired by the bombing of that Catalan town. Opposite his gate, built on the cellars of the former convent of the Grands-Augustins, is a restaurant now known as ⓯ the **Relais de Louis XIII**. A painted notice on the exterior wall explains that here, on May 14, 1610, shortly before his ninth birthday, the future Louis XIII learned that his father, Henry IV, had been assassinated, and he was now king. The restaurant dining room evokes that period with half-timbering, exposed stone, woodwork, stained glass windows and hangings.

Return to Quai des Grands-Augustins and continue to ⓰ **Place Saint-Michel**. This busy square, traditional gateway to the Left Bank, is flanked by cafés where, between the wars, one could sample specialties exclusive to this area. Paris itself produces no unique food, but did give its name to certain ingredients that appealed to the capital's tastes. Many Parisians disliked raw, wind-dried, chewy *jambon cru,* preferring a more tender, sweet, pale boiled ham, which was accordingly rebranded *jambon de Paris,* and since *girolles, cèpes* and other wild mushrooms were only available in season, entrepreneurs set up farms in tunnels under the city to supply chefs year-round with

16

The chestnut merchant, 1933

the white button mushrooms that became known as *champignons de Paris.*

In the 1950s, the official guide of the Left Bank Chamber of Commerce promised a chance to sample "Hare *à la Royale* at Montparnasse, roast piglet at the Odéon, *comfits* in the Saint-Michel square." Street vendors on Place St. Michel may no longer sell *comfits*—almonds or hazelnuts with a sugar crust—but it's still the case, as a visitor wrote in 1927, that "one of the most familiar odors of a winter day in Paris is that of roasting chestnuts." Then, as now, sellers used "a round brasier of glowing charcoal, with a mighty iron pan above," on which they baked the nuts until their shells cracked and charred. Today's vendors come from North Africa, unlike those of 1927, who were usually natives of the mountainous Auvergne, and no longer trundle their ovens on iron wheels, preferring supermarket shopping carts.

Enter rue St. Andre-des-Arts. A marker low on a wall opposite the intersection with rue des Grands-Augustins indicates the water level reached by the flood of 1910 which inundated the Left Bank. A secluded courtyard at **28 rue des-Grands-Augustins** hides ⓱ **Roger la Grenouille** (Roger the Frog), a busy, often noisy bistro with live music. Its glittering clientele has included painters Picasso and Balthus, who had studios nearby, as well as author Antoine de Saint-Exupéry and cabaret star Mistinguett, not to mention Britain's Queen Mother and Pope John XXIII.

Even after Haussmann rebuilt Paris, it wasn't unusual for people to keep goats, chickens and even cows in their courtyards. A few roamed the streets, tooting a horn and yelling their prices for eggs, milk and cheese, often milking an animal on the spot. As late as 1927, American journalist Janet Flanner wrote of "goat-herds, including our favorite Baptiste, whose flock parades the Quartier St. Germain at high noon." She relished in particular his homemade goat cheese, "at two [francs] fifty the cake, a remarkable luncheon dainty."

Continue along rue St. Andre-des-Arts to ⓲ **Passage du Commerce-St. Andre.** A century ago, the tables of street vendors lined such *allées* as this. In the morning, they sold coffee, hot milk, bread and rolls. At lunchtime, pop-up canteens appeared in vacant shop fronts. Business-like ladies heated large *marmites,* one containing *bouillon* with beef and vegetables, the other boiling fat in which bobbed both *pommes frites* and sweet *beignets,* ancestors of today's French fries and donuts. Sheets of tripe and whole beef tongues sometimes hung outside, still steaming from the *marmite.* In game season, butchers displayed pheasants in their plumage or even a *sanglier* or wild boar. Birds were sold unplucked, fish uncleaned. The better modern *poissoniers* will still gut and fillet your fish, a service for which, traditionally, one leaves a small tip, and, if you buy a chicken, the best butchers will ask if you want it "prepared." They will then "draw" it in front of you, asking if you wish to keep

18

Pommes frites!, 1915

the liver and other edible organs. A few even maintain a gas flame to singe pin feathers, the last flickering of a lost tradition.

Exit the passage onto Boulevard St. Germain, cross and enter the Carrefour de l'Odéon, where three streets meet: rue de l'Odéon, rue Condé and rue M. le Prince. Until 1750, this area was the estate of Louis II of Bourbon-Condé, the "Grand Condé," uncle of Louis XIV. Condé was famous for the feasts and accompanying spectacles at his château at Chantilly, directed by food and entertainment manager François Vatel. In April 1671, Condé ordered a banquet for a weekend visit by the king and his retinue of 500, with the additional requirement that, since Catholics ate no meat on Fridays, all dishes must use only vegetables, fruit or fish. The day before, Vatel purchased the entire catch from the nearest seaport, Boulogne-sur-Mer, and had it hauled fifty miles overland to Chantilly by night. When the fish had not arrived by dawn, Vatel, believing, wrongly, that it would not do so and convinced he was disgraced, committed suicide by throwing himself on his sword.[1-1]

Today, the busy *carrefour* or intersection houses a number of large *bistros,* in particular *Les Editeurs* (The Publishers) and *Le Hibou* (The Owl). On the corner with rue Monsieur Le Prince, the *Creperie Breizh* ("Breizh" is Brittany in the Breton *patois*) specializes in traditional buckwheat pancakes. Enter rue de l'Odéon. This street has numerous literary associations, in particular ⑲ **No. 12**, the site of Sylvia Beach's original **Shakespeare and Company** bookshop (English language bookshop). A plaque explains that James Joyce's novel *Ulysses* was published here. Diagonally opposite, ⑳ at **No. 7**, Beach's partner Adrienne Monnier had her own shop, La Maison des Amis des Livres (House of the Friends of Books—French language bookshop). For many years they shared ㉑ an apartment at **No. 18.**

Continue to Place de l'Odéon. ㉒ The theater, dating from 1782, was opened by Marie-Antoinette. Now one of the six theaters of the Comedie Française, the French national the-

Sylvia Beach and Adrienne Monnier

ater, it presents plays translated from other languages. During *les événements* of May 1968, dissident students seized it as their headquarters. In summer, the esplanade in front of the theater becomes a bistro.

Throughout the 19th and early 20th centuries, cafés occupied most of the premises facing the theater's Palladian-style portico. At the corner with rue de l'Odéon, a plaque marks ㉓ the site of the former **Café Voltaire.** Paul Gauguin and Stéphane Mallarmé were customers, and Paul Verlaine left unpaid bills when he died. Later patrons included André Gide, Anatole France and the actress Rachilde. It was one inspiration for the Café Momus in Puccini's *La Boheme,* where artists' model Musetta sings her famous waltz, boasting of her beauty and the admirers it attracts.

On the opposite corner with rue de l'Odéon, 22, the seafood restaurant ㉔ **La Méditerranée** has been popular with theater and film people

Meeting at Café Voltaire, 1894

Camille Desmoulins with family, 1792

since it opened in 1942. Jean Cocteau provided the lettering for its blue canvas awning and the design that appears on its plates, depicting his sexual ideal, a husky young fisherman, with a fish for an eye, and a stylized seascape in the background. His friend, the designer Christian Bérard, who lived on nearby rue Casimir-Delavigne, provided a mural for the interior, and cartoonist Raymond Peynet another. Famous patrons have included Charlie Chaplin, Orson Welles and Princess Margaret of Great Britain. American novelist Irwin Shaw wrote in 1953 that, "just after the Liberation, you could meet Jean Cocteau at that restaurant, and Christian Bérard, bearded and carrying a tawny, long-furred cat. You could also get a fluffy chocolate mousse there, made with American Army chocolate, whose availability was no doubt connected with the nightly presence of the smiling, well-fed American soldier at the bar who must have been a mess sergeant."

Camille Desmoulins and his wife Lucile lived in this building (2 Place de l'Odéon), until they were arrested and subsequently executed at the Place de la Révolution in April 1794.

Continue past the theater to rue de Vaugirard, and turn right, then right again onto rue de Tournon. At ㉕ **No. 18, Café Tournon** was a noted literary venue. Novelist Henry Roth, author of *Call it Sleep,* lived above, and drank in the café—to excess: "a page a *pastis,*" he told the proprietor. He died at one of its tables in May 1939, and is commemorated by a plaque on the façade. In the 1950s, expatriate African-American artists gathered here, in particular authors Chester Himes and Richard Wright, painter Beauford Delaney and sculptor Howard Cousins. They were joined by new arrivals from the Beat Generation, including Alexander Trocchi and Gregory Corso, as well as George Plimpton, who conceived the *Paris Review* at its bar. Later, Nobel laureate Patrick Modiano used it as a model for the Café Condé in his 2007 novel *In the Café of Lost Youth.*

Expatriate African-Americans had many reasons to prefer a café remote from the inquisitive eyes and alert *gendarmerie* of St. Germain and Montparnasse. Some used drugs, or had political or legal problems. Others had overstayed their visas. The Tournon also attracted French women seeking exotic sex partners. "All of us vocal blacks collected there to choose our white women for each night," wrote Chester Himes, "and the white women gathered about us and waited our selection." This was dangerous ground. Toleration was not approval, and only one careless act was needed to ignite the racism that smoldered just under the surface, even in liberal France. On October 17, 1961, scores of Algerian protestors would be massacred by Paris police, some of them thrown into the Seine to drown.

BOIS et CHA
Bouillon & Bœuf

Paul Newman and Duke Ellington in *Paris Blues* (1961)

In 1960, Duke Ellington, in town with his band to work on the film *Paris Blues,* played at the Tournon, but complained of the compromises forced on the film's writers and director by distributors wary of its mixed-race cast. April Ashley, formerly George Jamieson of Liverpool and a pioneer of transgender surgery, described her expedition into this corner of *bohéme,* of which her sense of exclusion made her a perceptive observer. She chatted up Richard Wright, who, she thought "looked sad, a long way from home." When she asked, "Then why don't you go back to Mississippi?" Wright snapped "And wipe spit off my face all day?"

Return to rue de Vaugirard, follow it to the intersection with rue Monsieur-le-Prince, turn left until ㉖ **No. 41**, home of **Crèmerie Polidor.** In Woody Allen's *Midnight in Paris,* screenwriter Owen Wilson is swept back to the 1920s, where he encounters his literary heroes and

heroines, among them Ernest Hemingway, who lectures him on life during a rendezvous at this classic restaurant, little changed since it opened in 1854. To one side of the main room, there is even a bank of lock boxes where regulars could leave their napkins until they accumulated enough stains to need laundering. "I love to go back to Paris," Hemingway said in 1960. "Want to go to cafés where I know no one but one waiter and his replacement. Find good, cheap restaurants where you can keep your own napkin."

The Polidor began as a *crèmerie,* selling only dairy products. The name "Polidor" has links to Normandy, which produces much of France's milk and cheese, so a Monsieur Polidor was probably its first proprietor. When it opened, the shop had no tables. Rather, shelves lined the walls, loaded with cheeses. Some were prepared in the large back room, while more pungent varieties matured in the cool of the cellar. Behind the counter, the Polidors sold eggs, *crème fraiche* (sour cream) or *fromage blanc* (cottage cheese). Butter, either *doux*—unsalted—or *demi-sel* was carved with a wire from a muslin-wrapped ten kilo mound shaped by the bowl in which it arrived from the farm. Specialties included the plump, round black-topped *gateau fromage*, its moist and crumbly interior revealing it as the ancestor of modern cheesecake. Polidor ceased to be a *crèmerie* around 1900. Ice boxes meant that housewives could stock up on dairy goods rather than buying them fresh each day. Once it installed tables, the transition to a restaurant was only a matter of time. Its menu reflects the tastes of the 19th century: country cooking, robust and unsubtle; sausage, paté, slow-cooked beef and pork, potato *purée*, lentils, cabbage.

The walk ends here. Return down rue Monsieur-le-Prince to **Metro Odéon**.

WALK 2

MONTMARTRE 1: THE BUTTE

START: Barbes-Rochechouart (Line 4)
FINISH: Metro Place de Clichy (Lines 2 and 13)

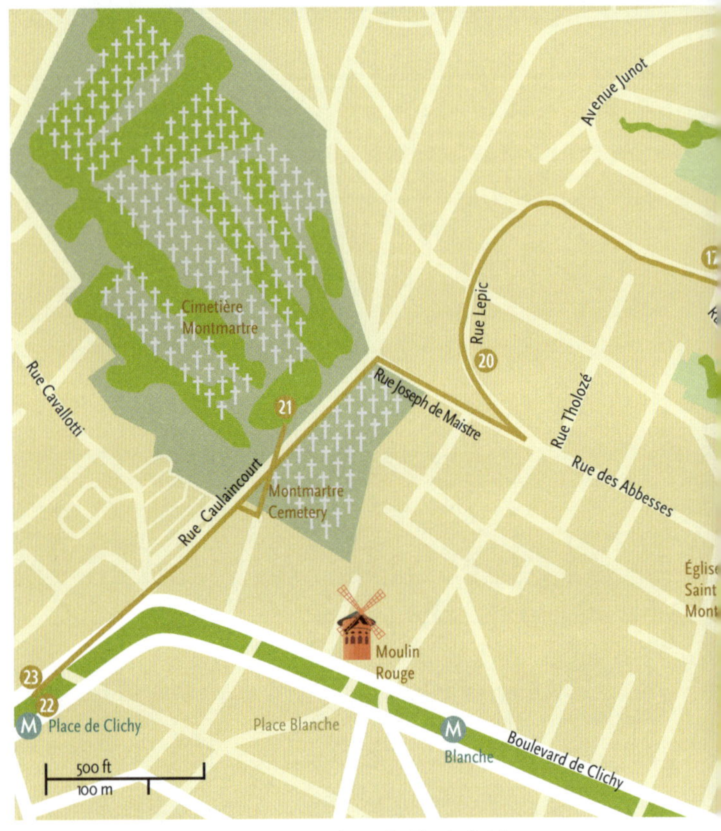

1. **Louxor Cinema**
2. **Anvers Metro station**
3. **Rue de Steinkerque**
4. **Place Saint-Pierre**
5. **Manège (carousel)**
6. **Funicular railway**
7. **Basilica of Sacré-Cœur**

Previous page: *Bal du Moulin de la Galette*, 1876, Pierre-Auguste Renoir

8. **Musée de Montmartre:** 12 rue Cortot
9. **La Mason Rose:** 2 rue de l'Abreuvoir
10. **Lapin Agile:** 22 rue des Saules
11. **Rue des Saules**
12. **Place du Tertre**
13. **La Mère Catherine:** 6 place du Tertre

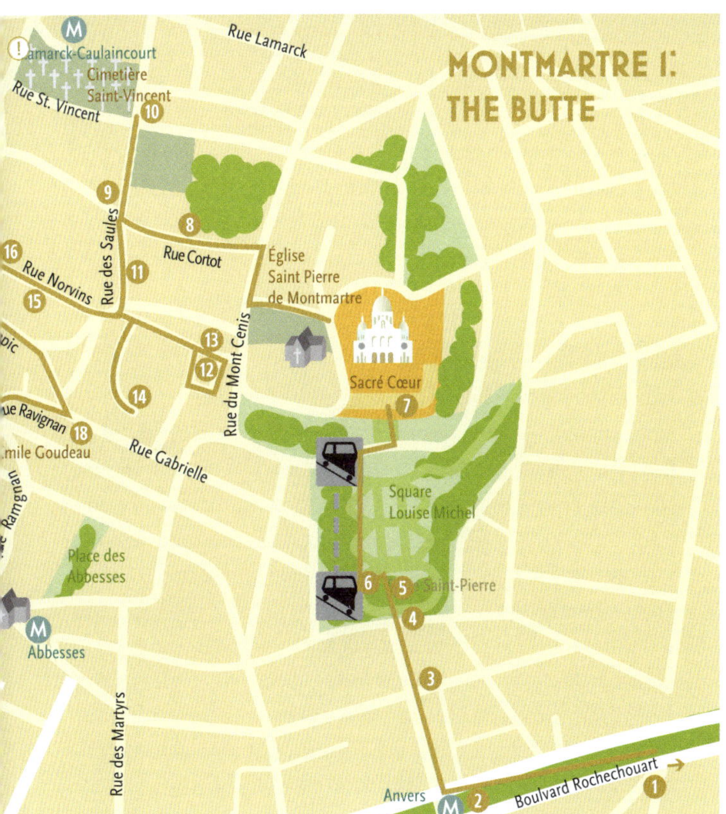

⑭ **Espace Montmartre-Salvador Dalì:** 11 rue Poulbot

⑮ **Hastings & Modigliani's Apartment:** 13 rue Norvins

⑯ **Statue of Le Passe Muraille**

⑰ **Moulin de la Galette**

⑱ **Picasso's Studio:** 49 rue Gabrielle

⑲ **Bateau Lavoir:** 13 place Émile-Goudeau

⑳ **Vincent van Gogh's Apartment:** 54 rue Lepic

㉑ **Montmartre Cemetery**

㉒ **Place de Clichy**

㉓ **Café Wepler:** 14 place de Clichy

(!) **Square Joël Le-Tac**

(!) indicates a place mentioned in the text, but not included in the tours.

The best time to visit upper Montmartre is when you feel adventurous. Perched on a bluff or *butte* high above the city, its lanes and staircases are steep. The winter winds whips down them, making the cobbles icy and treacherous, while in summer its narrow streets trap the air and heat it as in an oven. Your enjoyment will depend on the weather, the season, your expectations, but above all your stamina.

Originally, Montmartre was outside the city, popular with weekend visitors since alcohol there was tax-free. One of them described it as "a quiet, out-of-the-way village, to which few people climb. The buildings have a tumbledown air; they are old. The streets are narrow, twisting, and steep. They are roughly paved with cobblestones. There are great pieces of waste land on which grows grass and where dogs and children disport themselves." In the middle of the 19th century, Georges-Eugène Haussmann's renovations of Paris were indirectly responsible for its transformation. As his crews demolished whole districts, clearing space for shops and apartment blocks, thousands of working-class people, forced from their homes, relocated here. They created shanty towns from abandoned farm buildings, and made a living working the windmills that creaked in the persistent wind. A few shabby individuals in paint-stained clothing roamed the streets; artists attracted by cheap studio space.

Since Roman times, the chief industry of Montmartre had been the mining of gypsum. Also known as alabaster, this soft, white, marble-like stone was prized by sculptors. Ground to powder, it also became Plaster of Paris, an ingredient of such construction materials as sheetrock. But mining ceased in 1860, leaving the *butte* scarred

The Hill of Montmartre with Quarry by Vincent van Gogh

by open quarries and riddled with tunnels. Its meandering streets followed paths worn by miners to carry loads down the hillside. As the district became more prosperous, residents built wide staircases and lined them with apartment houses, one of the district's most distinctive features.

Our walk starts on the southern slope, at **Metro Barbès-Rochechouart (Line 4)**, where Boulevard Rochechouart meets Boulevard de Magenta. This noisy intersection, with its multi-racial crowds and the elevated Metro overhead, gives a taste of the *banlieue* (suburban Paris) which visitors seldom see. Cross to 170 Boulevard de Magenta and ❶ the **Louxor Cinema**. Once the flagship of the Pathé chain, this building, a rare survivor of the *art moderne/art deco* style, reflects the fad for Egyptian motifs that would intensify with the discovery of Tutankhamen's tomb in 1922—anticipated by the Louxor's architect Henri Zipcy, since the Louxor opened a year earlier. It flourished until television crippled the film-going habit. Repurposed as a West Indian boite de nuit, La Dérobade, and, briefly, in 1987, as Megatown, a gay nightclub, the building was dark from 1988 until 2013, when, now owned by the city of Paris, it reopened as a cinema. The murals in its main salle were restored, the original balconies rebuilt, and the auditorium dedicated to Franco-Egyptian director Youssef Chahine.

For decades until its 2020 liquidation, discount clothing and housewares store Tati owned most of the commercial property in this area. (It had intended to buy and demolish the Louxor until the government declared it a national monument in 1981.) A policy of "pile it high and sell it cheap" could lead to shoppers coming to blows in the hunt for bargains. The Tati brand become briefly fashionable after singing star Madonna shopped here for her retro-chic lingerie, including long-line bras and the panties she flung into the audience as part of her show.

Walk up the right-hand side of Boulevard de Rochechouart. The boulevard follows the line of the former Wall of the Farmers General which, until 1880, separated Montmartre from the city. Customs officers checked anybody entering to sell their produce, and exacted a toll, while bars and bordellos opened along the wall to service those waiting to enter. At the top of the slope, 2 the **Anvers Metro station** is a well-preserved example of the entrances designed by Hector Guimard, dating from 1902. (RATP, the authority that controls public transport, isn't noted for its sense of humor, but, since "Anvers" resembles "*envers*" (i.e., "reversed"), it has been known to invert the station's signs on April 1 as a *poisson d'Avril* (April Fool's joke.)

1

2

3

Turn right into ❸ **rue de Steinkerque**. This lane defines the term "tourist trap." Almost every store offers postcards, t-shirts and souvenirs. In the middle of the street, a few dubious characters are usually running the traditional con game of Three Card Monte, deftly shuffling cards or beer mats on a table improvised from cardboard cartons and inviting the gullible to "spot the lady." Do so at your peril.

At the top of the street, enter ❹ **Place Saint-Pierre**, which offers a first look at the park and cascade of stairs leading up to the basilica of Sacré-Coeur. Formerly named for Adolphe Willette (1857–1926), an illustrator who lived in Montmartre and designed the façade of the Moulin-Rouge, the park is now Square Louise-Michel. Michel (1830–1905), "the Red Virgin of the Commune," was a leader of the 1871 anarchist uprising. Branded by the press a "blood-hungry she-wolf," she was deported to New Caledonia but returned after seven years to continue campaigning. [2-1]

Louise Michel

On the rue Ronsard or downhill edge of the park, a plaque marks the entrance to the network of caverns and excavations created by centuries of mining. Fossils found here in 1798 inspired Frédéric Cuvier to formulate the foundations of modern paleontology. Place Saint-Pierre also boasts a traditional ❺ ***Manège*** or **Carousel**; ("*manège*" means "riding school," which the carousel with its wooden horses resembles). This Venetian example by

Bertazzon is in 18th century style, with two levels. To win a free ride, French children don't reach for a brass ring but for a gilded tassel.

Those who have the energy can climb the hundreds of steps to Sacré-Coeur, but since 1900, most have preferred, for the price of a Metro ticket, to take 6 the **Funicular railway**. The sloping plaza from which it departs is called Place Suzanne-Valadon (1865–1938), after the painter, and mother of Maurice Utrillo (1883–1955). At the summit, follow the *terrasse* to the forecourt of 7 the **Basilica of Sacré-Cœur**, which offers a sweeping panorama of Paris. The staircase below is invariably busy with tourists, as well as street performers, in particular "living statues," and musicians.

7

Of the ten million people who visit Sacré-Coeur each year, making it France's second most popular tourist attraction after the Eiffel Tower, few know anything of its tangled history. Begun

7

in 1875, on the site of a Roman temple, the building was intended as a monument to hostages executed during the Commune. However, by the time it was consecrated in 1919, public sympathy had shifted from that handful of murdered generals and church elders to the tens of thousands of communards killed or exiled in reprisal, and to the millions dead in the recent World War.

Engineers had to dig through a hundred feet of gypsum to find bedrock. To create the foundations, 83 wells filled with concrete and rubble were linked underground with masonry arches. The incongruous appearance of the building reflects the mixed motives of the seven architects who worked on it. Its bulbous domes suggest a Moorish influence, and the use of travertine limestone, which becomes whiter on exposure to the weather, gives the building an alien luminosity. Adding to the oddity, two equestrian statues atop the entrance, one of Joan of Arc, the other of Louis IX, canonized for leading the Seventh Crusade. The belligerence with which both flourish their swords sits oddly with the vision of a compassionate savior.

Outside the cathedral, turn right and take cobbled rue du Chevalier-de-la-Barre towards the center of Montmartre village. Turn right into rue de Mont-Cenis and follow it to rue Cortot and 8 **No. 12**, the **Musée de Montmartre**.

Situated on the highest point of the butte, dating from 1688 and built on the foundations of an abbey, this is reputedly the oldest building to survive from the original village. Suzanne Valadon and her son Maurice Utrillo lived here, and the studio welcomed Vincent van Gogh, Raoul Dufy, and composer Erik Satie. Auguste Renoir painted The Garden in the rue Cortot, Montmartre. The house later belonged to composer Gustave Charpentier, a descendant of whom acquired it in 1958.

Restored, it reopened in 1960 as the Musée de Montmartre.

The museum recreates the Valadon/Utrillo apartment, but its domestic calm reflects nothing of the drama that took place here. Valadon was only four when her father was sent to Devil's Island for counterfeiting. Joining a circus, she worked as an acrobat and trapeze artist. Since she had danced nude in private shows staged by the circus owner, modeling was a logical next step. Exceptionally, she showed artistic talent and, encouraged in particular by Edgar Degas, became an accomplished painter. Redhaired, sulky, and voluptuous, she posed for Degas, Renoir, and Toulouse-Lautrec, among others, and slept with many of them. When, in 1891, she gave birth to a son, she took the baby around the cafés, inviting her clients, any one of whom might be the father, to accept paternity. But Renoir, noted for his flesh tones, told her

Rue du Chevalier de la Barre, 1923

From left: Valadon and Utrillo; Renoir, c.1870; Degas c.1855–1860

"It can't be mine; he has a terrible complexion," and Degas, who excelled in painting skinny girls of the *corps de ballet,* protested "He's too lumpy." Finally a minor Spanish artist with whom, ironically, she hadn't slept, Miquel Utrillo y Morhaus, said "I would be glad to put my name to the work of either Renoir or Degas!"

Valadon left young Maurice with her mother, who followed the custom of *chabrot,* pouring wine into the dregs of his soup to float out the last morsels. By 16, the boy was an alcoholic. He also developed a morbid fascination with women—part lust, part fear. Encountering one in the street, he would tremble, whimper, and, if she fled, follow her, though always avoiding physical contact. Valadon, herself eccentric, wearing a bunch of carrots as a corsage and keeping a goat in the studio, to whom she fed her discarded sketches, resignedly placed him in a mental hospital. The institution encouraged painting as therapy, and Maurice showed talent. Valadon installed him in an upstairs room at rue Cortot. To prevent him from sneaking out to get drunk, she locked him in but urged him to paint what he saw—which, for him, meant the streets outside his window.

Providentially, illness imbued his canvases with a desolate beauty. Novelist Francis Carco praised their "leprous walls, livid skies, cold and mournful perspectives," a corrective to Renoir's sunny parties and picnics. Utrillo's mental health improved with age. Married off to a middle-aged widow, he moved to the country, away from feminine temptations.

The Swing, 1876. Renoir painted it at 12 rue Cortot.

Continue walking down rue Corot until you reach rue des Saules. At the corner, you'll find 9 **La Maison Rose**, a charming café famous for its appearance in Utrillo's paintings and its feature in the Netflix series *Emily in Paris*. Turn right onto rue des Saules. At the intersection with rue Saint-Vincent stands 10 the **Lapin Agile**, a historic cabaret named for the iconic rabbit mural painted on its façade by André Gill. In the early 20th century, it was a favorite haunt of Picasso, Modigliani, Utrillo, and other struggling artists of the Montmartre scene.

Retrace your steps and walk back up rue des Saules past La Maison Rose. Look closely, and you'll notice the setting of Paul Cézanne's painting 11 ***Rue des Saules, Montmartre.*** Turn left onto rue Norvins and follow it to 12 **Place du Tertre**. With its numerous restaurants, stalls selling postcards and prints, and caricaturists clamoring for clients, Place du Tertre retains little of its original charm. Its oldest restaurant, 13 **La Mère Catherine**, dates from 1793, and claims to have added a new word to the language. On March 30, 1814, Russian soldiers occupying Paris after Napoléon's exile to Elba shouted for food, and *bystri*—quickly. Soon, "bistro" came to signify a café that served light meals. Linguists, however, argue that it might just as well derive from *bistrouille,* meaning coffee that had been *corrigé*—corrected—with a shot of cognac. La Mère Catherine prefers its version, which appears on a plaque attached to its façade.

As Montmartre lost its aura of isolation, Parisians exploited its lofty location. During the 1871 siege of Paris, when Prussians sent

Rue des Saules, Montmartre, 1867, Cezanne

Catherine

LA BONNE

MOULIN ROUGE
GRANDE REDOUTE

LE CONSULAT

up hawks to kill pigeons bearing messages to the world outside, Parisians responded with hot air balloons launched from Montmartre. Carrying reports from stranded journalists, they drifted south over the encircling army and descended to earth around Tours or Poitiers. On December 24, 1898, Louis Renault drove one of his cars into Place du Tertre, proving its capacity to climb the highest hills, and inaugurating the French automobile industry.

Locals also realized there was profit in the area's reputation as a hangout for criminals and renegades. At such cabarets as the *Lapin Agile* and *Chat Noir,* balladeers sang of thieves and prostitutes. The most successful were **Aristide Bruant** (1851–1925), painted by Toulouse-Lautrec in trademark red scarf, black cape and high leather boots, and long-bearded, emaciated **Jehan Rictus** (1867–1933), whose funereal style suited his poems in Montmartre *argot* or dialect. One begins "*Merd'! V'là l'Hiver et ses dur'tés* (Shit! Here comes winter and its miseries.)" Both men were painted by **Théophile Steinlen** (1859–1923), whose posters for the popular cabaret *Le Chat Noir* featured an image of its eponymous black cat that became almost a trademark of

bohemian Montmartre. (Exceptionally, Steinlen is commemorated with a statue and a park on the western slope of the *butte*, at ⓘ **Square Joël Le-Tac**, 6 Place Constantin Pecqueur.)

Retrace rue Norvins to rue Poulbot and turn left to ⓮ **Espace Montmartre-Salvador Dalì**. The Spanish Surrealist never lived in Montmartre, preferring Montparnasse or, once he became rich, a suite at the Hôtel Meurice. The pieces on show were collected by an Italian gallerist and date from late in his career. Many are by other hands, including sculptures, furniture and glass that recycle his classic images: elephants on insect legs, and watches oozing like ripe Camembert (which gave Dalì the idea.) More showroom than museum, the gallery offers an introduction to the flamboyant Spaniard and to Surrealism which can be useful for newcomers and children.

Amedio Modigliani, 1915

Return to rue Norvins and turn left. The street narrows and dips downhill through what are now expensive private residences with walled gardens but, in harder times, were shacks and shanties. In 1915, painter **Amadeo Modigliani**, chronically broke and alcoholic, moved into ⓯ **No. 13**, the apartment of Beatrice Hastings. Beatrice, a British journalist, had come to Paris to write about the legend-

Beatrice, 1916, Modigliani

ary Parisian Bohemia for a newspaper. She described the artist upon their first meeting as "a complex character—a pig and a pearl . . . he looked ugly, ferocious, and greedy." Yet, by their second encounter, Beatrice admitted she found him charming, having already fallen for both the pearl and the savage. Modigliani painted Beatrice over ten times. Known for his womanizing ways, he immortalized many of his lovers through his art. Later, his relationship with Jeanne Hébuterne led to a tragic end.

Continue to Place Marcel Aymé and 16 the **Statue of Le Passe Muraille** (The Man Who Walked Through Walls). This bronze shows a man emerging from a stone wall. Half his body is free, but anyone who has read the story by Marcel Aymé (1902–1967) that inspired it will know that its subject, an otherwise placid civil servant named Dutilleul, is doomed to remain there indefinitely. Discovering he can move through solid matter, Dutilleul delights in entering the bedroom of his mistress without her husband being any the wiser, burgling the best-protected homes, even strolling out of the jail where he's imprisoned. All is going well until he experiments with ways of curing his condition, and is left permanently embedded. Actor Jean Marais, who became a sculptor in retirement, created the figure in 1989 to honor the writer, who lived nearby. The face is a portrait of Aymé, and visitors have worn the patina from his left hand.

Moulin de la Galette, c.1900

Continue to the next intersection and turn left onto rue Girardon, ascend the steep flights of steps until you arrive at rue Lepic and ⑰ the **Moulin de la Galette.** From the 15th century, windmills crowded the hilltop of Montmartre, the persistent north wind turning their sails. As well as milling corn and wheat for flour, they crushed grapes for wine, flowers for perfume, and gypsum for Plaster of Paris. The Debray family owned the largest. In 1809, they moved it lower on the city side and reopened as a wine shop or *guinguette* that also served *galettes*—tarts and pancakes. The Debray name disappeared, and the mill became known as the Moulin de la Galette.

In 1870, the besieging Prussians attacked Montmartre, strategically important as an observation point for artillery. Three Debrays died defending their mill. In revenge, the Prussians nailed the dismembered body of

17

Dancing at le Moulin de la Galette c. 1900

Pierre-Charles Debray to the sails. Its grindstones never turned again. Instead, the Debrays enclosed the mill floor to create a dance hall, leaving the old tower and sails as a monument and advertisement. A visitor of 1903 praised "the spacious ballroom, remodeled and redecorated with green lattice and crystal chandeliers. The orchestra is the best of its kind in Paris. The floor is kept in perfect condition. Adjoining the ballroom is a quaint summer garden. A flight of wooden steps leads from the garden to the table-like rock above, crowned by the ancient windmill bearing the date 1256."

Renoir's 1876 *Dance at the Moulin de la Galette* captured the pleasure of boys and girls enjoying a sunny weekend break. Appropriate to the Moulin's new status, they wear their Sunday best, the girls in striped cotton dresses, the men in the Panama straw hats so common among working-class Parisians that the suburbs where they lived were

Moulin de la Galette the only ball where you come to dance, 1898, René Péan

Moulin de la Galette. Restaurant. Lounges. Cabinets. Games garden, 1880, J. Jonchère

Christopher Columbus discovers the Moulin de la Galette, 1926, Maurice Neumont

Moulin de la Galette, 1897, Jérôme Auguste Roedel

Bateau Lavoir

known as Panam'. The dance hall and cabaret flourished but the mill itself deteriorated. In 1915, the Friends of Old Montmartre saved it from demolition. Moved to this more sheltered location in 1924, it became a restaurant, and in 1939 was declared a national monument.

Take rue Lepic back up the hill and turn right into Place Jean-Baptiste. you find the building with a plaque in front (18 **49 rue Gabrielle**). Upon arriving in Paris in 1900, Picasso had a studio here, which he shared with Carlos Casagemas, a close friend he had met in Barcelona.

Descend to rue Ravignan and 19 the **Bateau Lavoir** at **No. 13**, now renamed Place **Émile-Goudeau.** Artists lived and worked where they could, in this case a one-time piano factory. There was neither electric light nor heating, merchants stored potatoes and onions on the lowest floors, and in a storm it creaked like the floating laundries along the Seine, earning the name the Washerwomans' Boat or *Bateau Lavoir*. Tenants included Henri Matisse, Georges Braque, André Derain, Raoul Dufy, Marie Laurencin and Amedeo Modigliani. Pablo Picasso lived here from 1904 to 1909 and kept a studio until 1912, shared with model and companion Fernande Olivier. On leaving, he would lock her in, for fear other artists might lure her away. It was in this rickety ruin that he and Braque developed Cubism. The building sits on the summit of the hill, and falls away for four stories, not visible from the street. It was mostly destroyed by a fire in 1961, one year after being declared a national monument. Today, a shopfront displays images of its history.

While living at the Bateau-Lavoir, Picasso painted *Les Demoiselles d'Avignon* in 1907—widely considered the first Cubist masterpiece.

Retrace to rue Lepic and descend to 20 **54 rue Lepic**, where Vincent van Gogh lived with his brother Théo from 1886 until February 1888, when he left for Arles, leaving nearly 200 canvases behind.

Turn right onto rue Joseph de Maistre and left on rue Caulaincourt. Stay on the left side and walk down the stairs to the entrance of 21 **Montmartre Cemetery**.

Covering 48 acres, it dates from the 1789 revolution, when an open gypsum mine provided a convenient dumping ground for decapitated corpses. Afterwards, it became the last resting place of numerous celebrities, mostly of the 19th century, and the site of some striking monuments. Occupants include authors (Stendhal, Feydeau, Heine), composers (Offenbach, Delibes, Berlioz), artists (Degas, Picabia, Moreau), filmmakers (Truffaut, Clouzot, Autant-Lara), as well as society hostess Juliette Recamier, famously painted by David in 1800. Among perform-

Terrace of a Cafe on Montmartre (La Guinguette), 1886

In the Café: Agostina Segatori in Le Tambourin, 1887—Agostina, owner of the Café du Tambourin, was Vincent's lover. Their six-month affair ended on a bitter note.

View from Theo's Apartment, March-April 1887

Le Moulin de la Galette, 1886

Portrait de Juliette Récamier, 1800, Jacques-Louis David

ers buried here are dancer Vaslas Nijinsky and actor Frederic Lemaitre. The remains of Moulin Rouge dancer Louise Weber, aka *La Goulue*, were transferred from Pantin Cemetery. Her gravestone boldly credits her as "*créatrice du French cancan*." Nijinsky's tomb boasts a bronze statue of the dancer in costume for *Petroushka*. Adolphe Sax, inventor of the saxophone, is commemorated with a golden example of the instrument. A bust by Rodin tops the grave of art critic Jules Castagnary. Émile Zola rested here until 1912, when his remains were moved to the Panthéon, the highest compliment that can be paid to a French citizen. A monument marks the site of his original grave. And Marie Duplessis of *La Dame aux Camélias* sleeps here. Dumas is buried nearby. her grave is almost always decorated with fresh camellias. [2-1]

Exit the cemetery into rue Caulaincourt. Continue downhill to intersection with Boulevard de Clichy, marked by Frank Scurti's

MONTMARTRE CEMETERY

Degas

Nijinsky

Marie Duplessis

Zola

Berlioz

- A Stendhal (1783–1842)
- B Georges Feydeau (1862–1921)
- C Heinrich Heine (1797–1856)
- D Jacques Offenbach (1819–1880)
- E Léo Delibes (1836–1891)
- F Hector Berlioz (1803–1869)
- G Edgar Degas (1834–1917)
- H Jean Léon Gérome (1824–1904)
- I Gustave Moreau (1826–1898)
- J François Truffaut (1932–1984)
- K Henri-Georges Clouzot (1907–1977)
- L Claude Autant-Lara (1907–1977)
- M Juliette Recamier (1777–1849)
- N Vaslas Nijinsky (1889–1950)
- O Louise Weber, aka *La Goulue* (1866–1929)
- P Adolphe Sax (1814–1894)
- Q Dalida (1933–1987)
- R Émile Zola (1840–1902)
- S Marie Duplessis (1824–1847)
- T Alexandre Dumas fils (1824–1895)

20

Henry Miller

21

The Fourth Apple, a giant silver apple, etched with the countries of the world. It celebrates Charles Fourier (1772–1837), socialist theoretician and coiner of the term "feminism." Continue to busy 20 **Place de Clichy**, lined with cinemas and cafés. The central monument is to Marshal Jannot de Moncey, commander of the National Guard, who made a stand here against the Russians who invaded after the fall of Napoléon I.

American author Henry Miller (1891–1980), who lived in Clichy from 1932 to 1934, was unusual among expatriates in preferring Montmartre to more cosmopolitan Montparnasse. His 1956 book *Quiet Days in Clichy* celebrates the area and its people, particularly 21 the **Café Wepler** at 14 Place de Clichy. A haunt of gangsters before the war, it was sufficiently notorious to figure in popular songs. Music hall star Georges Guibourg, aka Georgius, sang of "Monsieur Bebert, gangster king, with two revolvers, who, when he takes coffee at the Wepler, steals the spoon." The Germans reserved the Wepler for use by its troops during World War II. Hardly had they left, however, than it resumed its old ways. "The rosy glow which suffused the place," wrote Miller, "emanated from the cluster of whores who

La Place Clichy, 1912, Pierre Bonnard

Ladies of Café Wepler, 1926, Albert André

Café Wepler, 1912, Edouard Vuillard

usually congregated near the entrance. As they gradually distributed themselves among the clientele, the place became not only warm and rosy but fragrant. They fluttered about in the dimming light like perfumed fireflies."

Pause to take a *café crème* and remember those days. Walk ends at **Metro Place de Clichy (Lines 2 and 13.)**

Un moment volé, Albert Guillaume

WALK 3

MONTMARTRE II: THE BOULEVARDS

START: Metro Pigalle (Line 2 and 12)
FINISH: Metro Saint Georges (Line 12)

MONTMARTRE II: THE BOULEVARD

1. **Place Pigalle**
2. **Site of Café de la Nouvelle Athenes:** 9 Place Pigalle
3. **Site of Le Rat Mort:** 7 Pl. Pigalle
4. **Avenue Frochot**
5. **Site of La Grosse Pomme** 73 rue Jean-Baptiste Pigalle
6. **Site of Cabaret de Néant:** 34 Boulevard de Clichy
7. **Site of La Lune Rousse** 36 Boulevard de Clichy
8. **Sites of Cabaret L'Enfer and Cabaret du Ciel:** 53 Boulevard de Clichy
9. **Place Blanche**
10. **Andre Briton's apartment:** 42 rue Pierre-de-Fontaine
11. **Site of Chez Joséphine:** 40 rue Pierre-de-Fontaine
12. **Site of Café Cyrano**
13. **Moulin Rouge:** 82 Boulevard de Clichy
14. **Cité Véron**
15. **International Visual Theater (Grand Guignol):** 20 bis rue Chaptal
16. **Musée de la Vie Romantique:** 16 rue Chaptal
17. **Hot Club:** 14 rue Chaptal
18. **Serge Gainsbourg birth place:** 11 bis rue Chaptal
19. **Headquarters of SACEM:** 10 rue Chaptal
20. **Salerooms of Goupil and Company and Iannis Xenakis's residence:** 9 rue Chaptal
21. **Museum of Gustave Moreau:** 14 rue Catherine de la Rochefoucauld

Moulin Rouge: La Goulue (detail), 1891, Henri de Toulouse-Lautrec

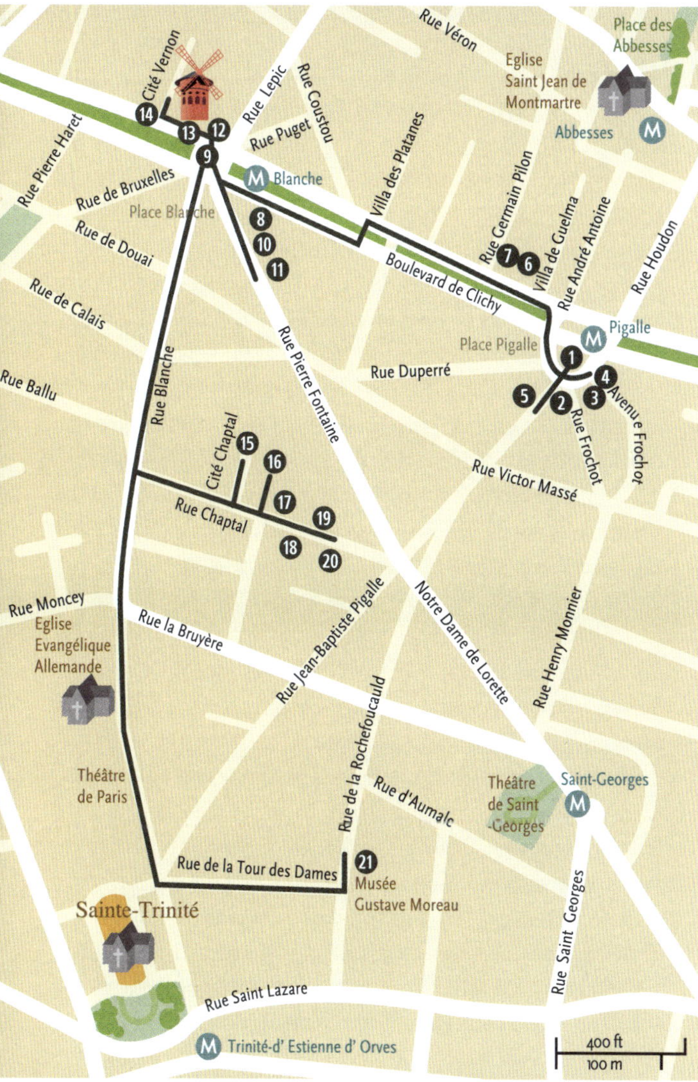
Rue Véron
Place des Abbesses
Eglise Saint Jean de Montmartre
Abbesses
Cité Vernon
Rue Lepic
Rue Coustou
Rue Puget
Rue Pierre Haret
Rue de Bruxelles
Place Blanche
Blanche
Villa des Platanes
Rue Germain Pilon
Villa de Guelma
Rue André Antoine
Rue Houdon
Rue de Douai
Boulevard de Clichy
Rue de Calais
Pigalle
Place Pigalle
Rue Duperré
Rue Ballu
Rue Blanche
Rue Pierre Fontaine
Avenue Frochot
Rue Frochot
Cité Chaptal
Rue Victor Massé
Rue Chaptal
Rue Moncey
Eglise Evangélique Allemande
Rue la Bruyère
Rue Jean-Baptiste Pigalle
Notre Dame de Lorette
Rue Henry Monnier
Rue de la Rochefoucauld
Théâtre de Paris
Rue d'Aumale
Théâtre de Saint -Georges
Saint-Georges
Rue de la Tour des Dames
Musée Gustave Moreau
Sainte-Trinité
Rue Saint Georges
Rue Saint Lazare
Trinité-d' Estienne d' Orves
400 ft
100 m

In the beginning, there was a wall. Called the Wall of the Farmers' General, it surrounded Paris from 1785 to 1880, cutting it off from adjacent villages. Its function wasn't military but commercial. Anyone with goods to sell was stopped at one of its gates, assessed and taxed. The duty on salt alone, known as *la gabelle*, accounted for six percent of the national income.

The wall created two Montmartres. One was the hilltop shanty town, the inhabitants of which lived off dwindling deposits of gypsum. Things were different at the foot of the hill, by the wall, along what is now Boulevard de Clichy. Bars and houses of prostitution sprang up as travelers loitered there, some to spruce up before entering the city, others to avoid tax by selling their goods—the first duty-free outlets.

Once the wall came down, Paris swallowed Montmartre. But the separation persisted. Our walk begins at **Metro Pigalle (Lines 2 and 12)**. Ascend into ❶ **Place Pigalle**, named for sculptor Jean-Baptiste Pigalle (1714–1785).

The conservative Pigalle, whose work decorates such churches as St. Sulpice, would have been startled at the changes to the area that bears his name. In the 1890s, the square hosted a "model market" each Monday. Models of every age, sex, social and racial type, often in costume, gathered around the central fountain, hoping to catch the eye of an artist. At night, many of the women doubled as prostitutes. Among the establishments "where great *cocottes* come every night," *Victor Leca's 1906 Secret Guide to Parisian Pleasures* recommended the Abbaye de Thélème, named after the abbey in Rabelais' *Gargantua* in which every pleasure could be satisfied; a sign over the café door urged patrons, "Do What You Like." In the ❷ **Café de la Nouvelle Athenes**, Edgar Degas

Rue Pigalle, 1952

Dans un Café (left); *At the Rat Mort Portrait of Lucy Jourdan, Private Room No. 7*

painted *Dans un Café*, aka *L'Absinthe*, showing drinkers numbed by this potent liquor, known to addicts as the *fée verte* (Green Fairy). Another café, ❸ **Le Rat Mort** (The Dead Rat), was so named because of the stink from the fountain where locals washed their dogs and clothes, and street-sweepers their brooms. In 1899, Toulouse-Lautrec painted *At the Rat Mort, Portrait of Lucy Jourdan, Private Room No. 7*. Seated on a red velvet banquette next to her client, seen only as an anonymous figure in evening dress, Lucy—a model for, and lover of, the painter Charles Conder—regards her world of vice with smug satisfaction.

By World War I, "Pig Alley," as servicemen called Pigalle, was synonymous with prostitution. At Christmas and Easter, a funfair and carnival took over the leafy promenade that divides the boulevard. The rest of the year it became a "stroll" for prostitutes. Even as people hurried to work, women loitered on street corners, alert for clients. By night, their numbers multiplied. Some buildings had an orange circle painted on the sidewalk. A man only had to stand there a few seconds for the woman who lived above to throw down a key. *Pierreuses* (Stonies) serviced clients on a vacant lot or a yard behind a bar. *Chandelles*

Café Scenes

Clockwise from top: *In the Café*, 1882-1884, Fernando Lungren; *Dinner with Friends*, 1903, Josef Engelhart; *Coffee Conversation*, 1877-1878, Giovanni Boldini; *Three Women in a Café*, 1916, Jules Pascin; *Cafe-Concert*, 1878, Edouard Manet

French Cancan (1955) and Cabarets

French Cancan (1955)

Divan Japonais, 1892-93, Toulouse-Lautrec

Trianon Concert, 1897, Georges Meunier

Bal Tabarin, 1904, Jules-Alexandre Grün

(Candlesticks), so named for their practice of standing under streetlights, patronized *hôtels de passe* which rented rooms by the hour. *Marcheuses* (Walkers) loitered around *Vespasiennes* (public urinals), catching the eye of clients over the skimpy metal screens that offered a minimum of privacy.

In the next block is located ❹ **Avenue Frochot**. Now an inaccessible "gated community," this narrow *allée* was the home of Pierre-Auguste Renoir before arthritis drove him to the warmer Cote d'Azur. His son Jean, who directed *French Cancan* (1955), a fictional account of how the dance made a fortune for the cabaret-owners of Pigalle, grew up here. Jazz guitarist Django Reinhardt lived here also. More recently, Avenue Frochot became popular with the worlds of fashion and design.

Retrace and walk into rue Jean-Baptiste Pigalle. American-born blues singer Adelaide Hall, who arrived in Paris with Lew Leslie's *Blackbirds* revue in 1928, stayed on to open her own nightclub, ***La Grosse Pomme*** (The Big Apple) at ❺ **No. 73.** Jazz and the sex trade are old friends. As Scott Fitzgerald wrote in *Echoes of the Jazz Age*, "the word 'jazz,' in its progress toward respectability, has meant first sex, then dancing, then music. It is associated

5

6

7

with a state of nervous stimulation, not unlike that of big cities behind the lines of a war." A girl who enjoyed a wild life was a "jazz baby" and "to jazz up" could mean speeding up the tempo of a piece of music or, equally, adding gaudy decorations to a dress.

Nearby No. 66 is the former site of the famous nightclub "Chez Bricktop" (1929–1961). Ada "Bricktop" Smith, a dancer from New York known for her fiery red hair and mixed-race heritage, rose to fame as a protégée of songwriter Cole Porter, who spent the war years studying music at Paris's Schola Cantorum. Spotting the red-headed Ada, he asked "Little girl, can you do the Charleston?" When she demonstrated vigorously, Porter exclaimed, "What legs! What legs!" He nicknamed her "Bricktop," and feted her so often at his parties that she opened her own club, Chez Bricktop, soon to become the most famous in Paris. In tribute, Porter wrote the blues-like "Miss Otis Regrets" specifically for Smith to perform. [3-1]

Return to Boulevard de Clichy, cross to the uphill side, and continue west. During the late 19th century, establishments known as *cafés concerts* presented programs of comic verse and sentimental *chansons*. The growing numbers of foreign tourists, however, didn't understand French, so entrepreneurs adapted the crypts and tunnels beneath the boulevard to create "ghost cabarets"; night clubs with eye-catching façades from which plaster figures of gods and monsters leered and gaped, while, in grotto-like interiors, reliefs of either angels in ecstasy or souls in torment decorated the walls.

Since the buildings themselves provided most of the entertainment, owners could economize on staff. The only food served was sandwiches, so they needed no kitchen or chef, and as there was no dancing, they could get by without a band. 6 **No. 34**, the ***Cabaret de Néant*** (Cabaret of Nothingness) opened in 1892. In its *Salle d'Intoxication,* clients sat under chandeliers made of human bones and drank at tables shaped like coffins. The ghost cabarets struggled once movies arrived, and other clubs began to offer more raunchy entertainment. In his 1931 story *Babylon Revisited,* Scott Fitzgerald's protagonist, returning to the Paris he knew in the drunken *années folles,* notices that "the two great mouths of the Café of Heaven and the Café of Hell still yawned—even devoured, as he watched, the meager contents of a tourist bus."

Cabaret de la Lune Rousse c.1904

At ❼ **No. 36**, now a theater, master of satiric lithographs Honoré Daumier lived from 1869 to 1873. In 1904, an entrepreneur from Marseilles, center of the French sex trade, opened ***La Lune Rousse*** (The Red Moon) at this address. Most of his customers came for sex, since pimps paid the proprietors to install girls here. Annual *Guides Roses* (Pink Guides) or sex directories not only gave the addresses of these cafés but often named the women and their attractions.

Painter Jules Pascin (1885–1930), painter of women and friend of Ernest Hemingway (see *With Pascin at the Dome* in *A Moveable Feast*), moved to this building in 1923, where he committed suicide in 1930.

Cross the boulevard to the downhill side, and continue to west. ❽ **No. 53** was the ***Cabaret L'Enfer*** (Cabaret of Hell) and, next door, the ***Cabaret du Ciel*** (Cabaret of Heaven). The entrance to the former, a gap-

From left: Jules Pascin; André Breton; Josephine Baker

ing mouth, with a doorman in a devil costume and holding a pitchfork, was one of the sights of Montmartre. (For more on the Ghost Cabarets, see a note at the end of this walk.)

Continue along Boulevard de Clichy to ❾ **Place Blanche.** Carts loaded with gypsum powdered these streets with its dust, earning the names "White Place" and "White Street." The Blanche metro station preserves Hector Guimard's distinctive *art nouveau* ironwork. Sinuous pillars and railings enameled in green suggest vines and long-stalked flowers, but also ancient bronzes covered in verdigris. Initially these entrances were much criticized. The newspaper *Figaro* called them "crooked chandeliers signaling the Metro stops with bulging frog's eyes." But Guimard's system of prefabricated elements was so economical it won the authorities over.

Turn left into rue Pierre-de-Fontaine. ❿ **42 rue Pierre-de-Fontaine** was André Breton's apartment. Breton had abandoned Montparnasse as too preoccupied with the pursuit of sensation, but found Montmartre just as bad, infested with prostitutes and what Guillaume Apollinaire called "hashish-eaters, opium smokers and the inevitable sniff-

Place Blanche: Moulin-Rouge and Café Cyrano, 1950

ers of ether." In 1928, to Breton's disgust, American singer, dancer and actress Joséphine Baker opened her night club, ⓫ **Chez Joséphine**, next door to his apartment.

Return to Place Blanche and look for the site of the ⓬ **Café Cyrano** on the uphill side of the boulevard right of the Moulin Rouge, the meeting place of the Surrealists from 1925 to the 1950s. Each evening, just before 5 p.m., the "hour of the aperitif," André Breton, founder and leader of the movement, strolled across the Place from his apartment. Attendance at the nightly *séance* was obligatory for members. The only acceptable excuse for absence was that one had been having sex, since desire was recognized as an irresistible force.

Place Blanche is dominated by ⓭ the **Moulin Rouge**. It looks like a windmill, but its crimson sails produce no flour. As an early star of its shows, Jane Avril, said bleakly, "All it ever ground was the customers' money."

In September 1959, Soviet Premier Nikita Khrushchev and his wife visited Twentieth Century-Fox in Hollywood. As Cole Porter's *Can Can* was in production, Shirley MacLaine and the *corps de ballet* treated them to a demonstration of the dance that made the Moulin Rouge famous. But its high kicks and splits left the Communist leader unamused. "The face of mankind is prettier than its backside," he grumbled. "The thing is immoral."

When the Moulin Rouge opened in 1889, respectable Paris agreed: the *can can* (pronounced con con) was a disgrace. A dance hall or *bal musette* on the site, *La Reine Blanche* (The White Queen), already had a bad reputation as a hangout for prostitutes and pimps. The new owner, Joseph Oller, exiled them to its basement and turned the ground floor into a cabaret. A park at the rear became a *guinguette* or beer garden, dominated by a larger-than-life plaster elephant salvaged from the 1900 *Exposition Universelle.* In the belly of this beast, a tiny theater presented attractions too racy even for the Moulin, among them

Posters by Jules Chéret, Henri de Toulouse-Lautrec and Charles Gesmar

Moulin-Rouge Palace (interior)

belly dancing, demonstrated by a Madame Zelaska. On the floor above, reached by a serpentine staircase, *salons privés* could be rented for intimate assignations.

Henri de Toulouse-Lautrec, who designed Oller's posters, could be found at a table next to the dance floor on most nights, sketching, and drinking—on the house. Oller called the Moulin Rouge "The Paradise of Women" but the title was misleading: only men could attend its shows. An American visitor praised (not very accurately) "a big, flashy revue here. 100 girls who do not wear even a bangle. A band plays in the foyer during intermission. Everyone leaves their seats, promenades and drinks. Also a roof garden on top of the building, and you can dine here. Also a naughty exhibition of Asian dancers. How tame by comparison is theater-going in America!" Titillation wasn't the only diversion on offer. Among the Moulin Rouge's biggest draws was Joseph

OULIN ROUGE
DU
LIN ROUGE
Féerie
ACHINE

Le Café de Paris (Can Can Dancers), 1880-1899, Jean Béraud

Pujol, aka Le Pétomane, a man "gifted," according to his publicity, "with a breathing arsehole." A virtuoso of the fart, Pujol could expel the sound of thunder and cannon-fire, "sing" in four octaves and, via a rubber tube attached to an ocarina, perform operatic arias and even *La Marseillaise*.

But what most came to see was the *can can*. To the *Galop Infernale* from Offenbach's *Orphée aux Enfers* (Orpheus in the Underworld), a crowd of women rushed onto the floor, whooping, turning cartwheels, and flourishing their petticoats. Barely a dance at all, the *can can* began when girls at a dance hall got bored and barged in among the dancers, creating chaos. It was all about behaving outrageously. Louise Weber, known as *La Goulue* (the Glutton) for her habit of snatching food from clients' tables, was notorious for *lése-majesté*. Spotting the future King Edward VII, then Prince of Wales, in the audience, she yelled "Hey, Wales, you invite us for champagne?" Her companions included *Nini Pattes en l'Air* (High-Kicking Nini), *La Môme Fromage* (Little Miss Cheese) and Lucienne Beuze, aka *Grille d'Égout* (Sewer Grating). The more limber girls threw spectacular flying splits and executed the *porte d'armes* (Shoulder arms), grabbing an ankle and raising a leg almost to the vertical, displaying everything their crotchless pantelettes didn't hide. (They also repeated these poses for photographs, on sale in the foyer.)

Other successes for Oller included the 1907 *Réve d'Egypte* (Dream of Egypt). In this adult pantomime with music, which every other theater turned down, the novelist Colette played a Pharonic princess in suspended animation. At the time, women needed police permission to appear in public wearing male clothing, so there was a sensation when the audience realized the archaeologist who revived her was actually Colette's female lover in drag. When the scene climaxed in a kiss, spectators rioted. "Insults are uttered that we cannot quote," said one report. "From two upper balconies, ladies throw various projectiles, even cushions, onto the stage; the whole room, standing up, boos the two performers in a final outburst of disapproval." Colette's husband fled, and filed for divorce.

Today's Moulin Rouge is a cabaret catering to the tourist trade. Troupes of dancers present elaborate shows that culminate in a prolonged exhibition of the *can can*. The performers are no less athletic than those of a century ago, though more discreet in the matter of underwear, and their whoops, splits

Toulouse-Lautrec

La Goulue

Edward VII

At the Moulin Rouge, 1892–1895, Henri de Toulouse-Lautrec

and high kicks come with an unexpected accent; many are recruited in Australia, where tall long-legged young women are the norm.

Outside the Moulin, turn right along Boulevard de Clichy and enter ⓮ **Cité Veron**. Once the haunt of petty thieves, this narrow *allée* developed into a community of rehearsal studios, public baths, workshops, and a few rooftop apartments. From 1953 to 1959, the third-floor at 6 bis was home to Boris Vian (1920–1959), novelist, trumpeter and partner with Juliette Gréco in running Le Tabou, the Left Bank's archetypal jazz club. Vian shared his terrace with poet and screenwriter Jacques Prévert (1900–1977). Seldom seen without a cigarette—he would die of lung cancer—and accompanied by his shaggy black dog Ergé, Prévert is remembered for his fragmentary and melancholy poems and in particular his screenplays for Marcel Carné's *Le Jour se Lève, Les Visiteurs du Soir, Les Enfants du Paradis* and *Les Portes de la Nuit*, including the pensive lyrics to Joseph Kosma's *Feuilles Mortes* (Autumn Leaves).

In the early 20th century, respectable hotels and stores along Boulevard de Clichy tried to stamp out the criminality that increasingly dominated their *quartier*. The *gendarmerie* raided the roughest establishments—pointlessly, since, as they kicked down the front door, the prostitutes, pimps, dope dealers and petty thieves disappeared out the back, melting away into a labyrinth of cellars and tunnels. In desperation, the council made it an offense for bars and cabarets to have back doors, only to backtrack after a few buildings caught fire, trapping customers without means of escape. Acknowledging defeat, the landlords withdrew to the downhill side of the boulevard. New zoning regulations reserved these streets for private residences. Bars, clubs, cafés, and cabarets were strictly excluded.

As their art became fashionable (and therefore saleable), newly prosperous artists moved down from hilltop Montmartre to more spacious and comfortable homes here. They included Camille Pissarro, Claude Monet, Paul Gauguin and Théodore Géricault. In 1823, a journalist called the sedate new suburb *La Nouvelle Athènes* (The New Athens). He meant only to stress how many residents were "Philhellenes": admirers of everything Greek, and supporters, like British poet Lord Byron, of Greece's struggle for independence from the Ottoman empire, but the name became a fashionable label.

Retrace to Place Blanche and descend rue Blanche and turn into rue Chaptal. Few streets in Paris possess such a variety of significant sites. At 20 bis, a narrow alley leads to the former premises of ⓯ the **Grand Guignol**, now the **International Visual Theater**, staging plays for the hearing-impaired. In 1896, Oscar Méténier, a police prosecutor turned pulp crime writer, opened a theater here in a converted chapel. Reasoning that violent death would always attract an audience, he presented short plays featuring the most grisly stage effects. Promoted as "the world's most murdered woman," his star, long-faced, wide-eyed Paula Maxa, boasted of having been "scalped, strangled, disemboweled, raped, guillotined, hanged, quartered, burned, dissected with surgical tools, cut into eighty-three pieces by an invisible Spanish dagger, stung by a scorpion, poisoned with arsenic, devoured by a puma and strangled by a pearl necklace."

The Guignol had private boxes for those who preferred to relish pain in secret, and prostitutes loitered in the lane outside, ready to satisfy anyone who found the show unbearably exciting. Hollywood even borrowed the idea. In the 1935 *Mad Love*, Peter Lorre plays a surgeon who spends every night at a "Theater of Horrors," relishing the lovely Frances Drake being tortured to death in a medieval dungeon. The Guignol closed in 1962. "We could never equal Buchenwald," said its last director. Meanwhile, "Grand Guignol" entered the language as a synonym for any scene of bloody horror.

⓰ **No. 16** houses the **Musée de la Vie Romantique.** Dutch painter Ary Scheffer, portraitist to emperor Louis-Philippe, also dabbled in politics until the excesses of Napoléon III drove him to abandon public life. His friends included Amantine Lucile Aurore Dupin, Baroness Dudevant, who, determined to break into the male-dominated trade of

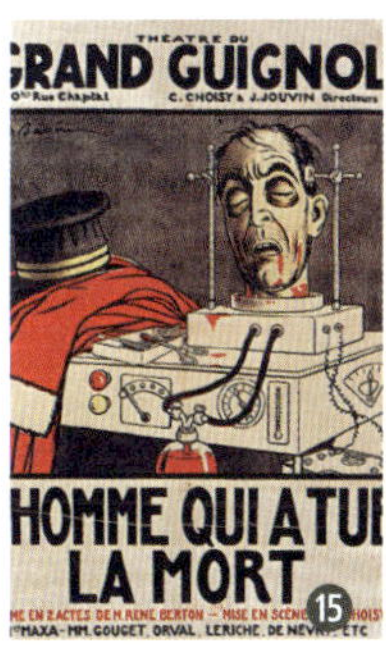

journalism, began dressing as a man and haunting the alleys of the Latin Quarter. Smoking cigars and buying drinks for the local riffraff, she wove their gossip into pieces for the newspapers, leading to a highly successful literary career under the male *nom de plume* George Sand.

For her male lovers, the bisexual Sand preferred sensitive young men, creative, but preferably in poor health, so she could play nurse. One of her first, the poet Alfred de Musset, suffered from a congenital heart condition that would kill him at 47. When he became ill during a holiday in Venice, she took up with his doctor, leaving Musset to return home alone. [3-2] After him, she beguiled the pianist Frédéric Chopin, a victim of tuberculosis. They lived in separate apartments on opposite sides of a courtyard, sufficiently distant so that both could work in peace. Eugène Delacroix painted a joint portrait of Chopin playing while Sand, incongruous in a gown, listens and, even more improbably, sews, but later cut the canvas in half, reflecting his belief that they would never make a couple. [3-3] On Sheffer's death, his home became the Musée de la Vie Romantique, one floor of which is devoted to Sand. A garden tearoom recreates the ambiance of the *belle époque*.

Joint portrait of Sand and Chopin by Delacrix was cut in half

From 1938 to 1947, ⑰ **No. 14** housed the **Hot Club of France**, which promoted the appreciation of jazz and published the magazine *Jazz Hot*. A plaque commemorates the official opening of the premises in April 1939 in the presence of Duke Ellington and Django Reinhardt. Formed in the early 1930s by critics Hugues Panassié and Charles Delaunay, the club also lent its name to the Quintet of the Hot Club of France, led by guitarist Reinhardt and violinist Stéphane Grappelli. Their laid-back style, influenced by *manouche* or Roma music, brought international success. Thanks to a German member of the Hot Club, jazz flourished in Paris during the 1940–1944 Occupation. Dietrich Schulz-Köhn had often visited Paris before the war, knew Delaunay and Reinhardt, and, as a member of the Luftwaffe, attached to the general staff, was able to secure special treatment for Jewish musicians and those of Roma or African descent. The grateful community assigned him the nickname "Doctor Jazz."

At ⑱ **No. 11 bis**, a plaque records that singer and actor Serge Gainsbourg (1928–1991) *né* Lucien Ginsburg, was born there. ⑲ **No. 10** houses the headquarters of **SACEM**, the Society of Authors, Composers and Publishers of Music which collects royalties on behalf of musicians and composers. High on its façade is a mask of Beethoven, flanked by muses playing a lyre and a violin, while *putti* sit in on tambourine and trumpet. At ⑳ **No. 9** were the salerooms of art dealer **Goupil and Company**, managed by Theodorus (Theo) van Gogh (1857–1891), who gave crucial financial and emotional support to his painter brother Vincent.

Also, at **No. 9**, a plaque records that French-Greek composer **Iannis Xenakis** (1922–2001), a pioneer in serialist music and electronic *musique concrete*, lived and died here. Trained as an architect and comfortable with most forms of technology, Xenakis interacted creatively with numerous artists, including composer Olivier Messiaen and architect Le Corbusier.

Return to rue Blanche and continue downhill until rue de la Tour des Dames, follow to its end, and turn left into rue Catherine de la Rochefoucauld. ㉑ **No. 14** is the **Museum of Gustave Moreau**. Religion and mythology preoccupied Moreau (1826–1898), one of the least typical residents of the New Athens. His symbolist canvases veered from ethereal to morbid: "chimeras, centaurs, dancing Salomés,"

wrote one critic, uneasily cataloging his subjects. "Orpheus charming the animals, Jupiter and Semele, bleeding Christ, unicorns, mystical flowers, Galatea, Pasiphaë, Herod: far-off characters from sacred, unknown, and mysterious lands." More enthusiastically, J. K. Huysmans wrote that "Gustave Moreau has given new freshness to dreary old subjects by a talent both subtle and ample: he has taken myths worn out by the repetitions of centuries and expressed them in a language that is persuasive and lofty, mysterious and new."

Dead Poet Carried by a Centaur, c. 1890

André Breton regarded Moreau as a precursor of Surrealism. In later life, he became an influential teacher. His students included Henri Matisse and Georges Rouault. Determined to be remembered, he redesigned his home as a museum, and bequeathed both house and contents to the nation, stipulating that it be kept exactly as he left it. Rouault became its first curator. The result is almost overwhelming, from scores of large canvases that crowd the walls to cabinets filled with thousands of drawings and preliminary sketches, an avalanche of art that reminds us of the ferment that was Montmartre in the *belle époque*. Exit onto rue Catherine de la Rochefoucauld. End of walk. For the nearest public transport, **Metro Saint Georges (Line 12)**, turn right onto rue de Bruyère, follow to rue Notre-Dame de Lorette and turn right.

ABOUT THE GHOST CABARETS

Customers who pushed through the black velvet curtains barring inquisitive pedestrians from the interior of these clubs had to endure a banteringly insulting welcome from a master of ceremonies who, at the *Cabaret de Néant*, wore the costume of a *croque-mort* or undertaker. Most took it with good humor, although a British journalist discouraged anyone "touchy, thin-skinned or squeamish, [who] holds death in awe, or understands French too well."

In the *Salle d'Intoxication*, where chandeliers of human bones cast a feeble light on tables made from coffins, a waiter took drinks orders. "Robed and cowled in black," wrote a visitor, "he will ask in lugubrious tones whether you will have Arsenic, Cholera, the Pestilence, or merely some fresh Sighs of the Dying." ("Cholera" was vermouth, "Pestilence" absinthe, and "Sighs of the Dying" a plate of sandwiches.) Once everyone had a glass, the master of ceremonies dimmed the lights and lectured about the paintings hanging around the room. All appeared innocuous until lighting from behind revealed devils and other horrors.

Following this, clients could visit the Chamber of Disintegration. In a dank crypt, as sepulchral organ music droned, a magician performed feats of transformation on volunteers from the audience. Wrapped in a shroud and placed in a coffin, a man was apparently reduced in seconds to a skeleton. Spectral figures gathered around those who joined the magician on stage, while women were menaced by a white-sheeted phantom; apparitions only the audience could see. Anyone familiar with music-hall magic would have recognized Pepper's Ghost, an antique stage illusion in which angled sheets of glass and directional lighting make objects and even people appear and disappear.

At the *Cabaret d'Enfer*, the drinks, except for their names—Molten Sins, Brimstone Intensifier—were identical to those at the *Cabaret du Néant*, as were the trick paintings in the bar. To accompany the lecture, a trio of devils seated in a cauldron, lit from below by theatrical hellfire, played eerie music. Just as clients were thinking of

Façade of the cabarets Le Ciel and L'Enfer, 1909

moving on, an actor appeared dressed as Satan in medieval doublet, Mephistophelean beard, and brocaded cloak.

Cabaret du Néant, c. 1900

Spotting a girl with her boyfriend, he paused by their table.

"Why do you tremble?" he growled. "How many men have you sent hither to damnation with those beautiful eyes, those tempting rosy lips?" Then he rounded on her escort. "You will have the finest, the most exquisite tortures that await the damned. For what? For being a fool." As he moved on, a waiter was at their side, suggesting a glass of Strychnine or even a bottle of Hemlock to help them recover.

Cabaret de L'Enfer customers

The show at the *Cabaret du Ciel* was less sinister and the atmosphere more benign. A towering Saint Peter holding an enormous key described the delights of heaven. Drinks were served, wrote one visitor, by "seraphim in frizzy blonde wigs, crowned with roses, light wings attached to their backs, pink tights on their legs and espadrilles on their feet." Thoroughly fleeced, clients were released to rejoin the crowds strolling along Boulevard de Clichy. Some may even have walked as far as the *Taverne des Truands* (Tavern of Criminals) at No. 100. Imagining it offered the same innocent fun, they passed under the giant plaster effigy of a Grim Reaper wielding a scythe, flanked by menacing creatures cascading to street level. However, they were in for a shock.

Taverne des Truands

Several shady clubs had already occupied this site, among them the Running Pig, the Porcupine, and the Spider Music Hall, but the *Taverne des Truands,* opened in 1914, set a new low. Tristan Rémy, a circus historian and member of Dada, launched it in the hope of reviving public interest in the skills of the circus. But jugglers and clowns attracted little attention, and it soon deteriorated into a clip joint, patronized by, according to one report, "pimps, cokeheads, morphine addicts, homosexuals, and whores." The singers who replaced Rémy's circus performers "obviously weren't concerned about censorship," grumbled one visitor, "because their songs were either nauseating or filthy." The Truands preyed particularly on servicemen on leave. "When an innocent individual wandered into this establishment," warned one report, "a villainous maître d'hôtel lost no time in placing him next to a young woman who persuaded him to consume as many drinks as possible and, if he had a fat wallet, to spend the night with her in one of the numerous local hotels." Not surprisingly, the police closed it in 1916.

WALK 4

PARIS ON PARADE: ART, FILM AND FASHION

START: Metro Trocadéro (Lines 6 and 9)
FINISH: Metro Franklin D. Roosevelt (Lines 1 and 9)

1783 1874 1911 1929

1. **Palais de Chaillot**
2. **Aquarium de Paris Cinéaqua:**
   5 Av. Albert de Mun
3. **Musée Guimet (Musée National des Arts Asiatiques):**
   6 Pl. d'Iéna
4. **Square Thomas-Jefferson**
5. **The Monument of Lafayette and George Washington shaking hands**
6. **The Monument to the American Volunteers**
7. **Maison Baccarat:**
   11 Pl. des États-Unis

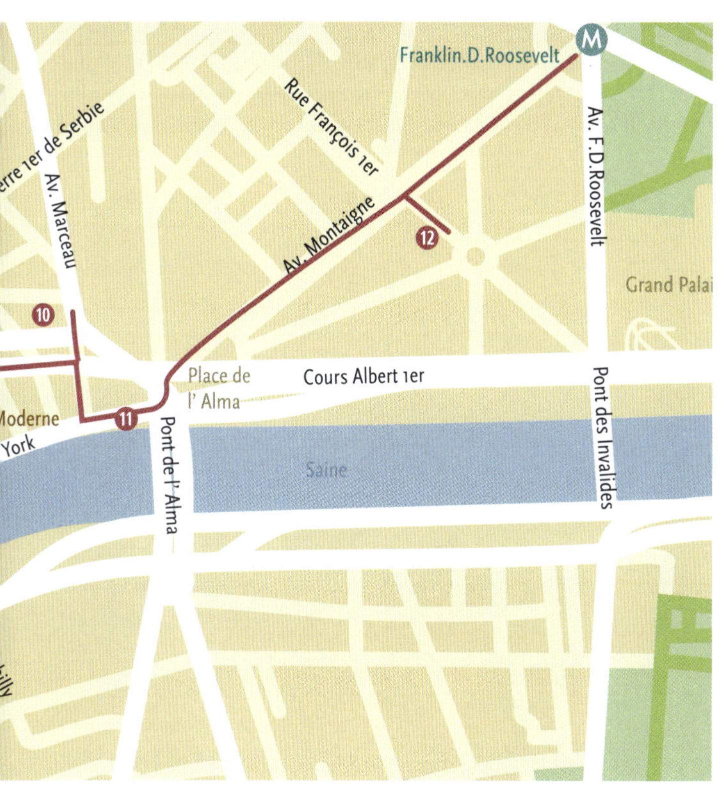

8 **Palais Galliera:** 10 Av. Pierre 1er de Serbie

9 **Palais de Tokyo:** 13 Av. du Président Wilson

10 **Musée Yves Saint Laurent:** 5 Av. Marceau

11 **Square Princess Diana**

12 **Offices of Christian Dior and La Galerie Dior:** 11 rue François-1er

P107: *Marie-Antoinette*, 1783, Vigeed Le Brun Louise-Elisabeth; *La Parisienne* ("The Blue Lady"), 1874, Pierre-Auguste Renoir; *Portrait de l'artiste*, 1911, Clémentine-Hélène Dufau; *La Musicienne*, 1929, Tamara de Lempicka

At the end of the 19th century, painters from around the world flocked to Paris to study Impressionism. After World War I, it was the turn of musicians, choreographers, and designers for the cinema, stage and fashion. Russian impresario Serge Diaghilev chose Paris to premiere the creations of his Ballets Russe. Their muscular, erotic dancing, designed and costumed in vivid color, with music that was often strident and percussive, electrified the city. French cinema welcomed experiment, embracing the *avant garde* concepts of Surrealism and Expressionism, while such couturiers as Paul Poiret and Coco Chanel revitalized fashion. [4-1] A showcase and laboratory for everything new, Paris, in Gertrude Stein's phrase, "was where the future was."

Costume study for Vaslav Nijinsky of Ballets Russes by Léon Bakst 1922

We begin in the Trocadéro district, at **Metro Trocadéro (Lines 6 and 9)**. The highest point of the Right Bank, this district is dominated by ❶ the **Palais de Chaillot**, built in 1937 for *the Exposition Internationale des Arts et Techniques dans la Vie Moderne* (International Exposition of Art and Technology in Modern Life). Replacing the dilapidated Palais de Trocadéro, a quasi-Moorish eyesore dating from 1878, the architects and decorators of 1937 embraced the style known as art moderne or art deco, noted for high ceilings, wide staircases and white walls, embellished with murals, statuary and reliefs.

The esplanade between its two wings, Trocadéro and Passy, offers a spectacular view across the Seine to the Eiffel Tower. Eight gilded figures flank the space, each representing a component of the good life: Flowers, Fruit, Birds, Youth, the Morning, the Countryside. A cascade of fountains and statuary falls away below the esplanade. When Adolf Hitler made his only visit to France in 1940, it was from here he chose to gloat over the city his armies had conquered.

Old Palais de Chaillot

Today's Palais houses the naval museum or *Musée national de la Marine*, the ethnographic *Musée de l'Homme*, the *Cité de l'architecture et du Patrimoine*, celebrating France's great buildings and feats of construction, and the *Théâtre Nationale de la Danse*. Much of the building is below street level, utilizing old stone quarries that honeycomb the hill. Some have been adapted into an aquarium. The 50 tanks of ❷ the **Aquarium de Paris Cinéaqua** house 13,000 fish and 35 sharks. (The entrance is around the corner, at 5 Avenue Albert-de-Mun.)

Buildings created specifically for exhibitions often struggle to find a role afterwards and the Palais de Chaillot was no exception. Before the United Nations had its own headquarters in New York, the General

Assembly convened here. In 1951, to mark the Universal Declaration of Human Rights, the esplanade was renamed *Parvis des Droits de l'Homme* (Plaza of the Rights of Man). Until 1972, the *Théâtre National Populaire* (TNP) or National Peoples' Theater, under charismatic left wing ideologue Jean Vilar, occupied the auditorium, while the Passy wing housed France's national film museum, the *Cinématheque Française,* headed by the equally iconic Henri Langlois, a hero to the young directors of the new wave, most of whom gained their cinema education in the basement cinema, the subterranean entrance of which sometimes appeared in their films, e.g., François Truffaut's *La Nuit Americaine* (Day for Night) and Bernardo Bertolucci's *The Dreamers.* In May 1968 it would become the site of a famous clash between the masked, baton-wielding CRS militia and demonstrators led by Truffaut's favorite actor Jean-Pierre Léaud.

Langlois co-founded the Cinématheque with Georges Franju and almost single-handedly maintained it in the face of official indifference. Overweight, untidy, impatient with paperwork, he was ill-suited to the civil service, and following a number of disastrous fires caused

André Malraux

Henri Langlois

François Truffaut

by the flammable nitrate film he stashed all over the city, nobody was too surprised when Cultural Affairs minister André Malraux fired him in 1968. The decision failed to take account of his enormous popularity. The day after, 3000 people gathered at the Palais to protest. Police charged the demonstration, leaving many injured, including directors François Truffaut, Jean-Luc Godard and Bertrand Tavernier. Langlois's dismissal contributed indirectly to the disturbances known as *les événements de '68* which reverberated around the world. [4-2]

(**JB:** I knew Langlois, who was generous with his assistance in my researches into film history. Once, as we were having coffee in a café opposite the Palais, I witnessed his legendary disorganization at first hand. When the proprietor politely asked us to settle the bill, I reached for my wallet, but Langlois stopped me. A hand dipped into the pocket of his rumpled suit, to emerge clutching dozens of unpaid checks. His other pockets were just as full. As he continued to excavate and a heap of paper grew before us, a waiter arrived with an adding machine to tote up the cost of numerous coffees consumed over the previous weeks.)

Exit onto Avenue du Président-Wilson, named for Woodrow Wilson, architect of the ill-fated League of Nations, precursor of the United Nations. Continue along the avenue and cross Avenue Albert-de-Mun (note entrance to *Aquarium de Paris Cinéaqua* at No. 5) to the intersection with Avenue d'Iena and ❸ the **Musée National des Arts Asiatiques** (Museum of Asiatic Art), otherwise known as the **Musée Guimet.**

France's long involvement with the orient is reflected in the treasures of this museum, the largest accumulation in the West of Asian

art. For centuries, European nations regarded Asia and Africa as places to plunder, justifying their looting as "ethnographic research." In 1923, André Malraux, later Minister of Cultural Affairs but at that time a member of the diplomatic service, was arrested in Phnom-Penh with a ton of Cambodian temple sculptures. Facing a three-year prison sentence, he sent his wife back to Paris, where she persuaded Louis Aragon, André Gide and André Breton, all eminent literary figures, to sign a petition demanding privileged status for "those who contribute to increasing the intellectual heritage of our country." The sentences reduced to a slap on the wrist, Malraux (and the sculptures) returned to Paris, where he claimed he'd been arrested because he breached the monopoly in antiquities smuggling enjoyed by the police themselves. (A pink sandstone porch from a 10th century Khmer temple is among the Guimet's exhibits.)

"Primitive" art caught the popular imagination. Picasso, Man Ray, Brancusi and Modigliani incorporated elements into their work. Entrepreneurs promoted jazz as "jungle music" and cinema churned out stories of white hunters in search of big game and explorers seeking

diamonds or gold. Painters, photographers and filmmakers joined the expeditions that scoured Africa and Asia. More than 3600 items of African sculpture and craftwork yielded by one such trawl became the basis of the *Musée de l'Homme*. At its opening in June 1933, the guest of honor was no distinguished scholar but Joséphine Baker, African-American star of the Folies Bergère, notorious for her stage appearance in a skirt of phallic bananas. [4-3]

The *Musée National des Arts Asiatiques* began as an attempt by French industrialist Émile Guimet (1836–1918) to document the variety of the worlds' religions. During an 1876 world tour, with stops in Japan, China and India, he accumulated quantities of votive art which he initially exhibited in his native Lyon. The locals showed little interest, so he offered everything to the nation, with the proviso that it be placed on permanent display in Paris. Guimet's museum, purpose-built, opened in 1889, with him as director for life. But the collecting urge soon outstripped any educational ambitions. When China, racked by civil war, began selling off its treasures and Japan admitted westerners after centuries of isolation, Guimet bought indiscriminately, and any reference to religion in the museum's title was quietly dropped.

Exit onto Avenue d'Iena and continue to Place des États-Unis and
4 **Square Thomas-Jefferson.** Before serving as the United States'

third president, Jefferson (1743–1826) followed Benjamin Franklin and John Adams to Paris to solicit France's help in the fight for independence from Britain. An enthusiast for the French way of life, he observed the storming of the Bastille in July 1789, and allowed the young Marquis de Lafayette to use his home to meet with other revolutionaries. In 1881, the United States' ambassador established a residence and legation here, naming the park for Jefferson. This attracted more Americans to the area, making it the preferred location for monuments celebrating the transatlantic friendship. On the east side, such a group shows ❺ **Lafayette and George Washington shaking hands**. The sculptor was Frédéric Auguste Bartholdi, who also created the Statue of Liberty, a bronze model of which was erected in the park in 1885, before being removed to the Luxembourg Gardens in 1888.

❻ **The Monument to the American Volunteers** dates from 1923, and celebrates 24 United States citizens who, before the U.S. joined the Allies, died fighting on the French side. The French initially rejected untrained foreign enthusiasts whom they feared would be a nuisance, and whose deaths, moreover, might discourage the United States' entry into the war. The few who persisted were redirected to the Foreign Legion, a near-mercenary unit that existed separate from the national army. Others found work

Hemingway in an American Red Cross ambulance during WW I in Italy, 1918

with ambulance companies and the Red Cross. They included future authors Ernest Hemingway, Dashiell Hammett and e.e. cummings, filmmaker Walt Disney, and Sylvia Beach, publisher of James Joyce's *Ulysses.*

Sculptor Jean Boucher based the central group, of an American doughboy shaking hands with a French *poilu,* on a photograph by one such casualty, the poet Alan Seeger, part of whose *Ode to the Memory of the American Volunteers Fallen for France* is engraved (in French) on the monument. Additional monuments on the square include, improbably, one to American Horace Wells (1815–1848), a pioneer of anesthesia. Another celebrates diplomat Myron Herrick, twice U.S. Ambassador to France (1912–1914, 1921–1929.) A plaque and an American oak also serve as a memorial to the victims of the terrorist attacks of September 11, 2001.

Of the buildings on the square, the most notable, at 7 **No. 11**, is the former Bischoffsheim mansion, later the home of Charles and Marie-Laure de Noailles, and now the **Baccarat Paris Crystal Room**. Commissioned in 1895 by Ferdinand Bischoffsheim, Belgian heir to a banking fortune, its furnishings include the ballroom from a palace in Palermo, complete with ceiling by Baroque painter Francesco Solimena.

In 1923, Ferdinand's granddaughter Marie-Laure married Charles, Vicomte de Noailles. Land-rich but cash-poor, the Noailles were one of the oldest and most distinguished families in France. The marriage provided them with much-needed capital, not to mention hopes of an heir. (In this they were disappointed: it produced two girls.) Charles, who was gay, showed less interest in procreation than in the history and design of gardens, on which he was an authority. Despite their incompatibility, he supported his wife's love of the *avant garde.* Jean Cocteau, a childhood friend, was a regular at their table, as were composer Francis Poulenc, film-makers Man Ray and Luis Buñuel, painters Balthus, Salvador Dalì and Max Ernst, and sculptor Alberto Giacometti.

André Breton, leader of the Surrealists, acknowledged that his group, like many others, "fed from the hand of the Noailles," but it was a hand they occasionally bit. As birthday gifts to his wife, Charles commissioned a series of experimental films, giving carte blanche to Cocteau, Man Ray, Dalì and Buñuel. In L'Age d'Or (The Golden Age), Buñuel and Dalì attacked the church, showing Jesus as one of the debauchees of Sade's The 120 Days of Sodom, the manuscript of which, written while Sade was imprisoned in the Bastille, was a treasure of the Bischoffstein family library. Charles de Noailles gave Cocteau a million francs to make Le Sang d'un Poet (Blood of a Poet) in 1932, in which he and some friends made a brief appearance as spectators at a theater. Cocteau then edited in a scene of a character committing suicide, which they appear to be applauding. A horrified Charles insisted the scene be re-shot. After The 120 Days of Sodom, Charles's colleagues in the Jockey Club demanded he resign. There was even talk of him being condemned by the church, said to have been forestalled by his mother with a bribe to the archbishop. "We

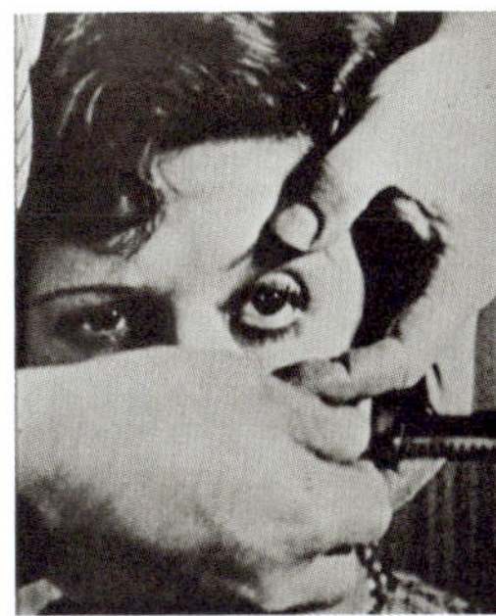

L'Age d'Or (1930)

are obliged to avoid all scandal in future," Charles wrote to Buñuel. "We must be forgotten. Will you please ask [your friends] *not to mention my name anymore!*" Marie-Laure died in 1970 and her daughters leased the building to crystal-makers Baccarat. Philippe Starck created a restaurant, and a museum displays pieces produced for international expositions, as well as for the Emperor of Japan, the Prince of Wales and Joséphine Baker. [4-4]

Exit the museum onto Square Thomas Jefferson, enter Avenue d'Iena and almost immediately take a left onto rue Freycinet and follow it to the entrance to 8 the **Palais Galliera**, home of the *Musée de la Mode de la Ville de Paris.* The Duchesse de Galliera, Italian widow of a property developer, commissioned the building in 1876 as a monument to her husband, intending to present it to the French nation, along with his art collection. Occupying spacious grounds in the city's most expensive *arrondissement,* with high painted ceilings, parquet floors and a landscaped garden, it deserved the label "palatial," even more so since the duchess insisted on using the same expensive materials and methods as the great palaces of the Italian Renaissance.

Duchess of Galliera

Lace exhibition, 1904

Construction was already well advanced when it emerged that, due to a clerical error, the building had been deeded not to the French state but to the city of Paris. The news coincided with a law that forbade any members of foreign nobility from residing in France. Deeply offended, the duchess decamped, with her art, to her native Genoa, leaving Paris with an opulent white elephant it could not afford to maintain. After standing empty for some time, it became a museum of industrial design in 1902, then a venue for occasional shows of modern art, and finally the headquarters of an auction house. In 1977, the city repurposed it yet again, as a museum of fashion.

Paul Poiret clothing

Among its 70,000 items of clothing are costumes worn by Marie-Antoinette and examples of the many hundreds of gowns commissioned by the empress Joséphine. (Maintaining her in imperial style following her divorce from Napoléon cost the state more than 30 million francs.) Designers represented include Balenciaga, Pierre Balmain, Christian Dior, Jacques Fath, Mariano Fortuny, Jean Paul Gaultier, Givenchy, Paul Poiret, Paco Rabanne, Yves Saint Laurent, and Elsa Schiaparelli. The museum also holds numer-

Legend of the Earth and Legend of the Sea

ous accessories—canes, fans, scarves, gloves, purses, jewelry—as well as a collection of undergarments, and an archive of graphic items: photographs, stamps, advertisements, etc.

Outside the museum, turn left into Avenue Pierre-1er-de-Serbie, return to Avenue du Président-Wilson and cross to 9 **Palais de Tokyo**, home of the *Palais des Musées d'art moderne*, the city's major showcase for contemporary art. This building, like the Palais de Chaillot, dates from 1937, and is also divided into two wings, with a central columned esplanade, looking out on the Seine. One wing houses the permanent art collection, which belongs to the city of Paris. The other, owned by the French state and formerly occupied by schools of cinema and photography, was redesigned in 2012 as a space for individual exhibitions. (Incidentally, the building has no connection with Tokyo or Japan. Avenue de New-York, the boulevard that separates the Palais from the Seine, was known from 1918 to 1945 as Avenue de Tokio.)

With its soaring colonnades and decorative reliefs, the complex is acknowledged as a masterpiece of late art deco. Alfred Auguste Janniot created the sculpted reliefs on the river-facing façade, a riot of wittily entwined human and animal figures representing the *Legend of the Earth and Legend of the Sea*. Convinced that "sculpture must be decorative before conveying an idea or expressing feelings," Janniot

Raoul Dufy's *The Electricity Fairy*

also designed interiors for the transatlantic liners *Ile de France* and *Normandie* and the gilded panel *Paris and New York Joining Hands Above Figures of Poetry, Beauty and Elegance* in New York's Rockefeller Center.

Most of the 15,000 items in the permanent collection, which include sculpture, furniture and photography as well as works on canvas and paper, are by artists who worked in or had an intimate relationship with the city, among them Picasso, Matisse, Braque, Derain, Modigliani and Raoul Dufy, whose massive mural *La Fée Electricité* (The Electric Fairy) occupies an entire room. A U-shaped wall of 2000 square feet shows the gods looking down from Olympus on the history of science and more than a hundred individuals, starting with Archimedes, who contributed to its refinement.

Exit the museum, cross Avenue du Président-Wilson, continue to intersection, and turn into Avenue Marceau, on which ⑩ **No 5** houses the **Musée Yves Saint Laurent**, devoted to one of the 20th century's most innovative couturiers. Opened in 2017, it occupies the mansion where Saint Laurent lived and worked for nearly 30 years, most of them shared with his partner Pierre Bergé, for whom an adjacent exhibition space is named. As well as displays of YSL's work, it offers a glimpse of the workrooms where visitors can watch the creation of new garments and the restoration of the old.

(**JB**: In 1992, I came here to meet Catherine Deneuve. Time had dealt unkindly with the decor of his showroom. Cigarette holes, neatly mended, marred the carpet and there were chips off the gilt of the nymph wafting eternally on a plinth by the big windows. No such damage, however, accrued to Madame Deneuve. The creamy Norman skin had settled over the bones of her face as paint grows to a canvas, enhancing its beauty. Those eyes had lost nothing of their flash, the voice none of its cello timbre. Even at 5 p.m. on a rainy afternoon, her navy blue linen pants suit, worn over a loose burgundy blouse, was as crisp as a new banknote. What garment would dare wrinkle on her?

YSL with Catherine Deneuve

Atelier d'Yves Saint Laurent

Except perhaps for Audrey Hepburn's partnership with Hubert de Givenchy, no designer was so intimately associated with a star as Deneuve with YSL. She acted as his hostess at public events. When he celebrated the house's 30th anniversary at the Opera Bastille in 1992, it was she, shimmering in sequins, who appeared on stage with him, comfortingly holding his hand. Beginning with *Belle de Jour* in 1966, he dressed her on screen and off. Nobody looked so well in his clothes. "He creates for women who lead double lives," she told me. "His day clothes are strongly tailored—good for me because I have big shoulders. Plus there's a masculine quality that's right for the woman who, by day, has to be assertive. For evening, however, his clothes make a woman more romantic—even a little devilish.")

Cross Avenue du President-Wilson, enter rue des Frères-Perier and turn left into Avenue de New-York, which, within a block, dips into the tunnel where, in the early hours of August 31, 1997, a car carrying Diana, Princess of Wales, pursued by intrusive photographers, was involved in a crash that killed the princess, her companion Dodi Al Fayed, and chauffeur Henri Paul. In 1989, to celebrate Franco-American friendship, the city had installed a scale model of the Statue of Liberty's torch on a small plaza just above the crash site. The monument risked becoming a white elephant until Diana's death gave it new purpose. The area was renamed ⓫ **Square Princess Diana**, and the torch, its American connection forgotten, became a reminder of a British life, passed, as Elton John sang at Diana's memorial service in Westminster Abbey, "like a candle in the wind." [4-5]

Exit the square onto Avenue Montaigne and continue to rue François-1er. The entire corner is occupied by ⓬ **the offices of Christian**

Dior and **La Galerie Dior** (entrance at 11 rue François-1er), celebrating the work of couturier Christian Dior (1905–1957). For fashion historians, the modern age began in February 1947 with Dior's first collection. By tradition, designers showed two groups of dresses each year, generally in their workshops. These *défilés* or parades were crowded, frantic, often slapdash. Clients squeezed in where they could. After five years of war, during which those design houses that remained open, including that of Lucien Lelong, for whom Dior worked, reserved their best for *collabo* wives and mistresses, most Parisians assumed the first peacetime collections would begin tentatively.

Instead, the diffident Dior, short, plump, polite, bald and shy, offered voluminous ankle-length skirts inflated by acres of petticoats. Swathing his models in the richest fabrics, he shaped the garments to magnify their femininity. "He immobilized them in exquisite dresses which contained between 15 and 25 yards of material," wrote British commentator Eric Newby, "with tiny sashed waists in black broadcloth, tussore and silk taffeta, each with a built-in corset which was itself a deeply disturbing work of art. By day, superb beneath huge hats that resembled elegant mushrooms, they were unable to run; by night, they needed help when entering a taxi. As these divine visions moved, their underskirts gave out a rustling sound that was indescribably sweet to the ear."

Despite a backlash from ordinary people, who struggled to find enough to eat—models and photographers on photo sessons were attacked in the street—Dior's audacity delighted the world of *couture.* Wrote one observer "The women wearing the frugal clothes imposed on them since the war years—short, narrow skirts and boxy jackets—started applauding early in the show and kept on applauding right through the final ovation." Evoking the roots of clothing in nature and seasonality, Dior called his collection *Le Ligne Corolle* (The Flower Line), but *Harper's Bazaar* editor Carmel Snow coined the name by which it became known and copied world-wide—The New Look.

Among the museum's numerous examples of Dior's clothing for both women and men, as well as his costumes for films and theater, a rusted metal star occupies a place of honor. Dior was superstitious, relying on the guidance of astrologers and fortune tellers. On April 18, 1946, on his way to see a possible financier, he found the star in the street. Since the investor did fund him, Dior kept it as a lucky charm and gave many subsequent designs and products motifs related to stars and the signs of the Zodiac.

Dior's New Look

Dior remained a force in fashion until he died in 1957, but by then the market was shifting to *prêt-à-porter* (ready to wear), an area dominated by newer houses such as that of Pierre Cardin, once a member of Dior's team. The stage was set for the modern world of *haute couture,* which has more to do with show business than clothing. No longer held in congested workshops, *défilés* take place in exotic venues—factories, warehouses, mansions—large enough to accommodate the hundreds eager for a first look at some theatrical but usually unwearable outfits. A few originals may be sold, but the creations are there to be written about, and to draw attention to what *really* makes money; the belts, bags, scarves, shoes, watches, jewelry and, above all, the fragrances marketed under the Chanel or Givenchy or Gaultier or Dior name. Of

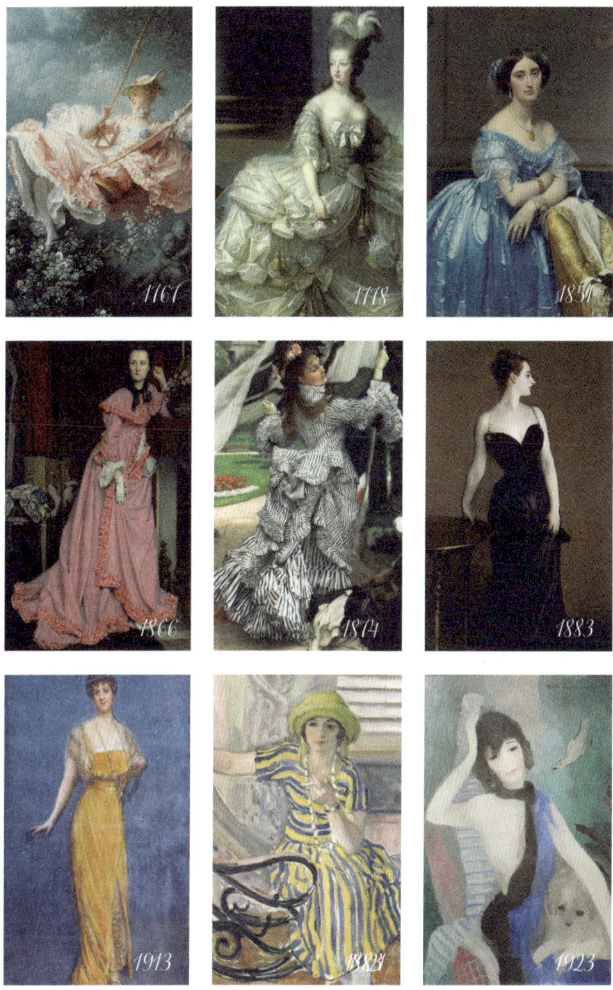
1767
1778
1851
1866
1874
1883
1913
1923

Harper's Bazaar: Fall Fashions 2023 cover, *Symphony in Black*, 1923, Etré

La Nouvelle Mode: A magazine cover from the June 28, 1896 issue

Femina: Women's lifestyle and literary magazine, October 1930, Léon Benigni

La Vie Parisienne: A blend of fashion, satire, art, and light eroticism, 1926

Vogue Paris: A vintage cover of a mannequin, 1926, Eduardo Garcia Benito

Elle: Brigitte Bardot's first cover for ELLE, photo by Jean Chevalier, January, 1952

Vanity Fair: *Cigarette Couple*, December 1919, Georges Lepape

Gazette du Bon Ton: Jeanne Paquin gown, 1914, George Barbier

the total revenue generated by the Yves St. Laurent empire, for example, perfumes contribute 83.5 percent.

Walk ends. Exit onto rue François-1er. Continue to Avenue Montaigne, turn right and follow to Champs-Elysées and **Metro Franklin D. Roosevelt (Lines 1 and 9)**.

WALK 5

THE LUXEMBOURG GARDENS: THE PEOPLE'S PARK

START: Metro Odéon (Lines 4 and 10)

FINISH: Metro Vavin (Lines 4, 6 and 12)

THE LUXEMBOURG GARDENS: THE PEOPLE'S PARK

1. Bust of Louis-Henri Murger
2. Fallen Students of the Resistance
3. Medici Fountain
4. Fontaine de Léda
5. Statue of *a Faune Dancing*
6. The Greek Actor
7. Statue of Clémence Isaure
8. Statue of George Sand
9. Le Grand Bassin
10. Medici Palace
11. Hommage à Eugène Delacroix
12. L'Effort (Hercules Diverting the River Alpheus)
13. Le Triomphe de Silène (The Triumph of Silenus)
14. Monument to Paul Verlaine
15. Liberty Enlightening the World
16. Monument to Frédéric Chopin
17. Le Poète: Monument to Paul Éluard
18. Monument to Watteau
19. Pavillon Davioud
20. Apiary
21. Little or Upper Luxembourg
22. L'Aurore (Dawn)
23. Midi (Mid-Day)
24. Institut d'Art et d'Archéologie
25. Le Crépuscule (Twilight)
26. La Nuit
27. Fontaine des Quatre-Parties-du Monde (Fountain of the Four Corners of the World)
28. Statue of Michel Ney
29. Le Closerie des Lilas
30. Gertrude Stein and Alice Toklas's Apartment: 27 rue de Fleurus
31. Sylvia Beach's Bookstore (Site of Shakespeare and Company): 12 rue de l'Odéon
32. Hemingway's Apartment: 6 rue Férou
33. Luxembourg Museum: 19 rue de Vaugirard
34. The Fitzgeralds' Apartment: 58 rue de Vaugirard
35. The Murphys' Apartment: 14 rue Guynemer

Previous page: *Luxembourg Gardens. Monument to Chopin*, 1909, Henri Rousseau, Hermitage Museum

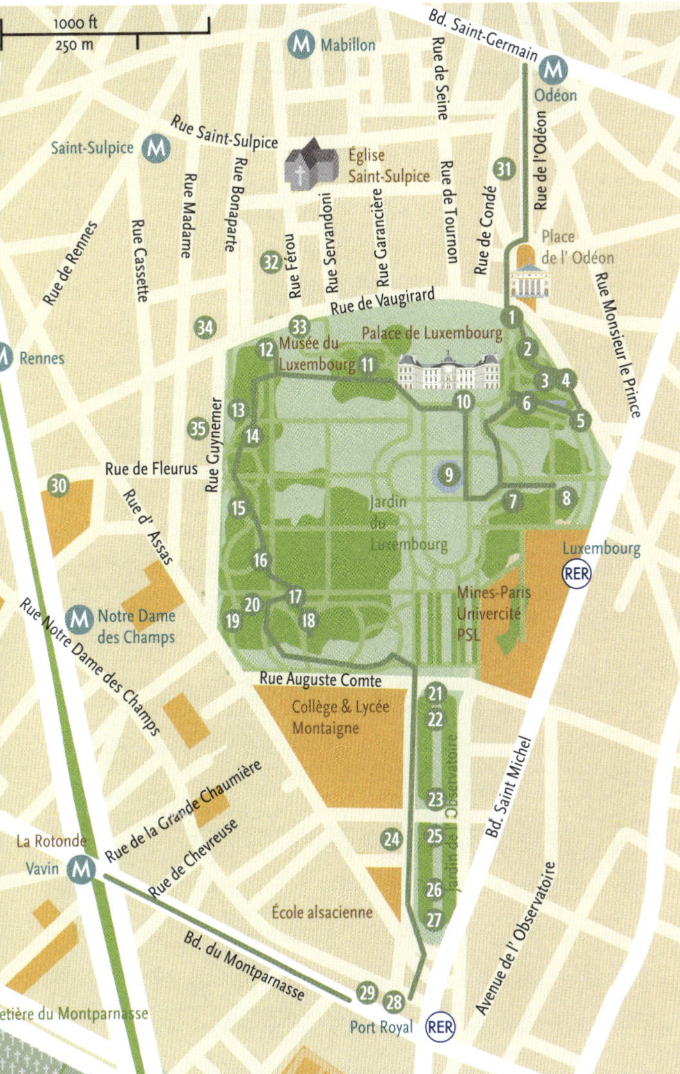
1000 ft
250 m
Mabillon
Bd. Saint-Germain
Odéon
Rue de Seine
Rue Saint-Sulpice
Saint-Sulpice
Église
Saint-Sulpice
Rue de l'Odéon
Rue Bonaparte
Rue Madame
Rue de Tournon
Rue de Condé
Rue Servandoni
Rue Garancière
Place
de l' Odéon
Rue de Rennes
Rue Cassette
Rue Férou
Rue de Vaugirard
Rue Monsieur le Prince
Palace de Luxembourg
Musée du
Luxembourg
Rennes
Rue Guynemer
Rue de Fleurus
Rue d' Assas
Jardin
du
Luxembourg
Luxembourg
RER
Mines-Paris
Univercité
PSL
Notre Dame
des Champs
Rue Notre Dame des Champs
Rue Auguste Comte
Collège & Lycée
Montaigne
Jardin de l' Observatoire
Bd. Saint Michel
Rue de la Grande Chaumière
Rue de Chevreuse
La Rotonde
Vavin
Avenue de l' Observatoire
École alsacienne
Bd. du Montparnasse
Port Royal
RER
metière du Montparnasse
1
2
3
4
5
6
7
8
9
10
11
12
13
14
15
16
17
18
19
20
21
22
23
24
25
26
27
28
29
30
31
32
33
34
35

For generations of visitors, as well as those who live in Paris, a walk through the *Jardin du Luxembourg*, sometimes called the *Jardins du Sénat*, has been central to an experience of the city, a chance to taste for a moment the world of four centuries ago. Though writers have described them, artists painted them, and invaders occupied them, the gardens will always belong to the people of Paris. Regiments of lovers have scuffed hand-in-hand through the leaves in November, thousands played *pétanque* or tennis or chess there, and a multitude of choirs and orchestras performed in its bandstand—not to mention the millions who walked or read or flirted or dozed. Each visitor finds his or her own Luxembourg. Now it's your turn.

The modern park combines two earlier gardens: those created for the palace of Marie de' Medici around 1612, and the grounds of a monastery that originally surrounded them. In 1796, the *Directoire*, a committee that ruled France from the end of the Revolution to the rise of Napoléon I, demolished the walls, and declared the combined area a

View of the Luxembourg Palace, 1750

place of recreation for the people. Later, the "Little Luxembourg," a strip of park, with wooded avenues, extended the gardens south to Montparnasse.

The walk begins at **Metro Odéon (Lines 4 and 10)**. At the top of rue de l'Odéon, walk along the side of the theater to rue Vaugirard, cross and enter the Gardens. A map on the kiosk just inside the gate explains the layout. The first statue you see, to your left, is ❶ a bust of **Louis-Henri Murger** (1822–1861). Stone roses straggle around his chest and trail down the plinth, an attempt by the sculptor to soften his grim expression. Murger inspired the myth of bohemian Paris. His 1851 *Scenes de la vie de Bohème* (Scenes of Bohemian Life), based on his own student days, describes how Rodolfo and his friends, hopeful writers and musicians, live in poverty in the bare, unheated *chambres de bonnes* (servants' rooms) in the attics of the buildings which Haussmann would soon demolish. They burn their manuscripts to keep warm, and call themselves "water-drinkers" since they can't afford wine. These conditions bred disease, in particular tuberculosis, from which Mimi, Rodolfo's lover, suffers. Murger died penniless, at only 38. *Scenes de la vie de Bohème* was his

Marie de' Medici

La Bohème poster, 1912

2

3

4

only success, but it wasn't until 1896 that Giacomo Puccini transformed his stories into the opera *La Bohème.*

Continue along the *allée,* avoiding any runners who pound past. (A jogging track runs around the periphery of the park, which also hosts an annual marathon.) The next statuary group on the left commemorates ❷ the ***Fallen Students of the Resistance.*** It shows a man standing over another who has fallen, above the inscription "Friend, if you fall, a comrade from the shadows takes your place." The line comes from *The Song of the Partisans,* written in 1943 in London, where Charles de Gaulle headed the Free French government in exile. It was sung again in December 1964, when the body of Jean Moulin, wartime leader of the resistance, was installed in the nearby Panthéon.

The *allée* ends at ❸ the **Medici Fountain.** Of the wall that once enclosed the gardens, all that remains is the grotto around which this fountain was constructed in 1860. Architect Alphonse de Gisors added the pond, the swags of ivy along both sides and an avenue of overarching *platanes.* The only connection with the Medicis is their emblem, the five-balled shield which surmounts the fountain, flanked by two women pouring water, representing

France's great rivers, the Rhone and Seine. Lower statues depict a faun and a huntress, and the masks of comedy and tragedy. In the main niche, statues by Auguste Ottin illustrate a story from the Roman poet Ovid. Polyphemus, a one-eyed giant, has just discovered Galatea, the sea nymph he loves, in the arms of her lover Acis.

Walk along the edge of the pool and around behind the fountain. For stability, Gisors placed this and the earlier and less ostentatious ④ **Fontaine de Leda** back to back. From a shaded pool, a single column of water bubbles before Achille Valois's relief of another incident from mythology, this time Greek. According to legend, Zeus, king of the gods, took the form of a swan to ravish Leda, a Spartan queen. Some artists show this as a rape but here it's depicted as a seduction. Despite the figure of Cupid shrinking, almost aghast, from what has just transpired, the graphically drooping neck of the exhausted swan (which impudently squirts a stream of water) and a languid Leda, exhibiting what

William Blake called "the lineaments of gratified desire," clearly show her as a willing participant. A shocked critic in 1812 urged the fountain be hidden because "the ideas it calls to the imagination [make it] hardly a suitable subject for a monument placed before the eyes of the public."

Continue along the fence and running track until 5 the statue of a ***Faune Dancing*** by Eugène-Louis Lequesne in 1850. Half human, half goat, he is playing a flute while dancing on a wine skin. Follow the *allée* downhill to another statue, 6 ***The Greek Actor*** by Charles-Arthur Bourgeois, dated 1868. He wears a sheep-skin, apparently his costume, and is studying his lines.

A stone balustrade with flower-filled urns defines the border between the former monastery and the gardens created for the palace. Following the fall of Napoléon I in 1815, Louis XVIII, in a belated tribute to Marie de' Medici, for whom the palace was built, commissioned the twenty statues of queens and other great women that encircle the formal gardens. All depict real people, except 7 the statue of **Clémence Isaure** by Antoine-Augustin Préault. Supposedly a 15th-century poet from a noble family in the city of Toulouse, Isaure never existed.

George Sand, 1905–1910

Préault may have suspected as much, since the form-fitting dress and provocative pose of the figure suggest more party girl than poet.

Take the steps down into the formal gardens. The perfectly aligned and color-coordinated flowerbeds do not occur by accident. Some mornings, you may see teams of gardeners working on them. One man uses a spade to lift a square of flowers and their roots. On the now bare earth, a second places a machine that forces steam into the ground, killing weeds and bugs. When he moves it away, a third drops into place a fresh block of flowers, hothouse-grown. The Luxembourg is not so much a garden as a décor, a backdrop, with flowers the furniture, to be changed before we, the performers, step on stage.

8 **George Sand** by François Léon Sicard. Amantine Lucile Aurore Dupin de Francueil (1804–1876) aka George Sand, was as widely read

Crowd around le Grand Bassin, 1926

in her day as Victor Hugo or Honoré de Balzac, but is remembered mostly for her affair with pianist/composer Frédéric Chopin, and for assuming male clothing and a male name. [5-1]

The octagonal pond, known as 9 **Le Grand Bassin**, is used today by children and, occasionally, adults to sail toy yachts. (A kiosk rents boats and the long rods to control them.) In 1925, American novelist William Faulkner (1897–1962) lived on rue de Vaugirard, opposite the palace. Intending to stay in Paris for a year, he left after three months. The last chapter of *Sanctuary*, his 1931 novel, is set near the grand bassin. His description of the gardens conveys his disappointment with the city. "It had been a gray day, a gray summer, a gray year. On the street, men wore overcoats and in the Luxembourg Gardens the women sat knitting in shawls and even the men playing croquet played in coats and capes, and in the sad gloom of the chestnut trees the dry click of balls, the random shouts of children, had that quality of autumn, gallant and evanescent and forlorn."

The Apotheosis of Henry IV and the Proclamation of the Regency of Marie de Médici on May 14, 1610, part of the Marie de Médici cycle, 1623-25, Peter Paul Rubens, the painting adorned the halls of Marie de' Medici's Palais du Luxembourg.(now in Musée du Louvre)

From the pond, one gets the first good view of ⑩ the **Medici Palace.** In 1612, Queen Elizabeth I of Great Britain had been dead for nine years and William Shakespeare had just finished writing *Hamlet* when Henry IV was assassinated. His new wife, Marie de' Medici, ruled on behalf of ten-year-old Louis XIII. The gardens were so planned as to ensure that, when she strolled in the morning or looked out the window, she saw nothing that suggested effort. Flowers were always in bloom, lawns trimmed to the smoothness of green felt. Gardeners would make a long detour rather than cross the gardens and risk being seen from the palace windows. The perfect servant was as unobtrusive as the statues that gave scale to the landscape in which Marie and her courtiers passed their perfect day. She never saw the palace completed. In 1617, her son came of age and demanded his throne. A three-year stand-off ended with him seizing power and imprisoning her. She escaped to Germany, where she died in 1642. Louis died the following year, to be

Donkey rides, 1932

Le Grand Bassin, 1913

Puppet theater, 1933

succeeded by Louis XIV, who moved the court to Versailles. With Paris no longer the seat of fashion, the palace was divided into apartments and, during the 1789 revolution, became a prison, while the gardens deteriorated into a wilderness.

In 1940, the Luftwaffe Western Command made the palace its headquarters. Blockhouses were built to protect its eastern and western approaches. The Medici Fountain became a swimming pool and lawns were dug up to plant potatoes and cabbages. *Reichsmarschall* Hermann Goering often visited the commanding General, Hugo Sperrle. "The Field Marshal's craving for luxury and public display ran a close second to that of his superior," Hitler's architect Albert Speer observed dryly. "He was also his match in corpulence." In August 1944, as Parisians retook the city, a contingent of SS seized the palace for a last stand. Sherman tanks bombarded the building from rue de Tournon, and the resistance commander threatened to call down an air strike. He probably wouldn't have done so, any more than Dietrich von Choltitz, outgoing military governor, obeyed Hitler's order to leave the city in ruins, but just the threat was enough. The Germans surrendered.

11 ***Hommage à Eugène Delacroix*** by Aimé-Jules Dalou. This twenty-feet-wide fountain with three larger-than-life bronze figures and a bust of the painter was unveiled in 1890. Funded by his friends, it shows a winged and aged Time struggling to lift a robust Glory high enough to place a palm branch before a bust of Delacroix, while Apollo, god of the Arts, has put aside his quiver and arrows to applaud.

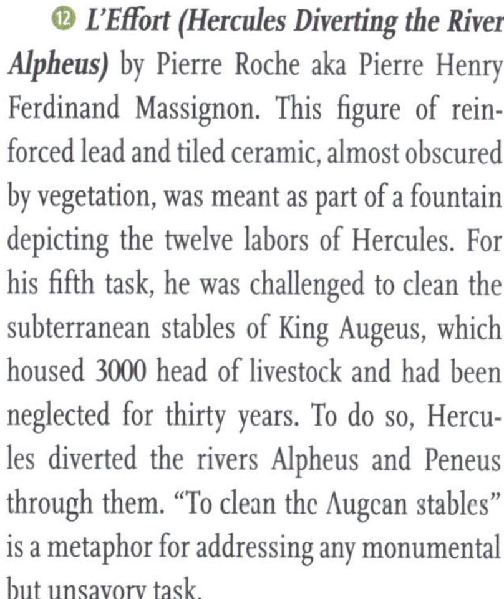

12 ***L'Effort (Hercules Diverting the River Alpheus)*** by Pierre Roche aka Pierre Henry Ferdinand Massignon. This figure of reinforced lead and tiled ceramic, almost obscured by vegetation, was meant as part of a fountain depicting the twelve labors of Hercules. For his fifth task, he was challenged to clean the subterranean stables of King Augeus, which housed 3000 head of livestock and had been neglected for thirty years. To do so, Hercules diverted the rivers Alpheus and Peneus through them. "To clean the Augean stables" is a metaphor for addressing any monumental but unsavory task.

Climb the steps into the western gardens, once part of the surrounding Carthusian monastery. Unlike the formal gardens, this part of the park acknowledges effort. Its amenities

The Drunken Silenus by Peter P. Rubens

include a créche, childrens' playground, puppet theater, tennis courts and a café.

(**JB**: We live only a short walk away, so our daughter Louise can claim to have been brought up in the Luxembourg. As a baby, we took her in her carriage for afternoon promenades. Once she learned to walk, she met other children on the swings and roundabouts of its playground, and cheered shows in the *guignol* puppet theater. On weekends, ponies give rides to children, thousands of whom had their first experiences of horseback on one of these patient Shetlands. Louise rode a horse for the first time on one of them, launching a lifelong enthusiasm for equitation.)

The statues of queens and saints continue. Further figures are scattered among the small tree-enclosed parks between the playground

and rue Guynemer. Of more than a hundred monuments in the Luxembourg, the following are of special interest.

⑬ ***Le Triomphe de Silène (The Triumph of Silenus)*** by Aimé Jules Dalou, after a painting by Peter-Paul Rubens. Silène (The Drunken Silenus), companion and tutor of wine god Dionysus (Bacchus), is often shown, as here, perched precariously on a donkey and supported by naked followers. Like the satyr, half man, half goat, he signifies how humans revert to animal behavior while drunk.

⑭ ***Monument to Paul Verlaine*** (1844-1896) by Auguste de Niederhäusern. Verlaine's importance as a poet is overshadowed by his affair with Arthur Rimbaud, for whom he abandoned his wife and child, and was jailed on charges of seducing a minor. Rimbaud moved to Africa and abandoned poetry, while Verlaine returned to Paris, where he died from alcoholism and syphilis. The monument shows an uncharacteristically glowering, almost malformed Verlaine on a plinth, decorated, puzzlingly, with three anonymous women. Described as "Prince of Poets," Verlaine was sentimentally attached to the Luxembourg. "I have no palace," he said, "but this is my royal park." [5-2]

⑮ ***Liberty Enlightening the World*** by Auguste Bartholdi. The 305-foot statue that stands on Liberty Island in New York Harbor was scaled up from this smaller bronze figure, first shown at the Paris Universal Exhibition of 1900, then donated to the Luxembourg Museum. It was placed in the gardens in 1906, but moved in 2012 to the Musée d'Orsay and replaced by the present facsimile. The American oak which shades it was planted on September 11, 2001, as a symbol of Franco-American friendship.

⑯ **Monument to Frédéric Chopin.** A bronze bust by Paul Dubois celebrating Polish pianist and composer Frédéric Chopin (1810–1849)

In the Luxembourg (Garden), 1889, Charles Courtney Curran

is supported by a plinth with the head and torso of an adoring woman in relief, possibly his mistress, author George Sand. The present bronze dates from 1992, and replaces the original, melted down in 1942 during the occupation.

⓱ ***Le Poète. Monument to Paul Éluard*** (1895–1952) by Ossip Zadkine. Éluard was a key member of the Surrealists, as well as one of the most active writers opposing the German Occupation. British bombers over France dropped copies of his 1941 poem *Liberté*, words from which are incised into the figure. In his private life, Éluard and his wife Gala shared a *ménage à trois* with artist Max Ernst, terminated when Gala became the life partner of painter Salvador Dalì. [5-3]

⓲ **Monument to Watteau** by Henri Désiré Gauquié. Jean-Antoine Watteau (1684–1721) is best known for his paintings of youthful courtiers enjoying a life of leisure and sexual dalliance in the open air.

The monument shows a fashionably dressed young woman of the period presenting roses to a bust of the painter.

People no longer play croquet on the lawns of the Luxembourg, but there's still an echo of the *clack clack* described by William Faulkner. It's the sound of people playing *petanque* or boules. The Romans played with clay balls. Before that, people used round stones or hard, unripe fruit, and on the roughest of ground. The less smooth, in fact, the better, since a skillful player exploits the terrain, aiming at a jutting pebble that will kick his ball against that of his opponent and send it skittering far from the marble-sized *cochonnet* (piglet).

Boules players, 1950

Kiosk

Most *boules* games are played on a longer pitch, and players take a three-step run before releasing the ball. However, in 1910, the owner of a café near Marseilles took pity on a friend who suffered from rheumatism and adapted the game, shortening the playing area by half and allowing the player to throw from a standing position. This new version, called by the locals "*pieds tanqués*" (feet planted), became more popular than the original. Today, the 300,000 members of the *Fédération Française de Pétanque et Jeu Provençal* are lobbying to have it included in the Olympics.

The gardens have two pitches, one next to the Orangerie, the other in a secluded corner near the Porte Croquet gate leading onto rue Guynemer. Signs warn that only members of the *Amicale Sportive de Jardins de Luxembourg* have the right to use this *piste*. There is formality in the way they play. Coats hang on a rack provided, next to the dark green painted kiosk inside which, in numbered boxes, the *boules* of regular players, made to order and calibrated to their taste, remain between matches. It may be a game, but that's no reason not to take it seriously.

18

Continue along the western fence of the park to 18 **Pavillon Davioud.** Constructed in 1867, this building with polychrome tiling and Moorish-style balconies was designed by Jean-Antoine-Gabriel Davioud. Originally a tea house, it housed classes in beekeeping before becoming the headquarters of the *Ecole d'Horticulture* (Luxembourg Horticultural School). Occasional exhibitions of contemporary art occupy it today. Next to the Pavillon is 19 the **Apiary.** The bee has special significance as the emblem of Napoléon I. Since 1856, a *Fete de Miel* (Honey Festival) has taken place here during two weeks in September.

19

Return to the formal gardens and turn uphill, into the 20 **Little or Upper Luxembourg.** In 1667, Louis XIV commanded the construction of an Observatory on the hill of Montparnasse, resting on the same meridian as the

Luxembourg palace. In Britain, an envious Charles II ordered a similar building at Greenwich, on the meridian which would become the point from which time in the British Empire was calculated.

To link Louis's Observatory to the park, Jean Chalgrin, architect of the Arc de Triomphe, created the Little Luxembourg. Two avenues of distinctively trimmed trees are divided by a wide graveled path and edged by Avenue de l'Observatoire. The trees are pruned in winter, so that, coming into leaf in the spring, the outer surfaces will line up precisely. Two identical lawns enjoy their shade, with one always off limits to visitors, allowing the grass to recover. Schools that border the park to the west, including the Lycée Montaigne and École Alsacienne, use the park as a playground, so expect to see children gathered around a teacher reading a story. Lovers habitually recline here. On Sunday mornings, *tai chi* groups, runners stretching their tendons, and other amateur athletes inhabit the space. The expanse of lycra, the grimaces, and the flexing of tanned, muscular flesh can resemble a work of contemporary dance.

The second half of the park, beginning at rue Michelet and known as the *Jardin des Grands Explorateurs* (Garden of the Great Explorers), celebrates Marco Polo (1254–1324), the Italian traveler who first brought China to the attention of Europe, and René Robert Cavelier de-La-Salle (1643–1687), one of the earliest explorers of North America. At 3 rue Michelet, the distinctive brick red 24 **Institut d'Art et d'Archéologie** has been called "the most curious building in Paris." It houses the *École d'Histoire de l'Art et d'Archéologie*, a department of the Sorbonne University. Designed in 1924, construction was finally completed in 1930. It took that long to create the terracotta sculptures that cover the exterior, the work of Paul Bigot, the ceramicist who also designed the studio building on rue Campagne-Premiere occupied by Man Ray. Crafted at the Sèvres factory, the reliefs replicate portions of the Parthenon sculptures from Athens, others from ancient temples in Rome, as well as figures from Assyria, Egypt and Angkor Wat.

Statues spaced through the *Jardin des Grands Explorateurs* symbolize the four stages of the day. In 22 ***L'Aurore*** (Dawn) by François Jouffroy, a sleeping man wakes as a woman, representing sunrise, stands over him. In 23 ***Midi*** (Mid-Day) by Jean Joseph Perraud, a hunter with a sling and a hunting horn is refreshed by a woman from an ewer. For 25 ***Le Crépuscule*** (Twilight) Gustave Grauk depicts a farming couple relaxing at twilight, he leaning on the plow, she holding a sickle. In the enigmatic 26 ***La Nuit*** by Charles Gumery, a man and his dog are about to be seduced by a mysterious robed figure representing Night.

At the end of the Little Luxembourg is the 27 ***Fontaine des Quatre-Parties-du-Monde*** (Fountain of the Four Corners of the World). Davioud commissioned the fountain in 1867 as part of Napoléon III's program to modernize Paris, but because of the Franco-Prussian War and the Commune, it wasn't completed until 1876. Four bronze figures by Jean-Baptiste Carpeaux surmount a globe by Pierre Legrain engraved with the signs of the zodiac. Louis Villeminot created the garlands that surround the pedestal. Below are turtles, dolphins and *hippocampi* (sea horses), the work of Emmanuel Frémiet. Carpeaux's figures represent Asia, Europe, America and Africa, with the chain around the ankle of Africa, crushed by the foot of America, signifying the United States' rejection of the slave trade after the Civil War.

A master at depicting the female body, Carpeaux bypassed the plump art school models with their repertoire of Greco-Roman poses and instead used young showgirls. Their slim

23

25

26

bodies were not to every taste. One critic called them "four undressed, gangly women [who] struggle with a bewildered and furious air under a large globe that they do not support." Another complained that "these thin, unhealthy women, with their wasted flanks, their elongated, furrowed thighs, are twisting around in a bizarre circle without any grace. One has to ask by what aberration of spirit, eye and hand one could compose such a group of wild, vulgar and wrinkled dancers." Carpeaux died in 1875, so never saw it become one of the most treasured ornaments of artistic Paris.

Exit the gardens at Place de l'Observatoire. The sky above the Observatory became the background to one of Man Ray's most memorable canvases, the 1934 *Á l'heure de l'Observatoire, les amoureux* (*The hour of the Observatory, the Lovers*). Painted to mark the end of Ray's relationship with his model and lover Lee Miller, it shows her elongated lips drifting through the sky like a crimson dirigible. [5-4]

(28) **A statue of Michel Ney** by François Rude stands at the intersection of Boulevards St. Michel and Montparnasse, next to (29) the

café/restaurant **Le Closerie des Lilas** (*The Lilac Hedge*). One of Napoléon's most able marshals, Ney rejoined the regular army after the emperor's exile to Elba in 1814, only to switch his allegiance back when Bonaparte escaped and returned to France for the "hundred days" that ended at Waterloo. Accused of treason, Ney chose to be judged by the army he'd deserted, and was shot in December 1815 against the wall (now a metal fence) opposite the Closerie. When the officer in command of the firing squad couldn't bring himself to give the order, Ney did so for him. In 1853, a penitent government commissioned this statue of Ney leading troops into battle, and added a plinth enumerating the achievements of a man Napoléon called "the bravest of the brave." Walk ends. Turn right on Boulevard du

The Execution of Marshal Ney (1868) by Jean-Léon Gérôme

ART GALLERY OF THE LUXEMBOURG GARDENS

Clockwise from top: *In the Luxembourg Gardens,* 1879, John Singer Sargent; *At the Luxembourg Gardens,* 1883, Pierre-Auguste Renoir; *The Luxembourg Gardens,* 1901, Henri Matisse; *Terrace in the Luxembourg Gardens,* 1886, Vincent van Gogh

From top: *Luxembourg Gardens*, 1906, William James Glackens; *A Nanny in the Luxembourg Gardens*, *c.1872*, Edgar Degas; *The Luxembourg Gardens*, 1887, Albert Edelfelt; *Jardin du Luxembourg*, c.1948, Lois Mailou Jones

Montparnasse and follow to intersection with Boulevard Raspail and **Metro Vavin (Lines 4, 6 and 12.)**

HEMINGWAY AND THE LUXEMBOURG

The Closerie des Lilas was a favorite writing location of Ernest Hemingway. He also admired the monument to Ney. "He looked very fine, Marshal Ney in his top-boots, gesturing with his sword among the green new horse-chestnut leaves." Hemingway (1899–1961) lived in Paris, on and off, from 1921 to 1928. [5-5] The park played an important part in both his work and life. After writing there all morning, he would stroll down to visit (30) **Gertrude Stein and Alice Toklas** on **27 rue de Fleurus** or (31) **Sylvia Beach** at her bookshop on rue de l'Odéon. As he couldn't afford restaurants, "the best place to go," he wrote, "was the Luxembourg gardens where you saw and smelled nothing to eat all the way from the Place de l'Observatoire to the rue de Vaugirard." He even claimed that, in hard times, he'd killed and eaten the Luxembourg's pigeons. Given the alertness of Paris's pigeons and Hemingway's lumbering frame, one has to view this story with suspicion.

In 1928, Hemingway and his second wife Pauline lived at 32 **6 rue Férou**, almost opposite 33 the **Luxembourg Museum**. Situated on the western side of the palace, next to the Orangerie, it's entered from rue de Vaugirard. Before the national collection of modern art was consolidated in the Musée d'Orsay, its paintings were shared among the city's galleries. This small museum held Impressionist works, mostly by Paul Cézanne. As part of her efforts to curb Hemingway's rambling descriptive style, Gertrude Stein urged that he study Cézanne, who contemplated his subjects for hours, then painted only those items with the underlying shapes—cylinder, sphere, cone—that, to him, carried some hint of the divine.[5-6]

Hemingway and Pauline, c.1927

Hemingway often had the museum all to himself. He was also sometimes a little drunk, having sampled Alice Toklas's *Confiture de vieux garcons* (Old Boy's Preserves). In a large ceramic or glass container, she placed strawberries, peaches, cherries and other soft fruit as they came into season. Sugar was added, and plentiful quantities of cognac. The fruit sank and, in the course of a year, created a compote, leaving a layer of sweet fruit-flavored alcohol, which she decanted and served

Gertrude Stein with Jack "Bumby" Hemingway, 1924

The Luxembourg Gardens, 1928

as an *aperitif.* Hemingway imbibed freely, often on an empty stomach, which may explain his somewhat incoherent praise of Cézanne. "I was learning something from the painting of Cézanne," he wrote, "that made writing simple true sentences far from enough to make the stories have the dimensions that I was trying to put in them. I was learning very much from him, but I was not articulate enough to explain it to anyone. Besides, it was a secret." The "secret" was what Hemingway called the "iceberg" effect or theory of omission; writing which articulated only a fraction of the meaning, the rest remaining hidden. Using this method, boasted Cézanne, one could "conquer Paris with a carrot."

F. SCOTT FITZGERALD AND THE LUXEMBOURG

Two sites adjacent to the Luxembourg figure in the life and work of Scott and Zelda Fitzgerald. In 1925, Honoria, daughter of their friends Gerald and Sara Murphy, introduced Zelda to her dancing teacher,

Lubov Egorova, a former principal dancer with Diaghilev, who had opened a school in Paris. Three years later, Zelda announced her ambition to revive her childhood ambition to dance. Hoping to join Diaghilev's Ballets Russe, now based in Monaco, she enrolled with Egorova.

The Fitzgeralds arrived back in Paris in April 1928. They usually lived in hotels, but the Murphys had leased a fourth floor apartment at 34 **58 rue de Vaugirard** while they waited for architect Michel Roux-Spitz to complete his art deco showpiece building at nearby 35 **14 rue Guynemer**, in which they'd bought the penthouse. (Scott used it as the basis of Abe North's home in *Tender Is the Night*.) As the rue de Vaugirard apartment was now empty, the Fitzgeralds moved in.

At 27, Zelda was well past the optimum age for the ballet, but Egorova assured her that, while she might never dance with Diaghilev, she could hope for a career, providing she followed the strict regimen of four hours practice seven days a week. Scott volunteered to pay the $300 a month for lessons, but Zelda refused, insisting she could make the money by selling stories and articles. Dancing was to be her declaration of artistic independence. As she wrote of herself later, "Reaching

Gerald and Sara Murphy

Scott and Zelda with daughter Scottie at their apartment in Paris

her goal, she would drive the devils that had driven her. In proving herself, she would achieve peace."

In July, Scott finally met James Joyce. Once he confessed his admiration to Sylvia Beach and his shyness about such a meeting, she invited both to dinner at the apartment on rue de l'Odéon she shared with Adrienne Monnier. Scott arrived drunk and, as with Edith Wharton and other writers he respected, behaved with grotesque effusiveness, kneeling before Joyce and praising him so extravagantly that Joyce asked Sylvia if he was mentally disturbed. As a souvenir of the evening, Scott inscribed a copy of *The Great Gatsby* to Sylvia, adding a sketch of the dinner. It shows Joyce simply as a pair of spectacles, a small moustache, and a halo.

The more Zelda practiced, the more friends were convinced she would never dance professionally. "There was something dreadfully grotesque in her intensity," wrote Sara Murphy. "One could see the muscles individually stretch and pull. Her legs looked muscular and ugly. One held one's breath until it was over. Thank God she couldn't see what she looked like." Theater producers visiting the school raised Zelda's hopes, only to crush them by admitting she interested them

Jardin du Luxembourg, 1878, Charles Marville

solely as a possible novelty dancer at the Folies-Bergère, demonstrating the current dance craze, the Shimmy. Life with an exhausted Zelda was reduced, in Scott's notes, to "drinking and general unpleasantness." In July and August, he was twice arrested for public intoxication, and spent the night in jail. He was bailed out by the only person he felt he could ask, the African-American club owner Ada "Bricktop" Smith.

He continued to struggle with *Tender Is the Night*. The Murphys, aware that they played some part in the novel, which he would dedicate to them, wearied of his intrusive scrutiny. He was still infatuated with young actress Lois Wilson, inspiration for the novel's Rosemary Hoyt, and wrote her romantic letters. The knowledge that she was seeing other men tormented him with jealous fantasies that he put into the mind of his alter ego Dick Diver. "Only the image of a third person, even a vanished one, entering into his relation with Rosemary was needed to throw him off his balance and send through him waves of pain, misery, desire, desperation. The vividly pictured hand on Rosemary's cheek, the quicker breath, the white excitement of the event viewed from outside, the inviolable secret warmth within."

WALK 6

FROM THE OPÉRA TO THE LOUVRE: THE BELLE ÉPOQUE

START: Metro Opéra (Lines 3, 7 and 8)
FINISH: Metro Palais Royal Musée du Louvre (Line 1)

FROM THE OPÉRA TO THE LOUVRE: THE BELLE ÉPOQUE

1. **Opéra de Paris**
2. **Grand Hôtel**
3. **Hôtel Scribe:** 5 rue Scribe
4. **Site of American Express office:** 11 rue Scribe
5. **Harry's New York Bar:** 5 rue Daunou
6. **Ciro's:** 7 rue Daunou
7. **Olympia:** 28 Boulevard des Capucines
8. **Church of the Madeleine**
9. **Lavatory Madeleine**
10. **Village Royale:** 25 rue Royale
11. **Christian Dior's Apartment:** 10 rue Royale
12. **Maxim's:** 3 rue Royale
13. **Place de la Concorde**
14. **Orangerie**
15. **Jeu de Paume**
16. **Hôtel de la Marine:** 2 Pl. de la Concorde
17. **Automobile Club of France:** 6 Pl. de la Concorde
18. **Hôtel de Crillon:** 10 Pl. de la Concorde
19. **Chancery of the United States Embassy**
20. **Hôtel de Saint-Florentin:** 258 rue de Rivoli
21. **Smith and Company Bookshop:** 248 rue de Rivoli
22. **Site of Swedish and Norwegian Circles:** 242 rue de Rivoli
23. **Meurice:** 228 rue de Rivoli
24. **Angelina:** 226 rue de Rivoli
25. **Galignani:** 224 rue de Rivoli
26. **Ivan Turgenevs Apartment:** 210 rue de Rivoli
27. **Leo Tolstoy's Apartment:** 206 rue de Rivoli
28. **Camille Pissarro's Apartment:** 204 rue de Rivoli
29. **Place des Pyramides**
30. **Palace of the Louvre**
31. **Carrousel du Louvre:** 99 rue de Rivoli

(!) **Maison Paquin:** 3 Rue de la Paix

Previous page: *Boulevard des Capucines*, c.1880–1890, Jean Béraud

Gal.Lafayette
Chaussée d' Antin La Fayette
Boulevard Haussmann
Rue Auber
Palais Garnier
Rue Halévy
Rue du Havre
Boulevard des Italiens
Quàtre Septembre
Opéra
Madeleine
Boulevard des Capucines
Avenue de l' Opera
Rue de la Paix
Rue Royale
Rue Cambon
Place Vendôme
Rue Saint Honoré
Pyramides
Concorde
Rue de Rivoli
Rue des Pyramides
Place de la Concorde
Palais Royal
Jardin des Tuileries
Pont de la Concorde
Palais Royal-Musée du Louvre
Saine
Musée du Louvre
Jardin du Carrousel
Assemblée Nationale
Musée d' Orsay
Musée d' Orsay
Pont Royal
Pont du Carrousel
Quai du Louvre
Quai Malaquais
Solférino
Beaux Arts Academy
Pont des Arts
Rue Bonaparte
Rue des Seine
1000 ft
250 m

Ascend from **Metro Opéra** (Lines 3, 7 and 8) into **Place de l'Opéra.** ❶ The **Opéra de Paris**, often called the **Palais Garnier**, announces its presence from eight blocks away. (Architect Charles Garnier persuaded town planner Georges-Eugène Haussmann not to plant trees along the Avenue de l'Opéra since they might block the view.) Up close, however, it doesn't disappoint. In 1875, the empress Eugénie had her first look at the building ordered by her husband, Louis-Napoléon III, as the *pièce de résistance* of the Right Bank's prestigious new *quartier.* "It's spectacular, M'sieur Garnier," she agreed, contemplating its gilded angels, rearing winged horses and naked Bacchantes, "but I don't recognize the style. It's not Renaissance; not Baroque; not Classical. What style is it?" Garnier, with a *savoir-faire* that belied his 35 years, responded imperturbably "Why, your imperial highness, it's *your* style!"

Almost a hundred sculptors, painters and mosaicists worked on the façade. Below the busts of composers are Charles Gumery's gilded *Harmony and Poetry.* Lower still are groups representing various arts: *Poetry* by François Jouffroy, Jean-Baptiste Guillaume's *Instrumental Music,* Jean-Joseph Perraud's *Lyric Drama* and, most notably, Jean-

Dance

The Opéra Garnier staircase, 1877, Louis Béroud

Baptiste Carpeaux's *Dance*. It was Garnier's suggestion that his friend Carpeaux create this group, showing Bacchantes celebrating the god of wine. They cavort drunkenly around the figure of Bacchus, crowned with vine leaves and waving a tambourine. Moralists at the time pelted the figures with ink. Some suggested that decent women would shun performances in the new building as long as they had to pass anything so outrageous. (For more about the Opéra and its famous Phantom, see the note at the end of this walk.)

Napoleon III and Eugénie

Nana, 1877 by Édouard Manet

Cross rue Auber to 2 the **Grand Hôtel.** When Eugénie opened this hotel in 1862, she said its luxury reminded her of the imperial palaces. In its 514 rooms and suites, courtesans met their lovers, flirted with the "green fairy" of absinthe, or used jeweled Pravaz syringes to inject heroin—legal, like most drugs, under this complaisant regime. In Émile Zola's novel *Nana*, its protagonist, once a star at the Opéra, now a prostitute, dies there of smallpox, while, below her window, crowds applaud troops leaving for the Franco-Prussian war that would end with France humiliated and Louis-Napoléon in exile. His fall ushered in the *belle époque* when, in the words of one historian, "European civilization achieved its greatest power in global politics, and also exerted its maximum influence upon peoples outside Europe." During those years, the Opéra and its surrounding hotels, cafés and department stores would come to seem, as some called it, "the center of the world."

Occupying the ground floor of the hotel, the Café de la Paix was popular with Oscar Wilde and Marcel Proust, both of whom lived nearby. Guy de Maupassant used it in stories, and Arthur Conan Doyle had Sherlock Holmes join Dr. Watson there. Edward VII, as

The Store Front Of Couturier Doucet, Jean Beraud (detail)

An Elegant Evening, c1890, Victor Gabriel Gilbert (detail)

Café de Paris, Albert Guillaume

ALPHONSE MUCHA'S ART NOUVEAU POSTERS

Prince of Wales, relished the parade of fashionable women on Boulevard des Capucines, though a 1927 guidebook for Americans took a more cynical view. "It is a great vantage point to watch the promenading tourists, the 'Ladies of the Boulevards,' the real Parisians, the Gigolos, the male Perverts, the taxicabs, the hawkers, the beggars. Old women and old men in rags and tatters picking up discarded cigarette stubs." The café figured in Ernest Hemingway's story *My Old Man,* although he had other—and humiliating—memories of the place. In December 1921, for their first Christmas in Paris, he and new wife Hadley dined there, but didn't bring enough cash to pay the check. While Hadley sat over her cold coffee, Ernest took a cab back to their hotel for more money. The experience convinced them to move from their already cheap hotel into an even cheaper apartment.

Café de la Paix, 1927

Hemingway and Hadley, 1920

Continue along Boulevard des Capucines to rue Scribe. The Second Empire façade of 3 the **Hôtel Scribe** dominates the area. A plaque on the wall records that the Jockey Club, a bastion of privilege and tradition, occupied the first floor from 1863 to 1913. During the winter of 1944-45, the foreign press corps congregated at the hotel since it alone had reliable hot water. New Yorker correspondent Janet Flanner rushed through her breakfast in order to enjoy a bath, only to find, as a friend put it, "her bearded friend Hemingway wallowing there."

Frantic (1988)

Roman Polanski used it in his 1988 thriller *Frantic*, which had Harrison Ford clambering over the roofs of Paris to rescue his kidnapped wife. On December 28, 1895, it was also the site of the first screening by Auguste and Louis Lumière of their films, an event from which most historians date the birth of cinema. The Lumières were instrumental in turning a carnival novelty into an industry that radically altered our vision of the world. Renting the basement Salon Indien, they hung a white sheet at one end of the room and, at the other, on a stepladder, placed their *cinématographe*, a combined camera and projector. Fewer than thirty people were present. Word quickly spread, however, and thousands attended in January. For the rest of 1896, the brothers toured world capitals with their films, while their cameramen demonstrated the *cinématographe* in Australia, China, Japan and South Africa, sending back films of each, the first steps towards an international cinema.

Lumière brothers cinematographe, 1896

At one time, the presence of 4 the **American Express office** at **No. 11** (now closed) made this short street one of the most important in Paris for expatriates. In its basement, they could meet friends, collect mail, change dollars into francs, cash travelers' cheques, and phone the US, a time-consuming and awkward business in contrast to today's technology. Stanley Donen's thriller *Charade* recreated the office in 1963 for a scene between Cary Grant and Audrey Hepburn, one of many movie connections with this address.

Cross Boulevard des Capucines and enter rue Daunou. Since 1911, 5 **No. 5** has housed **Harry's New York Bar**. American jockey Tod Sloan, believing Paris needed a place where visitors could drink in familiar surroundings, bought a Manhattan bar and shipped its fixtures and furnishings across the Atlantic. Everyone at Harry's spoke English, a fact promoted in its advertising, which urged clients to memorize a phonetic rendering of the address as "Sank Roo Da Noo." Celebrities who drank there include Humphrey Bogart, Rita Hayworth and the Duke of Windsor. Irish author Brendan Behan worked on the bar in 1948-9. Reputedly its barmen invented the Bloody Mary, Sidecar, Monkey Gland and other cock-

From left: Humphrey Bogart, Rita Hayworth; George Gershwin

tails. It's also claimed that George Gershwin composed *An American in Paris* on its basement piano, fueled by mugs of Black Velvet: Guinness stout and champagne. During World War I, Harry's attracted members of the American Field Service, including Ernest Hemingway.

Next door, at ⑥ **No. 7** (now a theater), was **Ciro's** restaurant and cabaret. Opened in 1912, it had branches in London, Monte Carlo, Deauville and other resorts. Popular with what restaurant critic Julian Street called in 1929 "prominent cigarette endorsers, beauty-cream endorsers, bedspring endorsers, eminent divorcées and jewel-wearers," Ciro's wasn't cheap. "If you must forget to bring either your platinum cigarette case or your pocketbook," he warned, "let it be the former, for however much you may need a cigarette you will need your pocketbook more."

Return to Boulevard des Capucines. In 1888, in the courtyard at ⑦ **No. 28**, Joseph Oller, founder of the Moulin Rouge, installed a *Montagnes Russes* (Russian Mountains) ride, an early version of the roller coaster. This undulating slide, four stories high, sent young men and their squealing girlfriends on a vertiginous trip back to the ground. When the police closed it as a fire risk, Oller replaced it with a 2000-

seat auditorium, the **Olympia**. Other theaters closed for the summer, but the Olympia stayed open to try out new talent. Hoping that *boulevardiers* would welcome light relief after a diet of grand opera, he presented contortionists, acrobats, dog and pony acts, and installed a wax museum in the basement where they could goggle at recreations of history's bloodier events and the latest murders.

In April 1893, the Olympia's debut presentation featured the Moulin Rouge's star can can dancer Louise Weber, alias *La Goulue* (The Greedy One). She shared the program with American dancer Loie Fuller, whose whirling dances in layers of chiffon made her a fountain of colored light. Oller's biggest star was Jeanne Bourgeois aka Mistinguett. Her legs, insured for half a million francs, and her saucy songs, often performed with much younger lover Maurice Chevalier, became a sensation. "Her voice, slightly off-key," said Jean Cocteau, "was that of the Parisian street hawkers—the husky, trailing voice of the Paris people." In the 1920s, Olympia, like most music halls, converted to cinema, but in 1954 returned to live performance under a new entrepreneur, Bruno Coquatrix, who would present the greatest French and international stars.

Ciro's menu cover, 1923

Olympia, 1914

Mistinguett

Olympia, 1893, Jules Chéret

Return to Boulevard des Capucines and continue to Place de la Madeleine, dominated by 8 the **Church of the Madeleine.** Political progress which, in most countries, occurs in an orderly manner, takes place in France in fits and starts, with periods of grumbling tranquility interrupted by outbreaks of violence and disorder. Public works become hostages to fortune, repurposed according to the fashion of the day.

In 1764, Louis XV ordered a church built at one end of newly-constructed rue Royale, looking towards Place Louis XV, now Place de la Concorde, and its centerpiece, his equestrian statue in the robes of a Roman general. Work began on a conventional building, but Louis died in 1774, and the next architect demolished most of it, in favor of a design which, in line with Louis's statue, evoked ancient Rome. The builders had completed a peristyle of Corinthian columns when the 1789 revolution again halted work. The revolutionaries, hostile to religion, considered completing the building but using it as a library, a public ballroom or a market. However, when Napoléon seized power, he decided it should be a temple to the glory of the *Grande Armée*, on which he relied to win his battles. His architect kept to the Roman theme, retaining the existing columns, but used hidden iron beams to support a single hall with three domes, inspired by Rome's Baths of Caracalla. After Napoléon's fall, the building became once again a political football. Louis XVIII suggested making it a symbol of penance for the sins of the Revolution. His successors briefly considered using it as a railroad

The Madeleine, 1837

MAISON PAQUIN: 3 RUE DE LA PAIX

Jeanne Paquin, a pioneer of Belle Époque fashion, transformed haute couture from her boutique at 3 rue de la Paix. While her name may not shine as brightly as Charles Frederick Worth or Paul Poiret, her influence on the fashion industry is undeniable.

Born Jeanne Marie Charlotte Beckers in 1869, she trained as a dressmaker and quickly rose to prominence with her creativity and ambition. After marrying Isidore Paquin in 1890, she launched Maison Paquin in 1895, establishing it as a hub of elegance and innovation.

Workers leaving the Maison Paquin, c.1900, Jean Beraud

Paquin revolutionized fashion marketing, being the first couturier to send models to public events like operas and horse races. Her designs, celebrating femininity and grace, became a favorite among the elite.

By the 1900 Exposition Universelle, Maison Paquin had gained international acclaim, with boutiques in London, New York, Madrid, and Buenos Aires. At its peak, her business employed over 2,000 people. In 1913, she became the first female couturier to receive the French Legion of Honour.

Paquin retired in 1920 and passed away in 1936. Although Maison Paquin closed in 1956, her innovative spirit and contributions to haute couture remain an enduring legacy.

Studio Paquin, c.1905, Isaac Israels

Five Hours at Paquin, 1906, Henri Gervex

Interior of the Madeleine

terminal, and it wasn't until 1842 that it was consecrated as a church, dedicated to the Madeleine, i.e., Saint Mary Magdalene.

A sculpted Last Judgment bridges the main entrance, above bronze doors with reliefs illustrating the Ten Commandments. Statues of 33 saints, including Geneviève, Joan and Denis, surround the exterior of the church. Unusually, Denis, who was decapitated by the Romans, is not shown carrying his head, although four statues at the rear lost theirs when a shell from Germany's massive *Paris Geschutz* gun landed nearby in 1918. Around the high altar, itself elevated on marble steps, statues show angels carrying the Madeleine into heaven, where, in Jules-Claude Ziegler's dome painting, *The History of Christianity*, she is seen being welcomed by Christ and the assembled saints—including, in his ermine coronation robes, Napoléon I.

Exit the church and circle it to find 9 the **Lavatory Madeleine**. Built in 1904, this subterranean restroom, now designated a national monument, is the most luxurious such public facility in Paris. Situated near the southeast corner of the church and originally reserved for women, it was designed by Porcher and Company, who proudly signed their work in art nouveau lettering embedded in the wall. It boasts individual stalls, each with a sink and mirror, as well as varnished mahogany woodwork, stained-glass windows, ornate ceramics, mosaics, brass fittings, floor-to-ceiling tiles, and a shoeshine stand. An attendant sits in a windowed office, a contrast to the *"dames pipis"* of cafés and hotels, stern guardians who once knitted stoically while male and female clients defecated on all sides, and grudgingly provided a scrap of towel and fragment of soap, pointedly presenting their saucer for a tip.

Continue into rue Royale. Until the 16th century, this was a muddy lane ending in the marsh which Place de la Concorde replaces. In 1746, the royal guard of Musketeers, made famous by Alexandre Dumas, built barracks nearby, and the street became the Marché d'Aguesseau, supplying produce to the garrison. Two years later, the creation of Place de la Concorde attracted civilian residents, and the lane was transformed

Rue Royale, 1915

into rue Royale. Today, it rivals Los Angeles' Rodeo Drive and London's Lower Bond Street for luxury, with branches of Chanel, Gucci, Dior, Prada and Lalique. The Dior boutique at **No. 25** also extends into the Cité Berryer passage, connecting rue Royale to rue Boissy-d'Anglas, which in 1992 became a shopping precinct, the 10 **Village Royale**, with further high-end boutiques and a bistro, Le Village. At 11 **No. 10**, couturier **Christian Dior** made his home for many years in a high-ceilinged apartment filled with plants and books.

At 12 **No. 3**, **Maxim's** restaurant opened its doors in 1893. By 1929, according to food writer Julian Street, "its name stood throughout the world as a symbol of nocturnal dissipation." He accused proprietor Eugéne Cornuché of "encouraging the presence of a class of woman, more or less attached to the establishment, whose business it was to attract male visitors." (Cornuché admitted this, and even boasted of seating the prettiest where they could be seen from the street.) Men went to Maxim's to show off their mistresses or look for new ones, which encouraged the *poules de luxe* to wear their most extravagant gowns. Jean Cocteau described these women as "an accumulation of velvet, lace, ribbons [and] diamonds. To undress one calls for three weeks' advance notice; it's like moving house." As the evening became less inhibited, items of clothing were sometimes discarded, and pieces of jewelry lost. Workmen renovating the premises in the 1960s, pushing the red plush banquettes away from the walls, "exposed," according to cultural historian Joseph Wechsberg, "heaps of jewelry, gold coins and garters that had been lost in the long wild nights."

Colette featured Maxim's in *Gigi* and her *Cheri* novels, but it was the decision of Franz Lehár to use the restaurant in his 1905 operetta *The Merry Widow* that launched its international reputation. His dissolute hero, Count Danilo, sings "At Maxim's once again/I swim in pink champagne/When people asks what bliss is/I simply answer, '*This*

The Belle Époque, The Bar at Maxim's, c.1890, Pierre-Victor Galland

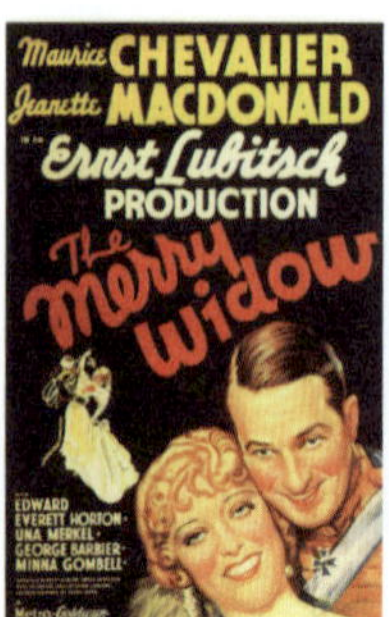

From left: A poster of The Merry Widow (1934), Aristotle Onassis and Maria Callas and the Duke and Duchess of Windsor

is!" Ernst Lubitsch's film with Maurice Chevalier as Danilo further established its credentials.

Such was the fame of Maxim's that revolutions and even wars left it unaffected. During World War I, a black market flourished at its bar. According to a police report, "At Maxim's, a fat man with the ribbon of the Legion d'Honneur explained to a couple of regulars how he got cigarettes via his member of parliament." In 1940, the owners came to an arrangement with the Occupation. Hermann Göering and Germany's ambassador to Vichy, Otto Abetz, were regular clients. A German manager guaranteed freedom from food rationing. The Resistance closed it down in 1944 but it opened again in 1946, its reputation even higher. When Pan Am started its New York-Paris route in February 1946, passengers enjoyed *haute cuisine* prepared by its chefs. Celebrities who ate at the Paris original included Aristotle Onassis and Maria Callas, the Duke and Duchess of Windsor, and millionaires Porfirio Rubirosa and Barbara Hutton. Otto Preminger also chose it for a scene in his film of Françoise Sagan's *Bonjour Tristesse*, with Jean Seberg musing on her meaningless life while Juliette Gréco murmurs George Auric's melancholy theme tune.

Under Cornuché's management, Maxim's had become a showcase of *art nouveau,* with varnished *boiserie,* a ceiling and screens of stained glass, and bronzes and lamps featuring beautiful women in flowing gowns, or no gowns at all. Julian Street scorned its "walls inanely appliqued with festoons and loops of wood and brass; those lighting fixtures tortured to the forms of calla lilies; those mural pictures, pale and wan." But modern taste re-embraced the style and in 1981, the interior was declared a national monument. By then, the Maxim brand was owned by couturier Pierre Cardin—who, ironically, had once been refused admittance to the restaurant because he was wearing a turtleneck instead of a shirt and tie. He licensed the name to a variety of luxury products and

Jean Seberg in *Bonjour Tristesse* (1958)

New Year's Eve party, 1949

also created a museum of *art nouveau* furniture and objects on its upper floors.

(**JB**: After the millennium, Maxim's gained a reputation as ostentatious and over-priced. I only ate there once but it was all one had feared. Champagne arrived, unordered, almost as soon as we sat down, and a strolling violinist paused by our table to play something soupily romantic. Of the food, I remember mainly that the quails' eggs which garnished the salad had been hard-boiled in a mold that gave them the same *art nouveau* fluting as the décor. Eggs as art? Only in Paris.)

The end of rue Royale opens onto ⑬ Place de la Concorde. With its obelisk and fountains, the Tuileries Garden on one side, on the other the Champs-Élysées, and with a view across the Seine to the Assemblée Nationale, this is one of the world's most majestic plazas.

A number of 17th and 18th century buildings fill the north and east sides of Concorde. They include (14) the **Orangerie** and (15) **Jeu de Paume**, (16) the **Hôtel de la Marine**, (17) the **Automobile Club of France**, (18) the **Hôtel de Crillon**, and (19) the **Chancery of the United States Embassy**. The Orangerie and Jeu de Paume, both now art galleries, are the only major buildings to survive from the former Tuileries Palace, destroyed in 1871 during the anarchist uprising known as the Commune. The Hôtel de la Marine, once the headquarters of the French Navy, is now a national monument and museum. Next to it is the Automobile Club of France, while the former residence of the Duc de Crillon was converted in 1909 into one of the world's most prestigious hotels. The last building looking onto Concorde is the Chancery of the United States Embassy. One of four Embassy premises in Paris, it houses the office of the ambassador. The four-story building follows 18th century style but was only built in 1931.

Since, during his long but troubled reign, weak, womanizing Louis XV (1710–1774) embraced any honor offered by his oppressed subjects, he was delighted when the merchants of Paris offered to pay for a mounted

From left: Automobile Club of France; the Madeleine; Hôtel de la Marine

statue in his honor. They hoped it would attract people to this empty area at the edge of the city, which was ripe for development. But it took 20 years for the octagonal square to be completed to Louis's satisfaction. He demanded stone balustrades to enclose the plaza, with a moat thirty feet wide and ten deep, to drain the site and also to keep out riffraff. Vain hope. Squatters turned the moat into a shanty town, and invaded the plaza to build shops and even houses.

Sculptor Edmé Bouchardon initially wanted his statue to show the king in ordinary dress, but after his victory at the Battle of Fontenoy in 1745, Louis preferred to appear as a conquering Roman general, complete with toga and laurel wreath. Finally erected in 1763, the monument survived only until 1792, after the common people, exasperated by the excesses of Louis's successor, rose in revolt. In August of that year they renamed the square Place de la Revolution. Louis's statue was melted down, and a guillotine erected

Statue of Louis XV, 1766

in its place. Of the 2,498 people executed in Paris during the Revolution, 1,119 died here, including its two early leaders, Georges Danton and Maximilien Robespierre, and both Louis XVI and his queen Marie-Antoinette. So much blood spilled onto the stones that the stench lingered for years, and even dogs shunned the place.

In 1790, the Pont de la Concorde connected the square to the Left Bank, and Place de la Concorde became a showpiece. Jacques-Louis David, favorite painter of the Revolution, suggested that two sculptures by Antoine Coysevox, of Fame and Mercury riding the winged horse Pegasus, which once stood at the entrance to Louis XIV's chateau at Marly, would look better over the gateway leading from the Tuileries. In 1836, the square acquired an obelisk of Rameses II, a gift from Egypt, and between 1836 and 1840 gained its most striking addition: two fountains, modeled after those of Saint Peter's in Rome, one devoted to rivers, with allegorical figures representing the Rhone and the Rhine, the oth-

Execution of Louis XVI on 21 January 1793, facing the empty pedestal where the statue of his grandfather, Louis XV, had stood, 1794

Fame riding the Pegasus

Fountain of the Seas

Nantes stone blockhouse

er celebrating the Atlantic and Mediterranean oceans. In 1838, eight stone blockhouses were installed around the periphery , each topped with a statue representing one of France's great cities. An entrepreneur leased that celebrating the city of Nantes, turning it into a bar and brothel. Drinks were served outside, and the interior provided a quiet and private place for the *poules* to do business.

Artists were never as attracted to the Hôtel de Crillon as to the nearby Meurice and Ritz. Ernest Hemingway mentions it in *The Sun Also Rises* and *The Snows of Kilimanjaro,* though it's unlikely he spent much time in this haunt of diplomats, crowned heads and oil sheiks (one of whom now owns it). After World War I, American delegates to the Peace Conference stayed here, and during the German occupation of World War II it housed the offices of Paris's military governor. More recently, the hotel enjoyed a brief scandal when it was learned that underage girls, known as *sucettes* (lollipops), from some of the better *lycées* would pedal over after school, lock their bicycles to the railings, take a seat in the bar, and wait for some nice gentleman to offer them an *eau-à-la-menthe* and invite them up to their room.

Place de la Concorde, c.1872, Joaquín Pallarés Allustante

In 1979, Margaret Thatcher, Britain's newly-elected Prime Minister, was staying here when she met President Valéry Giscard d'Estaing for the first time. She was all business—unlike the President, who was more interested in the view from her window. How many young couples, he mused, had looked out on Concorde after their first night of marriage? He himself had spent his honeymoon here. In fact, he realized belatedly, it had been *in this very suite*. Moved by the memory, he interrupted the "Iron Lady" to explain. She paused while he spoke—then continued, without comment, to lecture him on the economy. Giscard left the meeting with a clearer idea of the kind of woman he would be facing; one conspicuously lacking in the gentler emotions.

Enter rue de Rivoli. With this spacious avenue, half a mile long, running alongside the gardens of the Tuileries, Napoléon I hoped to cre-

Rue de Rivoli, 1855

ate an airy colonnade in the Roman style. For most of its length, it is now closed to traffic, except for taxis and commercial vehicles. This has restored some of its former tranquility, but the arcades are still marred by money changers, dubious art galleries and gift shops.

There are, nevertheless, many sites of historical interest. 20 **No. 258** is the **Hôtel de Saint-Florentin**; formerly Hôtel de Talleyrand. Plaques commemorate the 50th anniversary of the Economic Recovery Act of 1948, which was signed here. Named for Secretary of State George Marshall, the "Marshall Plan" provided economic assistance to restore stability in postwar Europe. 21 The **Smith and Company Bookshop** at **248** was formerly W.H. Smith's, a branch of the chain of British bookshops which opened here in 1903. Its first-floor tearoom was the favorite meeting place of Irish expatriate author Samuel Beckett. At 22 **No. 242**, arms manufacturer and philanthropist **Alfred Nobel** wrote the will setting up the annual Nobel Prizes.

At 23 **No. 228**, the **Meurice**, one of the most conservative of the city's 5-star hotels, has been the choice of many crowned heads visiting Paris, including Queen Victoria in 1855—an entire floor was renovated for the

From left: Samuel Beckett; Alfred Nobel; Salvador Dalì

occasion—and, in 1931, the exiled King Alfonso XIII of Spain, whose suite became the seat of government. Arguably influenced by this distinguished clientele, the military governors of Nazi-occupied Paris chose to live here. Postwar residents included Natalie Clifford Barney, doyenne of the prewar lesbian community, who died here in 1972, and Salvador Dalì, who occupied the former suite of King Alfonso for one month a year from 1959 to his death in 1989. Dalì was irate that the management replaced the toilet seat used by his majesty, and demanded its reinstatement. The Spanish Surrealist added another item of furniture when brothels were made illegal in 1946. He bought the elaborate copper bath from Le Chabanais, Paris's most luxurious *bordel*, in which the Prince of Wales, later King Edward VII of Great Britain, enjoyed watching a prostitute bathe in champagne while he and his cronies sat around and dipped out the occasional glass.

In 1926, Ernest Hemingway, having decided to leave his wife Hadley in favor of the younger and richer Pauline Pfeiffer, accepted Hadley's suggestion that the couple separate for six months. If, at the end of that time, they still wished to marry, she would raise no objection.

Leo Tolstoy, 1856

Pauline chose to spend the time in the United States. The night before she sailed, she booked a suite at the Meurice, where the couple enjoyed a night of lust and luxury, with a supper of grouse and caviar served in the room. If Hemingway had any doubts, they were swept away with this preview of married life with Pauline. They were married the following April.

The famous tea-shop 24 **Angelina** at **No. 226** is now the flagship of an international chain. Opened in 1903 and designed in *belle époque* style by Eduoard-Jean Niermans, architect of the Moulin-Rouge, it was a favorite of author Marcel Proust and couturier Coco Chanel. Its velvety *chocolat chaud* blends three kinds of African chocolate, but expect to stand in line for some time to sample it; there is almost always a queue. 25 The **Galignani** dynasty of booksellers and publishers have been in Paris since 1801 and at **No. 224** since 1856, although the interior was redone in the 1930s. A well-stocked English department has lured generations of Anglophones to its hushed, varnished premises. 26 **No. 210** was the home of **Ivan Turgenev** between 1860 and 1864. Fellow Russian writer 27 **Leo Tolstoy** lived at **No. 206** in 1857

The Garden of the Tuileries on a Winter Afternoon, 1899

and painter 28 **Camille Pissarro** at **No. 204** in January 1899.

The elegant 29 **Place des Pyramides** commemorates the 1798 Battle of the Pyramids during Napoléon's invasion of Egypt. The gilded bronze equestrian statue of Joan of Arc by Emmanuel Frémiet was erected in 1874, following France's ignominious defeat in the Franco-Prussian War. It reassured the nation that it had once been a military power, and might be again—a hope never realized.

Once you have crossed Place des Pyramides, the buildings opposite all form part of 30 the **Palace of the Louvre**. Ten statues in niches on the *façade* depict generals or marshals who fought under Napoléon I. Installed between 1840 and 1915, they are best seen from the upper level of a double-decker bus. Of particu-

La Place des Pyramides, 1875, Reconstruction of Marsan Pavillon

lar interest is Victor Peter's figure of cavalry commander Joachim Murat, distinguished by its self-satisfied look and snug breeches. Despite Napoléon naming him "First Horseman of Europe," historians assign to Murat part of the blame for the failure of the Russian campaign, since he omitted to fit horses with the cleated shoes they needed to grip on ice. Murat married the younger sister of Napoléon, who installed him as king of Naples, then an independent state. He reigned from 1808 but, following the fall of Bonaparte, was executed by firing squad on the orders of his replacement, Ferdinand IV. As a last request, he asked for a hot bath, perfumed with eau-de-Cologne.

Shopping arcade, 1907

30

Musée des Arts-Decoratifs

31

Of the galleries on this side of the Louvre, the ***Musée des Arts-Decoratifs*** (No. 107-111) contains costumes, furniture, ceramics, glass, and examples of advertising art, photography and interior decoration. Of particular interest are the galleries devoted to *art nouveau* and *art deco.* The 31 **Carrousel du Louvre** at **99 rue de Rivoli** is a subterranean shopping center and food court running under the Tuileries Gardens and the triumphal arch. Inside, an inverted glass pyramid echoes the upright one by I.M. Pei. A passage leading into the Louvre itself, via its capacious book and gift shop, pro-

The Tuileries Gardens and Rue de Rivoli from 5th floor of Musée des Arts Décoratifs

vides a more pleasant means of access than queueing in the courtyard above. The Carrousel also gives access to the ancient moat of the palace, a glimpse of its impressive construction. It contains statues rescued from the destroyed Tuileries Palace.

End of walk. The nearby **Metro Palais Royal Musée du Louvre (Line 1)** is decorated with facsimilies of statues and reliefs from the museum's collection.

ABOUT THE OPÉRA GARNIER

The Opéra attracted new enterprises to the area, from hotels and theaters to department stores Galeries Lafayette and Au Printemps, which seized whole blocks of nearby Boulevard Haussmann, using the swirls and curlicues of *art nouveau* to create cathedrals of commerce. Galeries Lafayette's domed roof of glass and iron was so strong that the store offered 25,000 francs to the first aircraft to land on it. They took the roof down during World War I, for fear it might be smashed by German bombing, but once it was reassembled, daredevil aviator Jules Védrines succeeded on January 19, 1919, at the cost of wrecking his plane and

Emilie-Louise Delabigne, 1879, Edouard Manet

By the time she posed for this portrait at age thirty-one, Louise Delabigne had reinvented herself as "Valtesse," a play on *Votre Altesse* ("Your Highness"). Born to a laundry maid in Normandy, Louise grew up in poverty and began working in a sweet shop by age ten, then in a Paris dress shop by thirteen. These fashionable boutiques were often frequented by wealthy men, and many young workers, known as *grisettes*, supplemented their income through sex work. The name came from the cheap grey fabric they used to sew their own dresses.

Louise soon became one of them. "I wanted to see, so I drew nearer to this world," she later wrote, "and I was swept up in a terrible chain." She fell in love with a young army officer, Richard Fossey, and had two daughters with him. Fossey promised marriage but ultimately abandoned her.

Determined to never marry and to control her own fate, she adopted the name Valtesse de la Bigne and declared herself a Comtesse. She became the mistress of composer Jacques Offenbach, appeared onstage, and gained access to elite artistic and social circles. Among her many admirers were Manet, Gervex, Courbet, and Boudin. Some called her *l'Union des Peintres*—the "union of painters."

She later caught the attention of Prince Lubomirski, who set her up in an apartment on rue Saint-Georges. But it was Prince de Sagan who famously built her a lavish mansion at 98 Boulevard Malesherbes—a financial move that eventually bankrupted him. Valtesse left him too.

She became a media icon, courting journalists, choosing blue as

VALTESSE DE LA BIGNE: THE BED THAT BUILT A LEGEND

State Bed of Valtesse de la Bigne, Paris, circa 1875, Édouard Lièvre, Musée des Arts Décoratifs (left), Mrs Valtesse de la Bigne, 1879, Henri Gervex

her signature color, and adopting the violet as her emblem. In 1876, she even published a semi-autobiographical novel titled *Isola*. Émile Zola based the heroine of his scandalous novel *Nana* (1879–80) on her. Manet and Gervex both painted her.

Valtesse retired to Ville-d'Avray, where she trained young women in the art of being a courtesan. When she fell ill at sixty-two, she wrote her own death announcement. Upon her death, she left her ornate bed (now at the Musée des Arts Décoratifs) and vast art collection to French museums—with one condition: her name must always appear on the label.

The Arrival of the Midinettes, 1901, Jean Béraud

injuring himself. A monument on the roof marks the spot where he landed.

In 1875, the Opéra de Paris was the last word in construction. [6-1] Garnier, realizing that the water table under his site was only a few feet below the surface, laid a concrete "raft" or caisson to block any water welling up. Throughout the 13 years it took to complete the foundations, steam pumps operated around the clock to keep them dry.

In 1871, the anarchist uprising known as the Paris Commune convulsed Paris. The police, overwhelmed with the volume of prisoners, held some in cellars under the Opéra site. Among the journalists covering their trial was Gaston Leroux, an author of crime stories. He saw the possibilities of a mystery set in the building, but, more importantly, beneath it. Garnier's problems with water seepage gave him the image of a subterranean lake, across which a cloaked and masked figure poled himself. For his plot, he pirated *Beauty and the Beast*, and reached back to such Gothic novels of the previous century as *The Castle of Otranto* and *The Mysteries of Udolpho*, in which helpless females were imprisoned under apparently haunted castles. Out of these emerged the story of disfigured composer Erik who knows the Opéra well enough to secretly move around and under it, materializing backstage, in dressing rooms and private boxes, and even appearing in costume at a masked ball as Edgar Allan Poe's Red Death.

The rest of the world discovered Leroux's story through the 1925 film starring Lon Chaney, who screwed metal rings into his eye sockets to create a spectral stare and wired back his nose to suggest a skull from which the flesh had been burned. So vivid was his performance that the existence of the lake was assumed. Some water did enter the foundations once the pumps were turned off, but only in one space, and then shallow enough for a man to stand upright. According to the Opéra's current historian, "the pressure of the water in the tank stops any more rising up through the foundations, and the weight of the tank stabilizes the building." Today, this cistern, inaccessible except through a grating, is visited only by fire-fighters to practice using underwater breathing apparatus in the dark.

Phantom of the Opera, 1911

Lon Chaney, 1925

The sole permanent residents are catfish, blind and white.

(**JB**: But phantoms are never far away from this vast edifice. Among my own memories is one from 1991. An archive and library had just been created in the wing where Louis-Napoléon and Eugénie once entertained before performances. For the gala unveiling, imperial guardsmen in silver breastplates lined the grand staircase, while, at the first landing, Culture Minister Jack Lang and historian Emmanuel Le Roy Ladurie waited to welcome guests. In the main foyer, as the glitterati sipped champagne, a figure appeared at the edge of the crowd. A true specter at the feast, his ragged appearance mocked the formal gowns and evening dress. A beret barely covered his near-hairless head, and a loose sweater and baggy corduroy trousers hung on his emaciated body. Many saw him but none acknowledged his presence. Finally he spotted some friendly faces and dived into the crowd, which parted silently and closed after him. Rudolf Nureyev, former director of the Paris Opéra Ballet, was dying of AIDS, and had little more than a year to live, but to those who had once cheered him on the stage of this building, he was already dead.)

WALK 7

THE LEFT BANK: A STROLL BY THE SEINE

START: Metro Pont Neuf (Lines 7)
FINISH: Metro Assemblée Nationale (Line 12)

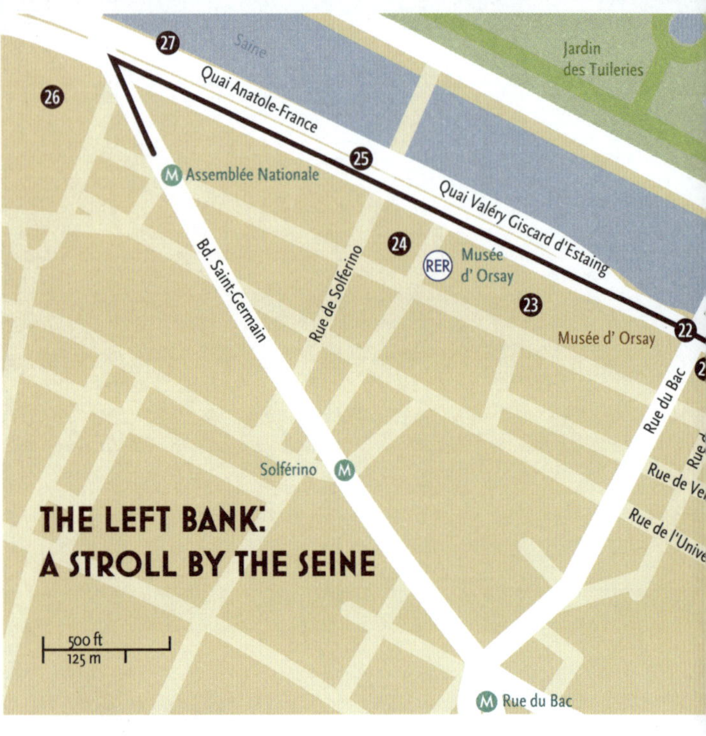

1. Pont Neuf
2. Statue of Henry IV
3. Square du Vert-Galant
4. Intersection of rue Dauphine and the Quai de Conti
5. Monnaie de Paris
6. Statue of Nicolas de Condorcet
7. Institut de France
8. Pont des Arts
9. Quai Malaquais
10. Ecole des Beaux-Arts
11. Place Mahmoud-Darwish
12. Promenade Marceline Loridan Ivens
13. Anatole France's Apartments: 15 & 19 Quai Malaquais
14. George Sand's Apartment: 19 Quai Malaquais
15. Mason Gainsbourg: 5 bis & 14 rue de Verneuil

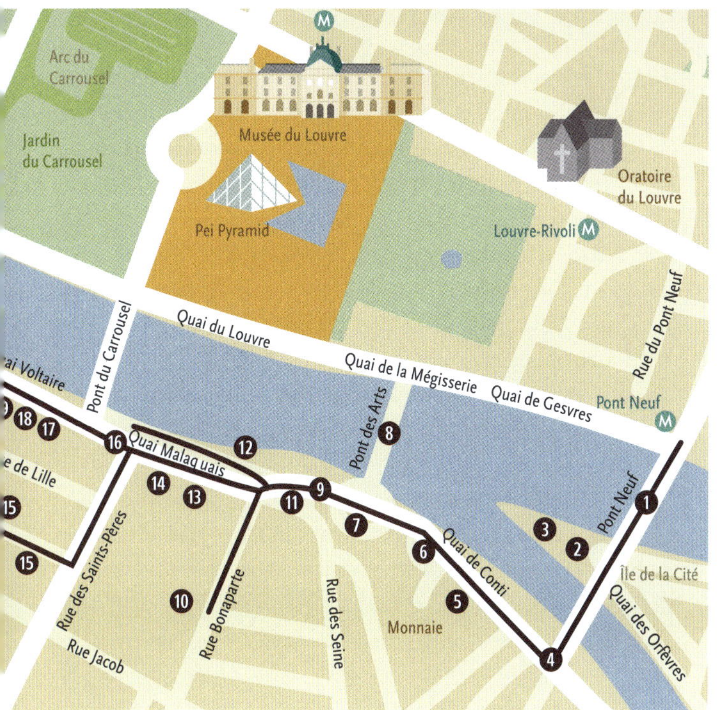

⑯ **Quai Voltaire**

⑰ **Jean-Dominique Ingres's Apartment:** 11 Quai Voltaire

⑱ **Eugène Delacroix and Camille Corot's Studios:** 15 Quai Voltaire

⑲ **Hôtel Wagner: Baudelaire, Wilde and Sibelius stayed here:** 19 Quai Voltaire

⑳ **Voltaire's Apartment:** 27 Quai Voltaire

㉑ **Site of Comte d'Artagnan's Home:** 33 & 35 Quai Voltaire

㉒ **Quai Valéry Giscard d'Estaing**

㉓ **Musée d'Orsay**

㉔ **Hôtel de Salm**

㉕ **Quai Anatole-France**

㉖ **Assemblée Nationale, and the Hôtel de Lassay**

㉗ **Piscine Deligny**

Previous page: *Paris Le Quai Malaquais*, c.1874, Auguste Renoir

"I do not know much about gods," wrote the British poet T.S. Eliot in his poem *The Dry Salvages*, "but I think that the river/Is a strong brown god—sullen, untamed and intractable." He might have been speaking about the Seine. One of France's two great rivers, it helped create the city of Paris, and dominates it still, a force both revered and feared. In 2006, the *Régie Autonome des Transports Parisiens* which manages Paris's public transport adopted the slogan *Aimer le ville*/Love the town. The accompanying logo featured a line resembling the Seine's route through Paris, redrawn to suggest a woman's face, upraised as for a kiss—a glimpse of how the RATP would like Parisians to regard a river often perceived as a threat.

The walk begins at **Metro Pont Neuf (Line 7)** The Seine rises on a plateau near Dijon and flows northwest to meet the English Channel at Le Havre. Our walk begins where it divides around the two islands, Île de la Cité and Île St. Louis, on which the first settlers built what would become, under the Romans, Lutetia, (the word means "swamp"), the ancestor of modern Paris. Our route takes us downstream, staying on the Left Bank, a name with both geographic and cultural significance. The Right Bank, older and more respectable, has the instruments of government, the luxury hotels: the power and the money. What does that leave for the Left Bank? A great deal, as we'll discover.

The city of Paris maintains and polices the river and its banks, but the bridges are under national control. ❶ **Pont Neuf** (New Bridge) is in fact the city's oldest, completed in 1607, but "new" need not mean only "recent." At the

time, this was a new *kind* of bridge for Paris; new in being built almost entirely of stone, and not encumbered with shops, houses or a roof. Moreover, it had sidewalks as well as a roadway, a novel idea for the time. Each generation finds a new use for its sturdy structure. One of the least likely took place in 1985, when artists Christo and Jeanne-Claude wrapped it in 40,000 square yards of golden fabric.

Cross as far as ❷ the **statue of Henry IV**, who reigned from 1589 to 1610, and take the steps down to ❸ the **Square du Vert-Galant**. Once known as the *Île aux Juifs* (Jews' Island), this triangular park, with its trailing willows and the river rushing by just a few feet away, was renamed in honor of Henry, who, because of his devotion to Gabrielle d'Estrées, the mistress with whom he fathered a number of

Gabrielle d'Estrées and one of her sisters, 1575-1600, unknown artist, Musée du Louvre

The sister is pinching Gabrielle d'Estrées' right breast, symbolizing Gabrielle's pregnancy with the illegitimate child of Henry IV.

children, was often tagged a "*Vert Galant*"—slang for an older man who still enjoys an active love life. Its closeness to the water has won the park an association with ritual. Jacques de Molay, Grand Master of the Knights Templar, and his lieutenant, Geoffroi de Charnay, were burnt at the stake here in 1314. An order of Catholic knights, the Templars gained great wealth and influence during the Crusades, but were suppressed when their power threatened that of the monarchy. Guy Debord (1931–1994), leader of the Lettrist and Situationist groups and formulator of the discipline known as Psychogeography, asked for his ashes to be consigned to the Seine from here.

Continue across the bridge to the Left Bank. On a sadder note, it was here, on a rainy April day in 1906, at ❹ the busy **intersection of rue Dauphine and the Quai de Conti**, that Nobel Laureate **Pierre Curie**, discoverer with wife Marie of radium, slipped and fell. The wheel of a horse-drawn cart ran over his head, killing him instantly.

Follow the Quai de Conti to the ❺ **Monnaie de Paris** or Paris Mint. Louis XV tasked architect Jacques-Denis Antoine with creating opulent premises for the factory that produced the nation's coinage.

It was officially opened in 1775. These days, currency is manufactured at Pessac, in the Gironde. The Monnaie de Paris houses the Coins and Medals division, which creates ceremonial medals, awards and other items of "metal art." It also demonstrates molten metal casting and pressure minting, offers classes for children in how to make medals from chocolate, and holds night-time tours of the building, conducted by the figure of Lady Fortune. A museum displays part of a collection of 170,000 items. The *Monnaie* also houses one of the city's most acclaimed restaurants, managed by Michelin-starred chef Guy Savoy.

Continue along Quai de Conti to ❻ the **statue of Nicolas de Condorcet** (1743–1794). The mathematician and pioneer of modern statistics died in prison during the Revolution. His statue was erected in 1889, but melted down in 1942 when Germany urgently needed copper. A plaster copy survived, from which this new version was cast in 1989.

The next building on the Quai, ❼ the stately **Institut de France**, with an esplanade opening onto the Seine, owes its existence to Car-

View of the Seine below Pont-Neuf, on the left the Hôtel des Monnaies, on the right the Louvre, 1782, Pierre-Antoine Demachy

dinal Jules Mazarin (1602–1661). A Latin inscription on the façade explains that "Jules Mazarin, cardinal of the holy Roman Catholic church, ordered the building of this church and this college in 1661." Born penniless in Rome, Mazarin rose to become aide to Cardinal Richelieu, whom he replaced as France's First Minister under Louis XIV, effectively ruling the nation for two decades. At his death, he was worth about $50 million, part of which went to build this College of Four Nations to educate young men from those provinces France acquired during his time in office. Napoléon I closed it in 1802 but it reopened in 1805 to house the elite of a Paris he hoped would rival ancient Athens or Rome.

The site had first to live down its sordid past as the location of the notorious Tour de Nesle. In 1314, France was ruled by Philip IV, known as Philip le Bel or Philip the Handsome. He married off his three sons to the daughters of Burgundian nobles, and his one daughter, Isabella, to Edward II of England. Unhappy in their marriages, two of the royal daughters-in-law, Margaret and Blanche, found alternative entertainment. Across the river from the Louvre was the Hôtel de Nesle, an old palace kept as an overflow residence

Cardinal Jules Mazarin

View of the Pont Neuf and Tour de Nesle, Jacques Callot(1592–1635)

for visiting royals. With the younger Blanche, Margaret, ("feisty and shapely," according to contemporary reports), turned it into a personal playground where they could party with their lovers, the brothers Gautier and Philippe d'Aunay. Servants combed Paris for likely young men, who, after a few depraved nights, were murdered by the Aunays and their corpses, each wrapped in a shroud weighted with a cannon ball, dropped into the Seine.

The scandal broke in 1313. On a visit from England, Isabella presented her sisters and their husbands with embroidered and jeweled purses of the sort that, before clothing had pockets, everyone wore hanging from their belt. (The criminal to watch for in a crowd wasn't the pick-pocket but the cut-purse.) Returning later that year to Paris, she saw the purses given to Marguerite and Blanche now being worn by the Aunays. Furious, she told her father, who, uncovering the scandal, had the Aunays tortured to death and his daughters exiled and imprisoned. The tower would be demolished, but its sulfurous reputation survives.

Frontispiece for the first edition of the Dictionnaire de l'Académie Française in 1694

Today, the Mazarin palace houses the prestigious *Academie Françaisc.* Its 40 members, known as "the immortals," award prizes for literature, and are responsible for policing the French language, publishing the definitive *Dictionnaire de l'Académie Française.* (It's a task they don't rush. The latest edition, the ninth, appeared in 2023, the previous one in 1935.) Membership is by application only. Most candidates offer their names a number of times before being selected, or giving up. They serve for life, and can't resign. Each receives an individually designed and engraved sword—female members can opt for a handbag or fan—and, as their first official act, deliver a eulogy on the person they succeed.

On ceremonial occasions, they wear antique breeches and a dark tailcoat, embroidered with olive branches in green and gold, and topped by a cocked hat. Jean Cocteau compared the Academy chamber filled with members in costume to "some underwater cave; an almost supernatural aquarium light and, on semi-circular stands, 40 mermaids with green tails and melodious voices." In 1910, those "mermaids" had real water with which to contend. On the rear wall of the building, a marker shows where the Seine flooded the Left Bank, in some places more than three feet deep. Civil servants rowed to work, and improvised walkways

Henri Robert admitted to the Académie Française 1924

A Windy Day on the Pont des Arts, c.1880-1881, Jean Béraud

bridged streets that had become canals. Residents who, protesting the squeal of iron wheels on stone, had insisted on having their street paved with wooden blocks, looked out in despair as it degenerated into a water-swollen jumble.

Opposite the Institute, ❽ the **Pont des Arts** connects the Left Bank to the Louvre. Built between 1802 and 1804, this iron bridge, wooden-decked, resting on masonry piers, was intended as a *passarelle*, a pedestrian promenade and garden, but tourists heading for the Louvre made it one of the busiest in Paris. Adding to its problems, not every bargee on the increasingly crowded Seine was able to thread the gaps between its arches. Frequent collisions, exacerbated by artillery and bomb damage during both world wars, weakened the structure. When, in 1979, a barge demolished almost 160 feet of the span, the bridge was rebuilt with wider arches.

Shortly after, lovers began to attach so-called *cadenas d'amour* or love locks to the bridge's wire mesh railings. To demonstrate fidelity, they wrote their names on a padlock, clipped it to the bridge, and threw the key into the Seine. By 2014, the number of locks was estimated at a million and their weight at 45 tons. When, in June 2014, part of a railing tore loose and fell into the river, glass panels replaced them, and the *cadenas* disappeared.

As sharks converge on reefs where fish are plentiful, Pont des Arts attracts panhandlers, pickpockets and petty thieves. For a time in the 1970s and '80s, women and children operated there in teams, the adult thrusting something under one's nose—a clipboard with a spurious petition was common—while the child, out of sight, groped for your handbag or wallet.

Another swindle involved a yellow metal ring which, at first glance, looked like gold. Pretending to pick it up from the pavement, a woman innocently asked a passerby "Is this yours?" Most ignored her but, out of every three or four tries, someone would stop and listen as the finder explained that, though she knew she should take this valuable item to the police, she might be willing to relinquish it—for a small payment, of course. Fortunately for victims, people skilled in this scam were rare. It was easy to spot the sudden stoop, apparently to pick up the ring but actually to drop it. Some did it so clumsily that one wanted to say "No, dear, don't let us *see* you putting it there. And pause for a second or two, as if you were wondering what to do." (**JB**: I tried this once, but the woman just muttered the equivalent of "Do I tell you how to do your job?" and went back to scanning the crowd for a new mark.)

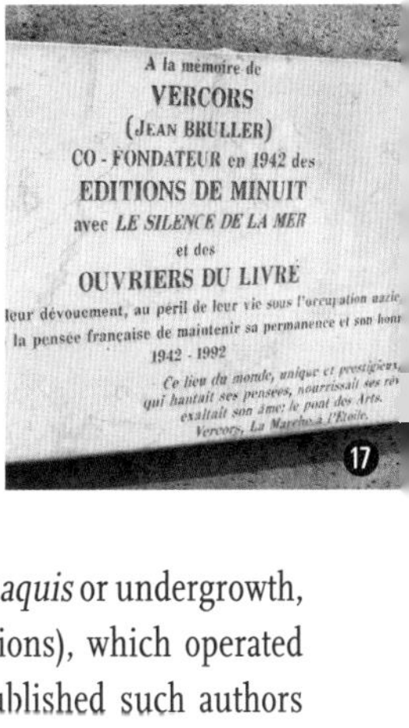

At the Left Bank entrance to the bridge, a plaque commemorates Jean Bruller, whose novel *Le Silence de la Mer* (*The Silence of the Sea*, published in English as *Put Out the Light*) depicted the refusal of a French family to socialize with an archetypal "good German" billetted on them during the Occupation. Bruller, who wrote under the *nom de guerre* "Vercors," named for the mountainous area in the *massif centrale* where resistants hid in the *maquis* or undergrowth, co-founded Editions de Minuit (Midnight Editions), which operated clandestinely throughout the war, and later published such authors as Samuel Beckett and Alain Robbe-Grillet. The plaque pays tribute to those "who, through their devotion, in peril of their lives under Nazi occupation, allowed French thought to retain its permanence and its honor," and adds a quote from one of Bruller's books: "This place in the world, unique and prestigious, which haunted his thoughts, fed his dreams, exalted his soul: the Pont des Arts."

Quai Malaquais, c.1890

After the intersection with rue de Seine, Quai de Conti becomes ❾ **Quai Malaquais.** Before houses were built along the riverbanks, this wooded area was known as the *Pré aux Clercs* (Clerks' Meadow). Its seclusion made it popular with duellists, including Cyrano de Bergerac.

Turn into rue Bonaparte. **No. 14** houses ❿ **L'École nationale supérieure des beaux-arts de Paris** (National School for Fine Arts.) For generations, its diploma was essential if you wished to teach art or make any kind of living as an artist. It was not easily won. Fees were high and women were not admitted. Applicants had to demonstrate superior talent; among those turned down was Henri Matisse. The four-year course followed rigid aesthetic rules based on classical painting and sculpture. The first year was spent drawing plaster casts of Greco-Roman statues. Even in life classes, so-called *modèles de profession* based their poses on these figures. When Édouard Manet demanded of one man "Is this how you stand when you go to the market to buy a bunch of radishes?", the model retorted indignantly that his poses had inspired more than one winner of the prestigious Prix de Rome.

Les Quat'z'arts, Adolphe Willette (1857–1926)

Once a year, students would let off steam in the *Bal de Quatz'arts* (Ball of the Four Arts), legendary for outrageous behavior. People competed to wear the fewest clothes and the ball climaxed in a parade of "Nude Works of Art." One conventionally dressed American journalist was refused entry with the suggestion that he try again but in just his underpants. Expatriate Harry Crosby attended in a loincloth and a coat of body paint, with a necklace of dead pigeons, and on another occasion spilled a basket of live snakes onto the dance floor. "The students are the pets of Paris," said one indulgent writer in 1899. He even justified the nudity as educational. "The artists and students see in these annual spectacles only grace, beauty, and majesty; their training in the studios, where they learn to regard models merely as tools of their craft, fits them, and them alone, for the wholesome enjoyment of the great ball."

Return to the Quai, which widens here to form ⓫ **Place Mahmoud-Darwish** (1941–2008), celebrating the Pakistani poet. A marble statue by Jean François Soitoux shows a female figure representing the republic of Napoléon III. She carries a drawn sword, warning of a readiness to defend the state, and, to signify the need for citizens to work together for the common good, guards a Roman fasces, the bound bundle of rods that symbolized strength in numbers (and gave its name to Fas-

Anatole France, 1910

cism.) Follow a ramp down to ⓬ **Promenade Marceline Loridan Ivens**. In 2019 this riverside walk, shaded by poplars, was named for the Holocaust survivor and filmmaker, widow of documentary director Joris Ivens. It offers a calm prospect of the river, a respite from traffic, and a means of avoiding the congestion around the entrance of the Pont du Carrousel.

The massive building from 11-17 houses the National Institute of Architecture. A plaque notes that **Anatole France** (1844–1924), writer, grew up in a house on this site (⓭ **No. 15, born at No. 19**) from 1844 to 1853. He was greatly admired by Scott Fitzgerald who, too timid to introduce himself, hung around outside for hours, hoping to run into him. At ⓮ **No. 19**, a plaque celebrates author **George Sand** (1804–1876). It reads (in French) "Here is the blue attic where Georges Sand lived from 1832 to 1836; she wrote *Lélia* there."

Turn away from the river into rue Saints-Péres, continue across rue de Lille and turn right into rue de Verneuil. The unmissable front wall of ⓯ **5 bis** with its gaudy graffiti was the home from 1969 to 1991 of singer, songwriter and actor **Serge Gainsbourg** (1928–1991). The interior, now a museum to his life, is almost as unconventional. Every surface is painted black. Gainsbourg, companion Jane Birkin and daughter Charlotte, both actresses, lived entirely by electric light, which burned day and night.

Gainsbourg ticked all the boxes to qualify as a *monstre sacré* (sacred monster), *i.e.*, a gifted individual whose excesses, rather than alienating his public, render him perversely attractive. His heavy tobacco and alcohol consumption, plus an aversion to shaving and bathing, were magnified when he assumed the character of an alter ego called "Gainsbarre." His appearances in this persona, in dark glasses, usually drunk, a smoking Gitane in hand, were invariably scandalous. He offended sensibilities everywhere by recording a reggae version of the *Marseillais.* To protest high taxes, he burned a 500 franc note on TV and, appearing on a talk show with singer Whitney Houston, informed her, in front of the national audience, "I want to f*** you." For Birkin, this was too much. "I could live with Gainsbourg," she announced as she left their home, "but not Gainsbarre."

His public was more forgiving. His more than 550 songs, ranging from the moaning dialog of a couple in the throes of orgasm (written for and performed with his sometime lover, actress Brigitte Bardot), to the lament of an employee on the Metro, condemned to spend his days punching holes in tickets, constituted the soundtrack to an era.

Return to rue des Saints-Péres and thence to the quai, which now becomes ⓰ **Quai Voltaire**, named for François-Marie Arouet, a.k.a. Voltaire, (1694–1778), best known for his satire *Candide.* High-end antique dealers favor this area. If you don't fancy window shopping

Voltaire, c.1720s

Ingres, 1860

(called in French *lèche-vitrine* — literally "window licking"), cross to browse the secondhand booksellers or *bouquinistes* whose green-painted stalls line the parapet. They have suffered in the migration from print to digital. Many diversified into selling posters and other tourist items, and their future is uncertain.

Plaques along the quai include: No. 1 Thomas Robert Bugeaud, Marquis de La Piconnerie, Duke of Isly, French soldier (1784–1849.) No. 7 Hubert de Lagarde, (1898–1945), military officer, writer and resistance fighter, Cécile Sorel, actress, (1873–1966), and Dominique Vivant, Baron Denon (1747–1825), artist, writer, diplomat and archaeologist.

At ⓱ **11 Quai Voltaire** the painter **Jean-Dominique Ingres** lived here until his death of pneumonia on 14 January 1867, at the age of 86. (**JB**: I never see his name without remembering the trouble the actor **David Soul** gave us while recording the commentary for a documentary. No matter how often we explained that the painter's name should sound something like "Ang'r", he always pronounced it to rhyme with "fingers.")

The most distinguished address on this street is ⓲ **15 Quai Voltaire.** On its 5th floor,

La Liberté guidant le peuple, 1830, Eugène Delacroix

two great painters worked: **Eugène Delacroix** (1829 to 1835) and **Camille Corot** (1849 to 1875). Delacroix painted *La Liberté guidant le peuple* (Liberty Leading the People) here.

At ⓳ **No. 19**, originally an abbey and later a hotel from 1851, **Richard Wagner** composed parts of *The Mastersingers of Nuremberg* (1861 to 1862), while **Charles Baudelaire** worked on his poetry cycle *Les Fleurs du Mal* (1856 to 1858). **Oscar Wilde** stayed here in the summer of 1874 and spring of 1883, and Finnish composer **Jean Sibelius** visited in March 1909.

The enlightenment philosopher and writer **Voltaire** died on the first floor of ⓴ **No. 27 (Hôtel de Villette)** on May 30, 1778 after return-

ing Paris in February for the first time in 25 years. According to one story of his last words, when the priest urged him to renounce Satan, he replied, "This is no time to make new enemies."

At 21 **Nos. 33** and **35** (the intersection of rue du Bac and Quai Voltaire: the plaque on 1 rue du Bac) was the home site of **Charles de Batz de Castelmore, Comte d'Artagnan**, immortalized in Dumas's *The Three Musketeers.* His death in 1673 ended an era of swashbuckling swordsmanship. Paradoxically, he didn't die in a duel but was killed by a musket ball at the siege of Maastricht in the Netherlands.

At the Pont Royal bridge, Quai Voltaire becomes 22 **Quai Valéry Giscard d'Estaing**, named for the President from 1974 to 1981. At 48, he was the youngest to hold the post until Emmanuel Macron, elected at 39. Urbane, aloof, he lacked the common touch, and only lasted one term.

Follow the quai to 23 **Musée d'Orsay**. Originally a railway terminal, this building, deceptively designed in Beaux Arts style, is constructed of iron, with a thin stone *façade.* As there was no room for new lines to attach it to the existing network, trains terminated at the Gare d'Austerlitz and carriages were towed

Hôtel de Villette,1904

here by electric engines through a tunnel running along the Seine. The terminal closed after its platforms became too short for modern main-line trains. (Of the few features retained from its earlier days, the most striking is the giant glass-faced clock that dominates the façade.) A portion was leased as an auction house and occasional movie location; Orson Welles used it for his 1962 version of Franz Kafka's *The Trial.* In 1972, Jean-Louis Barrault, fired from the Théatre de l'Odéon after the *évenéments* of 1968, relaunched his career in a circus tent pitched on the station's vast concourse.

At the time, the national collection of modern French art was scattered across a number of galleries. Planners realized that the Orsay building's opulent style, incongruous as a railroad terminal, might provide these treasures with a suitable home. The museum opened in 1986. It holds mainly French art dating from 1848 to 1914, including the world's largest collection of impressionists and post-impressionist paintings. Fortuitously, daylight streaming through the glass roof provides the ideal environment for statuary. Among its 2,200 pieces in stone and bronze are works by Auguste Rodin, anguished figures by his protegée and lover Camille Claudel, and studies of action by another Rodin apprentice, Émile-Antoine Bourdelle. Three life-sized *animalier* statues decorate the esplanade outside the main entrance. They are *Rhinocéros* by Henri Alfred Jacquemart, Emmanuel Frémiet's *Jeune Éléphant pris au Piège* (Young Elephant Trapped) and *Cheval à la herse* (Horse with Harrow) by Pierre Louis Rouillard.

Next door to the Musée, across rue de la Légion-d'Honneur, ㉔ the **Hôtel de Salm** houses the headquarters and museum of the Légion d'Honneur. Thomas Jefferson wrote in 1787 "I was violently smitten with the Hôtel de Salm, and used to go to the Tuileries almost daily to look and admire." Legion membership is the highest honor the French state can confer, and is awarded to soldiers and civilians who have rendered "eminent services." Approximately a million people have been honored since Napoléon I established the Légion in 1801, and at any one time about 100,000 individuals are entitled to display its discreet red ribbon on their lapel. Many are citizens of other countries, including the United States. Bob Dylan, Clint Eastwood, Dwight D. Eisenhower, David Lynch, James Baldwin: the list is as long as it is varied. Under what other cir-

The Crosbys, 1922

Palais Burbon, c.1810

Hôtel de Lassay

cumstances might one find Jesse Jackson rubbing shoulders with Jerry Lewis, or test pilot "Chuck" Yeager with Orson Welles?

Continue along ㉕ **Quai Anatole-France.** In 1920, people on the river stared as a boat rowed by a young woman in a swimsuit would pull up to the quai here each business day, allowing a tall man in a tailored suit to step ashore. Harry Crosby was on his way to the office of Morgan Guaranty, the bank of his uncle J. Pierpont Morgan. The rower was his wife, Polly, who, on moving to Paris, changed her name to Caresse. They soon became the most visible of all expatriate Americans, only for their marriage to end in a sensational murder/suicide. [7-1]

Our walk ends at the center of national government. The former **Palais Bourbon** houses the 550-strong ㉖ **Assemblée Nationale**, and the **Hôtel de Lassay**, official residence of its President. Before we conclude, however, another site of significance along this stretch of the Left Bank deserves mention, even though, paradoxically, it no longer exists.

In 1785, Barthélemy Turquin, also credited with inventing the life jacket, opened the city's first *école de natation* or swimming school. Between 1801 and 1803, the school, housed on a floating jetty, was towed to this location where, as ㉗ **Piscine Deligny**, it served generations of Parisians as a public swimming pool.

Asian-style terraces and cafés created the atmosphere of a Turkish café. Timber for their construction came from the steamer *Dorade,* which, when Napoléon's body was brought from Saint Helena to Paris in 1840, carried it up the Seine for reburial. During the *belle époque, boulevardiers* strolled to the Deligny in the afternoon to smoke, drink coffee, and admire the women bathers in their clinging wool *maillots de bain.* Marcel Proust's mother was among the swimmers. He remembered her "splashing and laughing there, blowing him kisses and climbing again ashore, looking so lovely in her dripping rubber helmet, he would not have felt surprised had he been told that he

Piscine Deligny, 1934

was the son of a goddess." Private cabins were provided for changing clothes, but, as one *habitué* reminisced, "American girls learning French at the Alliance Française, just three Metro stops away, would come down to the pool. They seemed to enjoy perfecting their French with me. Sometimes I would take the girls into my cabin to continue their French lessons. It was charming, if not altogether comfortable."

So much garbage was dumped into the Seine that, in 1844, the water had become "*sale, trouble, souvent fétide et malsaine*" (dirty, cloudy, often foul-smelling and unhealthy.) People continued to swim in it until 1923, when young novelist Raymond Radiguet succumbed to typhoid fever after doing so. The 1900 Olympic Games used the Deligny and better filtering was installed in 1919 but it took the German Occupation to achieve a real upgrade. The *Wehrmacht* and *Luftwaffe* officers who had exclusive use of the facility demanded it. In the 1960s, the Deligny became a popular gay hangout. A member of the National Assembly complained that, crossing the bridge on his way to a sitting, he was distracted by the sight of near-nude boys sunbathing below. Rather than suggesting he avert his eyes, the owners screened off the terrace, but these indignities were too much for the timbers that had borne the bones of Napoléon, and, in the early hours of July 8, 1993, the Deligny, possibly from shame, sank ingloriously into the mud. The walk ends at **Metro Assemblée Nationale (Line 12)**.

WALK 8

MONTPARNASSE: A WALK ON THE WILD SIDE

START: Metro Vavin (Line 4)

FINISH: Metro Vavin (Line 4)

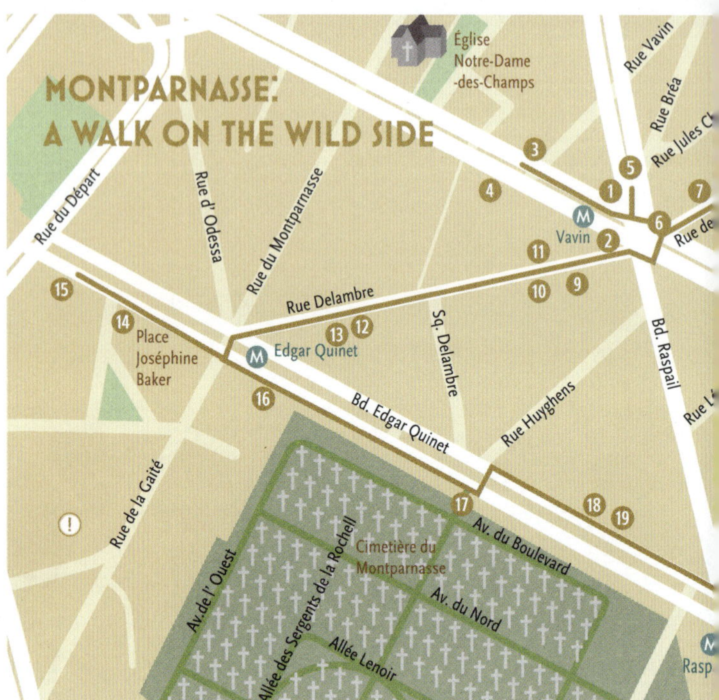

❶ **La Rotonde:** 105 Boulevard du Montparnasse
❷ **Le Dôme:** 108 Boulevard du Montparnasse
❸ **Le Select:** 99 Boulevard du Montparnasse
❹ **La Coupole:** 102 Boulevard du Montparnasse
❺ **Statue of Honoré de Balzac:**
❻ **Model Market**
❼ **Académie de la Grande Chaumière:** 14 rue de la Grande-Chaumière
❽ **Modigliani's and Mucha's Studios:** 8 rue de la Grande-Chaumière
❾ **Foujita's Studio:** 5 rue Delambre
❿ **Isadora Duncan's Studio:** 9 rue Delambre
⓫ **Dingo Bar:** 10 rue Delambre
⓬ **Hôtel des Bains:** 33 rue Delambre
⓭ **Hôtel Delambre:** 35 rue Delambre
⓮ **Place Joséphine Baker**
⓯ **Site of Sphinx:** 31 Boulevard Edgar-Quinet
⓰ **Le 2plus2 :** 9 Boulevard Edgar-Quine

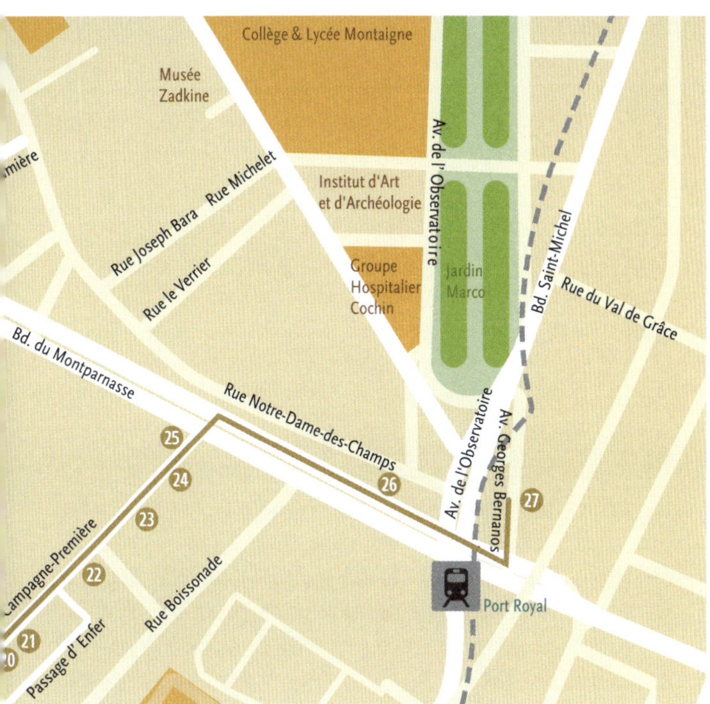

17 **Cimitière de Montparnasse**
18 **Le Monocle:**
14 Boulevard Edgar-Quinet
19 **Cabaret Maldoror:**
12 Boulevard Edgar-Quinet
20 **Man Ray and Kiki's Studio:**
31 bis rue Campagne-Premiere
21 **Hôtel Istria:**
29 rue Campagne-Premiere
22 **Eugene Atget:**
17 bis rue Campagne-Premiere
23 **Cité Taberlet:**
9 rue Campagne-Premiere
24 **Chez Rosalie:**
3 rue Campagne-Premiere
25 **Le Jockey:**
146 boulevard du Montparnasse
26 **La Closerie des Lilas:**
171 boulevard du Montparnasse
27 **Bal Bullier:**
39 avenue Georges Bernanos
! **Bobino:** 20 Rue de la Gaité

Previous page: *Le Bal Bullier (detail)*, 1931, Jules Flandrin

Visitors to Paris seldom see its secret side. Online travel sites emphasize its least disturbing aspects, and direct attention away from anything sordid or dangerous. A hundred years ago, the situation was reversed. Foreigners came to Paris looking for adventure. And while few had the experience of the writer in Woody Allen's film *Midnight in Paris,* who goes walking alone at night and miraculously encounters Ernest Hemingway, Scott Fitzgerald and Gertrude Stein, many who set out at dusk to find the "real Paris" returned to their hotels the next morning looking disheveled, often with a hangover, and always with a tale to tell.

(**JB**: My own grandfather was among them. During World War I, he experienced Paris as many young soldiers did, during a few days' leave from the trenches. Of what he did and saw there, he never spoke, but for the rest of his life scraps of French peppered his conversation, and when I first moved here, my father told me conspiratorially, "Don't be surprised if you see someone in the street who looks just like you." He didn't elaborate. Did I have FrancoAustralian cousins in Paris? It was a tantalizing prospect.)

So let's take a walk and see Montparnasse as the visitor of a century ago—as my grandfather—might have done.

We begin outside ❶ the **Rotonde Café** at the corner of Boulevard Raspail and Boulevard du Montparnasse, only a few yards from **Metro Vavin (Line 4)**. Of the four great Montparnasse cafés, only ❷ the **Dôme**, on the opposite

Modigliani, Picasso and André Salmon (above), Moise Kisling, Paquerette, and Picasso, at the Café de la Rotonde, photos by Jean Cocteau, August 1916

corner, is older, dating from 1898. The Rotonde opened in 1911, ❸ the **Select** in 1925 and ❹ the **Coupole** in 1927. Students from the Academie Colarossi and other art schools on rue de la Grande-Chaumière patronized the Rotonde, since the owner, Victor Libon, sometimes accepted paintings as payment, and allowed Amadeo Modigliani to dash off portraits of café patrons for a franc a time. His and other art works hung in the large upstairs room, which for a time served as a dance hall.

Once such artists as Pablo Picasso moved to Montparnasse after World War I, the Rotonde became their preferred meeting place. Hispanics held an afternoon *peña*

or salon where both locals and visitors congregated. The proliferation of foreigners irritated longtime residents, known as *Montparnos*, even though most were foreigners themselves. Polish poet Guillaume Apollinaire grumbled about this invasion from "the Montmartre of artists, singers, windmills, cabarets."

After World War I, a devalued franc drew the first wave of Americans. By 1923, 32,000 United States citizens lived in Paris. Most worked for banks, import/export companies, or the diplomatic service and had homes in one of the more respectable arrondissements. Only artists and bohemians lived in Montparnasse. They called it "the Quarter," as in "Diplomatic quarter" or "Native quarter," implying an area where normal rules no longer applied. Most people in The Quarter spoke a little English, one reason why the demi-monde congregated there. In 1922, Ernest Hemingway, after less than a year in the city, complained that "the scum of Greenwich Village, New York, has been skimmed off and deposited in large ladles on that section of Paris adjacent to the Café Rotonde. A first look into the smoky, high-ceilinged, table-crammed interior gives the same feeling that hits you as you step into the bird house at the zoo." A 1927 guide-

Menu for La Rotonde, Albert Fernand Renault, c.1930: La Rotonde, 1929

book suggested tourists go there for the same reasons as people of the 19th century toured insane asylums. "You see all the Nuts and all of the Freaks, plain and fancy, broke and affluent, mangy and modish, glassy-eyed and goo-goo-eyed; long-haired and bald-domed; Van Dyke-bearded and pasty-faced; decorous and degenerate; pious and perverted; mademoiselle-ish young men and young-men-ish mademoiselles. Every sort, type, and figured male and female you ever beheld, inside or outside a side-show."

Cafés were never simply places to relax and chat. During the 1920s, a person's preferred café was their contact address. One of Man Ray's models, Jacqueline Goddard, told me that "after a day of work, the artists wanted to get away from their studios, and get away from what they were creating. They all met in the cafés to argue about this and that, to discuss their work, politics and philosophy. We went to the bar of La Coupole. Bob, the barman, was a terribly nice chap. As there was no telephone in those days, everybody used him to leave messages. At the Dôme, we also had a little place behind the door for messages." She sighed nostalgically. "The telephone was the death of Montparnasse."

The café La Rotonde, a popular meeting place for artists in the Montparnasse district of Paris in the early 20th century, Illustrations of Paris, 1927, Léonard-Tsuguharu Foujita

With hiring halls unknown and private telephones a rarity, certain cafés became informal clubs and meeting points for professionals who worked by the day, even the hour. Band musicians gathered in one, each carrying an object signifying their instrument; a trumpet mouthpiece, or a few clarinet reeds tucked into a hatband. They spent the day reading or playing cards, waiting for a band leader who needed extra men in a hurry. Small-part actors gathered in another, some wearing the costume of their preferred role: policeman, butler, tramp. Cafés where prostitutes loitered were listed in the annual Guides Roses (Pink Guides) that outlined the capital's clandestine pleasures.

From the Rotonde, cross Boulevard Raspail to the central garden island and 5 Auguste Rodin's **statue of Honoré de Balzac**. Balzac died in 1850 so Rodin had only a few drawings of the short, pot-bellied novelist to inspire him. He decided to call the statue *Monument to Balzac*, and base it less on the writer's physical appearance than his work. Early versions showed Balzac nude, symbolizing his courageous confrontation of reality, but the Société des Gens de Lettres who commissioned it objected, and Rodin created a wax robe to drape over the figure. Shown at the 1898 Salon, it was execrated as nothing but a lump of clay with some dents in it, and a mask on top. It wasn't until 1939 that the statue, recognized as a masterpiece, was cast in bronze and placed in its present site.

Continue across the intersection and along Boulevard du Montparnasse to rue de la Grande-Chaumière. From the late 19th century,

❻ a **"model market"** convened on this corner each Monday. Modeling paid well: five francs for three hours, at a time when a laborer was lucky to earn that in a week. One reporter described the crowd that gathered here. "Italian *modelos,* matrons from Naples and elsewhere, Levantines and blacks, *Carmencitas* and ex-seamstresses; a seething carnival with its pretty girls and proud adolescents, its decrepit peasants and old men with white beards nursing their grandchildren, all ready to inspire painters and artists." The market closed in 1914 after café owners complained that the crowd blocked foot traffic. An increase in tourism had highlighted the commercial possibilities of *la vie de boheme* and they wanted it for themselves.

Turn left onto rue de la Grande-Chaumière, a quiet little street steeped in artistic history. At ❼ **No. 14**, you'll find the **Académie de la Grande Chaumière**, founded in 1904. As the plaque reveals, renowned artists such as Ossip Zadkine, Lucien Simon, and Claudio Castelucho once taught here.

In June 1919, painter Amedeo Modigliani, his mistress Jeanne Hébuterne, and their newborn daughter moved into what would be-

Gauguin at Mucha's studio, c.1893

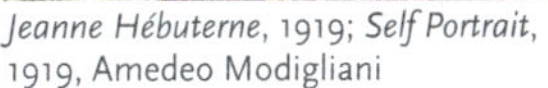

Jeanne Hébuterne, 1919; *Self Portrait*, 1919, Amedeo Modigliani

come his final residence: a top-floor studio at ⑧ **8 rue de la Grande-Chaumière**, arranged by his dealer and friend Léopold Zborowski. The move was likely marked by optimism—Modigliani finally had a home of his own, and his work was beginning to gain recognition.

By autumn, however, his health had deteriorated, worsened by his drinking and the squalid conditions of the studio. The lack of coal, damp and dripping walls, and insufficient food took their toll. In January 1920, after several days without hearing from him, a neighbor visited and found Modigliani delirious in bed, clinging to Hébuterne. He was taken to the Hôpital de la Charité, where he died on January 24, 1920, at the age of just 36.

The tragedy deepened the following morning when, at 4 a.m., Jeanne Hébuterne threw herself from the fifth-floor window of her parents' home, ending her life and that of her unborn child. [8-1]

Café du Dôme, 1936

Gauguin preceded Modigliani, working in the same building during 1893–1894 in the studio of Art Nouveau poster artist Alphonse Mucha.

Retrace and cross Boulevard du Montparnasse and Raspail to **Café du Dôme**. Americans relocated here while the Rotonde was being renovated and found they preferred it. The first thing Ernest Hemingway wrote in Paris, the poem *Montparnasse*, was inspired by the Dôme, and concluded "Every afternoon the people one knows can be found at the café." Cab drivers with an American fare too drunk to remember his hotel could drop him off at the Dôme, confident that someone would see him home safe. "And we sit outside the Dôme Café," Hemingway wrote in a letter to Sherwood Anderson, "warmed up against one of those charcoal brazziers and it's so damned cold outside and the brazzier makes it so warm and we drink rum punch, hot, and the rum enters into us like the Holy Spirit." Loitering on the *terrasse*, drinking *vin rouge* and eavesdropping on the conversation, a new arrival felt that they might become an artist just by *being* there. "My dear," murmured one giddy visitor in 1929, "at first, I was uncertain whether the Dôme was a place or a state of mind or a disease. It is all three!"

Continue into what Swedish playwright August Strindberg called "dark and quiet rue Delambre, a street that more than any other in the neighborhood can make you miserable." He may have been thinking of the few soberly dressed individuals who lingered over cold coffee or the dregs of a beer at this end of the Dôme café. They were watching for funerals heading to the nearby cemetery. As a cortège appeared, they hurriedly paid the bill and joined those walking solemnly behind the hearse. It was usual for bereaved families to invite the mourners, even strangers, to join them for a meal after the interment.

In fact Delambre today is quite cheerful, since many small businesses unable to afford premises on the boulevards relocated here, preserving the village atmosphere. It's still a place where locals come

Rue Delambre, 1920

to buy fruit, vegetables, fish and cheese. At 9 **No. 5**, a plaque identifies the former home of Japanese painter **Léonard Tsuguharu Foujita** (1886-1968.) He and his Belgian wife and model Lucile, a.k.a. Youki (Japanese for "snow": she had unusually white skin) occupied a converted coach house on the ground floor of this former *hôtel particulier.* Man Ray had the adjacent studio before moving to his more permanent home on rue Campagne-Premiere. Ray's lover Alice Prin, a.k.a. Kiki de Montparnasse, boldly posed nude for Foujita in the courtyard.

From 1926, dancer **Isadora Duncan**, then in her late forties, lived at 10 **No. 9**. No longer able to command large sums for her performances, she famously complained "I don't know where the next bottle of Champagne is coming from." She gave private lessons to, among others, her neighbor Foujita. In 1927, she would die dramatically in Nice, her neck broken when her scarf caught in the wheel of an automobile. [8-2]

11 **No. 10**, now the Auberge de Venise, was the **Dingo Bar**, a popular *Montparno* meeting place. Its French owner made it a mecca for expatriates by poaching ex-boxer Jimmie Charters as barman from the Falstaff

on rue du Montparnasse, and renaming his establishment with a corruption of the slang word *dingue* (crazy). “The crowd would begin to drift in any time after noon,” wrote Charters. “Sad individuals with hangovers, or small and quiet sober groups of earnest men and women discussing art, which seemed to be an inexhaustible subject. The hangovers took pick-me-ups, and the others sipped their drinks slowly, but by five o’clock the crowd was in full swing. Excited women, amorous couples, jittering fairies, gay dogs, over-serious young men expounding theories, and a few quiet, observing souls who took it all in and appreciated it.”

The American Dingobar in Paris, 1925, George Grosz

Former Ziegfeld showgirl Angela Martin, known as “Flossie” because of her tangled hairdo, and noted for her use of profanity, was a feature of the Dingo. Two American dowagers, searching for the authentic Montparnasse, overheard her cursing, looked at one another, and said “This must be the place”—the title Charters gave to his memoirs, for which Hemingway wrote a preface, comparing the barman’s observations, favorably, to those of Gertrude Stein, with whom he was feuding. Increasingly, Montparnasse seemed to Hemingway “more a state of mind than a geographical area. This state of mind is principally contempt. Those who work have the greatest contempt for those who don’t. The loafers are leading their own lives and it is bad form to mention work. Young painters have contempt for old painters, and that works both ways too. There are contemptuous critics and contemptuous writers. Everybody seems to dislike everybody else."

It was at the Dingo that he and Scott Fitzgerald first met. With *The Great Gatsby* just published, to indifferent reviews and sales, Fitzgerald's reputation was in decline, while Hemingway was poised for success. Humor writer Donald Ogden Stewart, a bigger name than either at the time (and one model for the perennially tipsy Bill Gorton in *The Sun Also Rises*), introduced the two men, who became immediate friends. Hemingway even asked Fitzgerald to read his manuscript, and incorporated most of his suggestions. They might have remained close had Zelda Fitzgerald not undermined the relationship, implying that Hemingway was a closeted gay with designs on Scott: "a fairy with hair on his chest." As Hemingway wrote perceptively of her behavior in *A Moveable Feast*, "hawks don't share." The Auberge has a small display of Hemingway memorabilia but, of the original décor, only the bar itself survives. A plaque, placed, puzzlingly, at ankle level, explains the connection, including the dubious claim that Ernest invented that potent concoction of gin, tequila, white rum, Cointreau and Coca Cola known as Long Island Iced Tea.

Continue up rue Delambre to ⓬ **No. 33**, now the **Hôtel des Bains**. Keeping clean was difficult in as crowded a district as Montparnasse. Foujita at No. 5 was one of the few artists to have hot running water, which made him popular with models eager for a bath. Itinerant bathmen cruised the streets, pulling handcarts with a collapsible bath and large copper boilers. Most people, however, went to a public bathhouse—the original function of the Hôtel des Bains (Odessa bath house). Some, like this one, became gay meeting places. Jean Cocteau was a frequent visitor, as was bisexual Louis Aragon, who went there with fellow author Pierre Drieu la Rochelle. "Each time I hear the word 'bains'," said Aragon, "I break out in a sweat." One of its 12 private bathrooms was fitted with a two-way mirror, an amenity appreciated by Cocteau, who had a fetish for young sailors and fishermen with wet skin, an image that recurs in his work. Volunteering for ambulance service during World War I, he took a special interest in the showers where common soldiers or *poilus* ("hairy ones") enjoyed their first bath in weeks.

Next door at ⓭ **No. 35** is the **Hôtel Delambre.** Plaques in the entrance identify this as the former home of painter Paul Gauguin and writer André Breton. Gauguin lived here in 1891, the year of his first voyage to Tahiti, which would inspire his best work, and where he would die of syphilis contracted from a Montparnasse prostitute. Breton, the son of a policeman, scorned the area's triviality and relocated in Montmartre—which, he acknowledged to Louis Aragon, was "no better—the same prostitutes and drug addicts." All the same, it was in Montmartre, at Café Cyrano on Boulevard de Clichy, that he convened the first of the Surrealist *séances* which became a daily event.

Louis Aragon, c.1924

Mural at the intersection

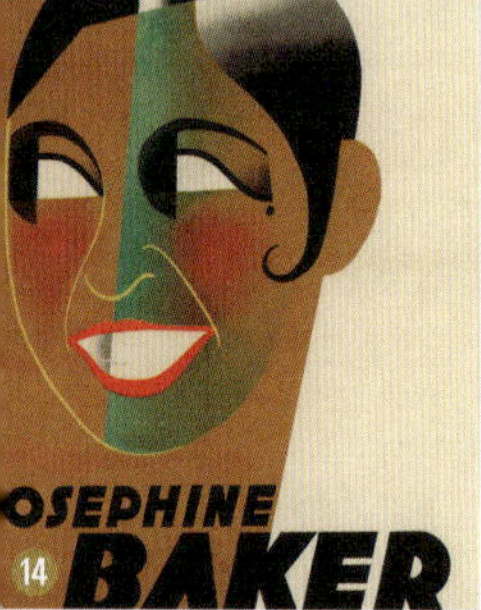

Maison Close, c.1916, Atget

At the intersection of rue Delambre, rue de la Gaité, and Boulevard Edgar-Quinet, cross the boulevard, turn right, and continue along the south side to the next intersection with rue Poinsot, rue Jolivet, and Boulevard Edgar-Quinet. This area has been designated ⓮ **Place Joséphine Baker** in honor of the African-American dancer, singer, and actress. The location is close to several of Baker's favorite haunts, including Bobino (20 rue de la Gaité), where she gave her final performance in April 1975, and La Coupole, where she spent countless evenings.

In November 2021, a memorial was inaugurated in her honor at the Panthéon in Paris, following her "election" to the mausoleum by French President Emmanuel Macron in August of the same year. [8-3]

Boulevard Edgar-Quinet cuts through the heart of Montparnasse, from the Gare Montparnasse to Boulevard Raspail. For part of its length, it adjoins the Cimitière de Montparnasse, a fact that discouraged conventional businesses from opening here but recommended it as a "red light" district. (In fact, France never adopted the convention of a red lamp to designate a brothel. Napoléon I legalized prostitution and the licensing of so-called *maisons closes* or *maisons de tolérance* with the proviso that they not stand out or allow anyone to see inside. Most were referred to by their addresses—"rue Chabanais" or "*le 122*"—or some name without sexual connotations, *e.g., Les Belles Poules,* and occasionally by the name of their proprietor; *e.g., Miss Betty's,* the St. Germain establishment, opposite the church of St. Sulpice, which reserved its facilities for Catholic priests.)

At ⑮ **No. 31**, a building, since demolished, housed Montparnasse's busiest *maison close,* **The Sphinx**. Some guidebooks for American tourists of the 1920s encouraged them to visit a brothel. "The 'ladies' see no harm in you coming merely to inspect them," one advised. "They will parade before you in frankest nudity, and dance with one another in a mirror-walled room, so that of their charms you may miss nothing." Paul Carbone and François Spirito, who financed Le Sphinx, were the first to see the possibilities of a brothel aimed at foreign-

Le Sphinx, 1937, James Boswell

Le Sphinx closed in 1946

ers. Opening at 3 p.m. and closing at dawn, the Sphinx imitated American nightclubs in imposing a cover charge to enter. Once inside, visitors found themselves in a spacious cabaret. A band played for dancing and a bar served cocktails. It might have been the first-class lounge on a transatlantic liner—except for the dozens of beautiful women who wandered among the tables, all half-undressed, and some naked except for high-heeled shoes. From time to time, a group of them, in a version of the classic brothel "parade," appeared on a stage at one end of the salon. A payment to one of the female "supervisors" who cruised the floor bought an hour with the woman of one's choice in a mirrored bedroom upstairs. To explain the system, the proprietors produced a brochure in five languages, the English section written by American author Henry Miller.

Until it closed in 1946, Le Sphinx attracted the cream of society and show business, including writers Colette, Jean-Paul Sartre, Simone de Beauvoir and Jacques Prévert, artists Man Ray, Moise Kisling, Leonard Foujita, Jules Pascin and Kees van Dongen, who painted its faux-Egyptian murals, and movie stars Gary Cooper, Humphrey Bogart and Errol Flynn. Marlene Dietrich also used it as a cover for assignations with her lover Madeleine Sologne. When bandleader Duke Ellington visited, friends urged him to choose a companion from among the lovelies parading on stage. "OK," Duke said. "I'll take the three on the end."

During the Occupation, the Sphinx was reserved for the Nazi high command and its collaborators. In 1946, the government, as part of a postwar reform movement, made brothels illegal. A public relations triumph, the decision was in other respects disastrous. Forced back onto the streets, prostitutes were no longer subject to health checks, which increased the incidence of sexually-transmitted diseases. They also became prey to pimps, who took their money in return for "protection." Brothels got a little of their own back by publicly selling off their furniture and fittings, noting in the catalogs which politicians and religious leaders had enjoyed the house's hospitality. [8-4]

Retrace and continue on Boulevard Edgar-Quinet. At ⑯ **No. 9**, ***Le 2+2*** claims to be the oldest *échangiste* or sex club in Paris but has only been so for a few years, since another club, much older, called the Vortex, shut its doors. A journalist wrote, "The upper classes have invented a new vice. All these blasé individuals no longer take great pleasure in doing what you think; the greater pleasure, for them, is watching each other do it. We call it '*La Partouze*', [defined as] a party during which the participants (whose number generally exceeds four) practice the exchange of partners and engage in collective and simultaneous sexual activities." Serious *par-*

Paris Plaisirs, November 1925

tousiers distinguish between such *échangiste* or *libertin* clubs as the 2+2, which require no invitation, and the more social *partouze*, where participants know one another or have been introduced by a member. The *partouze* lifestyle made headlines in 2002 with the publication of *La Vie Sexuelle de Catherine M*, in which art historian and media personality Catherine Millet documented a lifetime spent in pursuit of sexual sensation. [8-5]

Continue towards Boulevard Raspail to ⑰ the **Cimitière de Montparnasse.** Created from farmland in 1824, this is the resting place of numerous figures from literature, politics and the arts. These include the shared grave of Jean-Paul Sartre and Simone de Beauvoir, the plain black marble slab of Samuel Beckett, Man Ray's monument with its reticent epitaph "Unconcerned, but not Indifferent," the grave of Alice Prin, a.k.a. Kiki of Montparnasse, and the photograph-decorated grave of singer Serge Gainsbourg. Gays or personalities of gay interest buried here include actress Delphine Seyrig, camp icon Maria Montez, Pierre Louys, author of the spuriously Sapphic *Songs of Bilitis*, photographer Gisele Freund, and film director Jacques Demy.

Signs at the main entrances indicate the general position of most celebrity graves, but you may need to ask one of the attendants for specific directions. Exit the cemetery onto Boulevard Edgar Quinet, cross the boulevard and continue towards Boulevard Raspail.

(18) **No. 14** is the former premises of **Le Monocle**, Paris's premier club for cross-dressing females. Clients were encouraged to wear male evening dress, with, ideally, a monocle.

(19) **No. 12** has housed a number of enterprises, including, briefly, in 1930, **Cabaret Maldoror**, with décor by Egyptian artist Dida Mayo. It took its name from *Les Chants de Maldoror* of the Comte de Lautréamont, an author revered by the Surrealists. Their leader, André Breton, had already led a raid on the theater at which German dancer Valeska Gert presented a program of what she called "Surrealist Ballet." In a similar attack on Cabaret Maldoror, Louis Aragon sustained a minor knife wound. The next day, Breton apologized to the owner in a letter on Surrealist stationery, marked with a symbolic drop of blood.

Cross Boulevard Raspail, turn right, then left to (20) **31 bis rue Campagne-Premiere**. Dating from 1911, this building, designed by André

Man Ray, 1934

Arfvidson, contains 20 duplex studio apartments. Oriented to take advantage of the north light artists prefer, it is faced with tiles to which *art nouveau* ceramicist Alexandre Bigot, by firing them at intense heat, gave a glass-like surface. The furthest left ground-floor studio was occupied by Man Ray, shared with model and mistress Alice Prin, a.k.a. Kiki, and, later, Lee Miller. His bed, perched on a mezzanine, overlooked the tiny salon. Film was developed and printed in a former closet. [8-6] In 1960, Jean-Luc Godard chose the street outside to film the climax of his first feature *À Bout de Souffle*, with would-be gangster Jean-Paul Belmondo shot by police, watched by girlfriend Jean Seberg.

A plaque on 21 the **Hôtel Istria** next door reads, "In the creative effervescence of the 1920s, the Hôtel Istria welcomed, among others, Francis Picabia, Marcel Duchamp, Moise Kisling (painters), Man Ray, (photographer), Kiki de Montparnasse, (model and muse), Erik Satie, (composer), Rainer Marie Rilke, Tristan Tzara, Vladimir Mayakovsky (poets) and Louis Aragon, who met Elsa Triolet here." Aragon and Triolet remained together for the rest of their lives, becoming the senior literary couple of France. (For more about the relationship of Aragon, Triolet and Mayakovsky. [8-7])

Moise Kisling 1924

Tsuguharu Foujita, 1925

Gustaw Gwozdecki 1920

Moise Kisling 1925

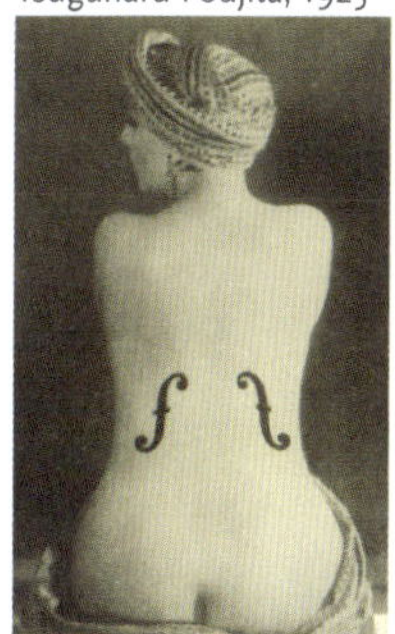
Man Ray, 1924

Maurice Mendjizky, 1921

Kees van Dongen c.1922–24

Jacqueline Marval, 1921

Man Ray, 1923

22 **No. 17 bis** was formerly the home and studio of pioneering photographer Eugene Atget, who meticulously documented the streets and buildings of old Paris.

Inspired by Montmartre's *Bateau Lavoir*, formerly a piano factory, Montparnasse landlords converted workshops and stables into studio complexes known as *cités des artistes*. Where no suitable buildings existed, they constructed them, using recycled materials. Trade expositions were a prime source, since their often elaborate pavilions were broken up and sold as scrap. In 1889, a builder purchased doors, windows and other fittings from that year's *Exposition Universelle* and reassembled them along an *allée* at what is now 23 **No. 9. Cité Taberlet**, a complex of 128 studios, was named for the architect who designed it. Modigliani, Whistler, Foujita, Giacometti, Kandinsky, Miro, Ernst and Friesz all worked here. Among its tenants were poet Rainer Maria Rilke, one-time secretary to Auguste Rodin. His *Notebooks of Maltes Laurids Brigge* describe, unflatteringly, the disorientation of living with disproportionate and oddly placed doors, and mismatched walls still bearing marks of former plumbing. In the bitter winter of 1946, American photographers Elliott

Le Jockey, Tableaux de Paris, Chas Laborde, 1927

Erwitt and Robert Frank shared a studio here with a Romanian sculptor who, to conserve heat, slept in a crate of the sort used to ship Jeeps.

Artists working at Cité Taberlet habitually ate at 24 **Chez Rosalie** at **No. 3**, a modest restaurant founded on this location by retired model Rosalie Tobia. (The building has since been demolished.) This was one of Modigliani's favourite places to go because Rosalie, who was Italian just like him, served many dishes from their national cuisine and Modigliani was sometimes allowed to pay in drawings or paintings. Later Rosalie said, "When he became famous, I searched for them, but the mice had nibbled them."

Continue to the intersection with Boulevard du Montparnasse. At the western, *i.e.*, left-hand corner stood 25 **Le Jockey**, now demolished, which Ernest Hemingway called "the best nightclub that ever was." It inspired numerous anecdotes: Hemingway dancing with Joséphine Baker, who, before stepping out into the night, opened her long fur coat to show him she was naked under it. Or the proprietor, American artist Hilaire Hiler, interrupting a client about to take his life in the toilets, and persuading him to kill himself instead at the Dôme and so ruin business for a competitor.

Turn right into Boulevard du Montparnasse and continue to the intersection with Boulevard St. Michel. On one corner stands 26 the **Closerie des Lilas**, on the other 27 the **Bal Bullier**. Tourists who pass through the hedge surrounding the Closerie des Lilas seldom know more beyond Hemingway's praise of it as "one of the best cafés in Paris. It was warm inside in the winter and in the spring and fall it was fine outside with the table under the shade of the trees on the side where the statue of Marshal Ney was, and the square, regular tables under the big awnings along the boulevard."

Fifty years before, the Closerie was mainly patronized by drinkers of absinthe, known, because of its grassy opalescence, as *la fée verte*: the green fairy. Distilled from wormwood, fennel, licorice and anise, bolstered with as much as 74 percent alcohol, it was the hardest of hard liquors. Charles Baudelaire and Paul Verlaine drank it here, Verlaine staggering home to die in a rooming house at 39 rue Descartes—the same building, by coincidence, where Hemingway rented a work-room in 1922. Another absinthe addict, Swedish playwright August Strindberg, confided to his diary for May 17, 1904, "Absinthe at six o'clock on the terrace of Brasserie des Lilas behind Marshal Ney has become my only vice, my last joy." Increasingly addicted, he became prey to hallucinations. Shortly after Verlaine succumbed to its effects, Strindberg showed composer Frederick Delius an unremarkable photograph of the poet on his death-bed and asked what he saw.

Couples in a lively dance at the Closerie des Lilas, popularly known as the Bal Bullier, c.1860–1869

"Such as?"

"Well, the huge animal lying on his stomach," Strindberg said, puzzled at his obtuseness, "and the imp crouched on the floor!"

The Closerie began as a *relais* or coach stop on the road to Fontainebleau. Its first proprietor, François Bullier, planted a lilac hedge to shelter patrons from the dust of the road and mask the smell of horses. He also built the Bal Bullier, a dance hall/bar or *bal musette.* Invariably jammed, such places offered no room for fancy steps. Instead, couples jigged round the crowded floor in the *java,* a dance separated from vertical sex only by a few layers of fabric. Cigarettes wedged in the corner of their mouths and berets or *casquettes* jammed on brilliantined heads, men stared over their partners' shoulders and, clutching the other's buttocks with both hands, ground their pelvises together, intent only on a few minutes of sensation. They did so without speaking since the etiquette of the establishment forbade conversation. The original Bal Bullier was demolished to build the monolithic *Centre Sportif Universitaire Jean Sarrailh.* Bullier relocated the *bal,* now a café, on the corner opposite the Closerie des Lilas. It's still called Bal Bullier but dancing there is discouraged.

Walk ends. Turn right onto Boulevard du Montparnasse and continue to intersection with Boulevard Raspail and **Metro Vavin (Line 4.)**

WALK *9*

PARIS AT WAR: THE NAZI OCCUPATION

START: Metro Sevres-Babylone (Lines 10 and 12)
FINISH: Metro Hotel de Ville (Lines 1 and 11)

❶ **Hôtel Lutetia:** 45 Boulevard Raspail

❷ **Square Boucicaut**

❸ **Site of Secret Meeting of NRC:** 48 rue du Four

❹ **Site of Communal Oven:** 43 rue du Four

❺ **Place Mehdi-Ben-Barka:** 35 rue du Four

❻ **Le 22:** 22 rue du Four

Previous page: *The Astronomer,* 1668, Johannes Vermeer. In 1940, following the German invasion of Paris, the painting was seized from the Rothschild family mansion by the Nazis and given to Adolf Hitler. After the war, it was returned to the Rothschilds before being acquired by the French state in 1983 as payment for inheritance taxes. It has been exhibited at the Louvre ever since.

- ❼ **Church of St-Germain-des-Prés**
- ❽ **Placc Julicttc-Gréco**
- ❾ **Les Deux Magots:** 6 pl. Saint-Germain des Prés
- ❿ **Sartre's Mother's Apartment:** 42 rue Bonaparte
- ⓫ **Le Chai:** 26 rue de Buci
- ⓬ **Hôtel la Louisiane:** 70 rue de Seine
- ⓭ **Pablo Picasso's Studio:** 7 rue des Grands-Augustins
- ⓮ **Place St. Michel**
- ⓯ **Mémorial des Martyrs de la Déportation**
- (!) **Le Bon Marché:** 24 rue de Sèvres
- (!) **Church of Saint-Séverin**

(!) indicates a place mentioned in the text, but not included in the tours.

Few speeches are more deeply engraved on the French national memory than Charles de Gaulle's address in August 1944 after his return from four years of English exile. "Paris! Paris outraged! Paris broken! Paris martyred! But Paris liberated! Liberated by itself, liberated by its people with the help of the armies of France, with the support and help of the whole of France, the France that fights, the only France, the true France, the eternal France."

In fact, the liberation of which he spoke was only a week old. The people of Paris waited until the Allies were in the suburbs before they attacked the last remnants of the German garrison. Before that, only about two percent of the population put up any serious resistance. In his novel *The Fall,* Albert Camus, himself editor of the underground magazine *Combat,* suggested cynically that most people thought of such activity as like "being asked to do some weaving in a cellar, for days and nights on end, until some brutes should come to haul me from hiding, undo my weaving and then drag me to another cellar to beat me to death. I admired those who indulged in such heroism of the depths but couldn't imitate them."

Boulevard Saint-Germain, 1941

General Charles de Gaulle addressing crowds in Chartres, France, August 24, 1944

Resistance was not part of the French national character. Conquered by Rome, colonized by Christianity, invaded by England, inherited by the Bourbons, from whom they liberated themselves in the revolution of 1789, only to be swept up in the imperial ambitions of the Napoléons, they endured not through opposition but acquiescence. If France was, as de Gaulle said, eternal, it was because it had learned to accept foreign domination, keep silent, and resist in the only way that really mattered: by surviving. [9-1]

De Gaulle, who served as president until 1953, and again from 1958 to 1969, fostered the legend of a courageous resistance, selfless and united, but the typical resistant was already an outsider who would have opposed authority in any form. De Gaulle was such a man. Stiff, pompous, resentful of being passed over, he appointed himself head of a "Free French" government in exile and, notwithstanding the official collaborationist administration of Marshal Philippe Petain, persuaded the world to accept his leadership. The backbone of the resistance was loners and renegades. Communists comprised the largest contingent. They were joined by separatists fighting for regional independence and young men on the run from being sent to Germany as forced labor. Criminals also joined. The wartime *equipe* of Corsican Jean Jehan would become the hero in smuggling operation dramatized in the film *The French Connection.*

We start the walk at **Metro Sevres-Babylone (Lines 10 and 12)**, the closest to ❶ the **Hôtel Lutetia**. In 1940, the *Abwehr* counter-intelligence service of Admiral Wilhelm Canaris made its headquarters here. Had their roles been reversed, Charles de Gaulle would have done the same: he stayed here in May and June 1940 before relocating in London. It was already popular with show business people such as Joséphine Baker, after whom a new bar was named in 2020, but also with the more intellectual expatriates; James Joyce sang Irish ballads in its lounge, accompanying himself on the piano. With interiors that recall a transatlantic liner, the hotel, as imposing as the *Normandie* or *Ile de France*, dominates a wide intersection within sight of the world's first department store, Bon Marché. The placement is no accident. Store owner Marguerite Boucicaut built the hotel "so that important provincial customers could be accommodated in a nearby establishment corresponding to their lifestyle."

Hitler intended postwar France to become a major source of food for the Reich. Its entertainment, wine and fashion industries would also continue, and Paris and the Côte d'Azur remain tourist Meccas. Meanwhile, he systematically looted the nation, and, in a final indignity, forced the French to bear the costs of maintaining the occupying forces. At the Lutetia, foreign entrepreneurs eager to share the plunder met with Otto Abetz, Berlin's ambassador to Vichy, and his court of collaborators. They drank in its high-ceilinged bar, negotiated over dinner in its restaurants, then dallied upstairs with one of the *poules de luxe* attracted by these high-spending invaders. Staff watched impassively as even the enlisted German soldiers went shopping, "returning," recalled one employee, "with armfuls of boxes for their dear wives, shouting, *'Ooh la la'*: shoes, and a lot of other things at incredible prices." In a small act of rebellion, the hotel walled up its wine cellar. If someone ordered any, the waiters told them, straight-faced, that they were all out.

Exit Lutetia onto Boulevard Raspail. In August 1944, de Gaulle pointedly designated the hotel a repatriation center for survivors of the

James Joyce,1928

Marguerite Boucicaut

Bon Marché ad, 1933

Oh-la-la, between 1940–1944, Gefreiter G. Schmitz

concentration camps. Pale and emaciated, dressed now in rags, they shuffled through the hotel that once welcomed them as guests. Relatives scanned notice boards for news of loved ones. Singer and actress Juliette Gréco, whose mother and sister survived Ravensbruck, wrote "We came every day, hoping to find our loved ones, a bit like the arrivals of the tide. The lounges downstairs were hell or heaven. And that smell? It was the bland scent of death. They all wore it in their striped dresses, with nothing underneath."

A plaque on the wall facing Boulevard Raspail commemorates the hotel's role in the liberation, but not its discreditable part in the Occupation. It reads "From April to August 1945, this hotel, which had become a reception center, received the greater part of the survivors of the Nazi concentration camps, glad to have regained their liberty and their loved ones from whom they had been snatched. Their joy cannot erase the anguish and pain of the families of the thousands who disappeared who waited here in vain for their own in this place." Although the Germans commandeered most other luxury hotels in Paris, in particular the Crillon, Meurice and Ritz, the Lutetia is the only one to display an admission of guilt, even one as half-hearted as this.

The Lutetia as a repatriation center

Cross the intersection of Boulevard Raspail, rue de Sevres and rue Babylone to ❷ **Square Boucicaut**. The park itself celebrates Marguerite Boucicaut, who built the Lutetia and Bon Marché—there is a large monument—but the central path or *allée* is dedicated to writer and

Jean Moulin

resistant Pierre Herbart (1903–1974). A prewar friend of Jean Cocteau and André Gide, and an active communist, Herbart joined the resistance and, as "General Le Vigan," helped set up a network in the southwest of France for young men fleeing deportation. Later he headed the resistance movement in Brittany.

Exit the park onto rue de Sèvres and follow until it becomes rue du Four at the intersection with rue du Dragon. At ❸ **48 rue du Four**, a plaque reads "Here was held on May 27, 1943, during the German oppression, the first secret meeting of the **National Council of the Resistance** under the presidency of Jean Moulin, delegated by General de Gaulle."

Before the war, Moulin had been *Préfet* of the city of Chartres. Refusing to collaborate with the Germans, he even tried to cut his throat rather than sign a false declaration as they demanded. In September 1941 he travelled to London and offered his services to de Gaulle, who asked him to return to France and unify the resistance. "A great man," the general wrote of him after their meeting. "Great in every way."

Moulin chose the location for the meeting with care. Five Metro stations nearby allowed participants to arrive individually from different directions and, should something go wrong, escape over the roofs. But many factions declined to send a representative, and before he could make much headway in uniting the disparate groups, another resistant betrayed him to the Gestapo in 1943. His body was never found. When, on the 50th anniversary of the liberation, his "presumed ashes" were installed in the Panthéon, the greatest honor the nation can confer, the coffin was empty.

Rue du Four, off rue Bonaparte, c.1867, Charles Marville

Before Haussmann rebuilt Paris in the 1860s, streets in this area were narrow and malodorous. One account called them "dirty, muddy and filled with trash, [with] quantities of manure combined with sludge." Few houses had kitchens. People cooked soups and stews in pots over an open fire, but needed an oven for anything more complicated, such as bread. For their use, the Abbey of St. Germain maintained a communal oven at ❹ **No. 43**. "Rue du Four" means literally "Street of the oven."

The association of Paris with intrigue didn't end in 1944. ❺ **Place Mehdi-Ben-Barka** at **No. 35** is named for the outspoken opponent of France's occupation of Morocco who disappeared during a visit to Paris in 1965. Israeli intelligence helped Moroccan agents and French police kidnap and murder him. ❻ **No. 22**, now a perfume shop, has an

7

9

even more significant pedigree in public violence. Formerly the café **Chez Moineau**, then the bookshop **Le 22**, this was the postwar meeting place of the Lettrists and Situationists, whose radical theories, elucidated by Guy Debord, helped spark the student revolution of May 1968.

Return and turn right into rue Bonaparte and continue untill it intersects with Boulevard St. Germain at a point dominated by ❼ the **Abbey Church of St-Germain-des-Prés**. The esplanade in front of the church, at the intersection of rue Bonaparte and rue de-l'Abbaye, was renamed ❽ **Place Juliette-Gréco** in 2020. Nearby is ❾ **Les Deux Magots**, one of the city's most popular literary cafes, a wartime meeting place of Jean-Paul Sartre, Simone de Beauvoir and Albert Camus. (The two *magots* or Chinese figurines survive from when this was a shop selling porcelain and toys. Founded in 1812 at 23 rue de Buci, it was

Juliette Gréco

Sartre and de Beauvoir

transferred to Place St-Germain-des-Prés in 1873. The statues now adorn the café interior.) In 1947, Sartre, following the death of his step-father, moved into his mother's apartment at ⓾ **42 rue Bonaparte.** In the 1960s, he relocated in Montparnasse after the *Organisation armée secrete* (OAS), supporting French rule in Algeria, twice bombed the building in protest at Sartre's opposition.

Return to Boulevard St. Germain and continue east to rue de Buci. At the intersection of Buci and rue de Bourbon-le-Chateau, ⓫ the café **Le Chai**, formerly *Au Chai de l'Abbaye*, marks the site of the wine store of the St. Germain abbey, destroyed during the Revolution of 1789. The café was popular both before and after World War II with political exiles from the Balkan countries. They sat at the back, invisible to new arrivals but able to watch the front door in mirrors on the rear wall.

After Hitler promised that anyone who wore the German uniform could expect a week's leave in Paris, young Germans eager for a good time crowded the cafés on this and surrounding streets. Proprietors turned their *caves* or cellars into *boites de nuit*—literally "night boxes"—with girls and music. The Luftwaffe officer in charge of en-

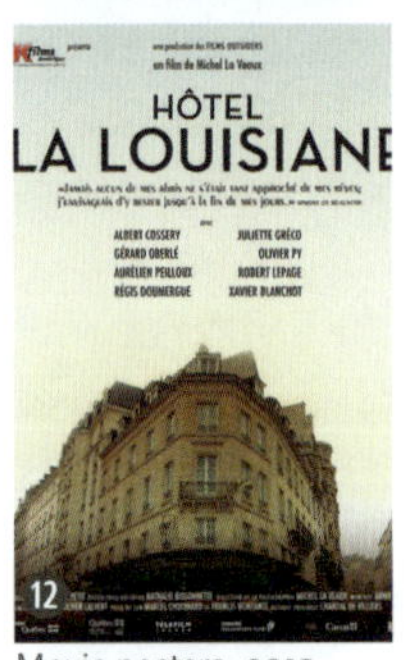

Movie posters, 2015

tertaining the troops, Dietrich Schultz-Köhn, was a familiar figure in Paris prewar jazz circles. Faced with the problem that Hitler had declared jazz "decadent" and, in addition, that the best players were Jewish, Roma or African, all proscribed under Nazi racial laws, he resourcefully designated them *wirtschaftlich wertvolle* (economically valuable), removing the risk of deportation. Grateful musicians named him "Doctor Jazz." [9-2]

Well into the 1960s, the Saint-Germain-des-Prés neighborhood was a major hub for jazz, attracting both French and American musicians. Such eminent musicians as pianist Bud Powell played in its cellar club, which Bertrand Tavernier recreated for his film *Round Midnight*.

With almost all produce shipped to Germany, Parisians struggled to feed themselves. Actress Leslie Caron, then a child, remembered the experience vividly. "We ate animal fodder: salsify, rutabagas, Jerusalem artichoke. Fruit was as rare and expensive as tobacco. Children had one glass of milk a day. We were each given an ever-shrinking ration of butter; it eventually amounted to an eggcup-full per person, per week. By the end of the war, bread was down to one slice a day per person—two-

Women waiting in line outside a grocery store to buy food during rationing, 1940s

thirds flour, one-third wood shavings. Meat was also extremely scarce: about two hundred grams a week each. Cats and dogs disappeared—they were stolen and eaten. As a pharmacist, my father received cocoa butter to make suppositories, and it became the substitute for butter and oil in our cooking. Everything at our table had a faint cocoa flavor." Adults fared even worse. Jean-Paul Sartre subsisted on a diet of cigarettes, sausages, and as many as 50 amphetamine pills a day.

Cross to the corner of rue de Buci and rue de Seine. On April 4, 1942, as part of a Resistance plan to protest food shortages, a group of women invaded the Eco food store at this intersection, the window of which displayed cans of sardines, then a luxury. Looting the store, they distributed the food to a growing crowd, with a leaflet explaining, "If we raise our voices more, we will obtain more. Let's help ourselves. Our children are hungry, that comes first." The police intervened and a gunfight ensued with resistance members in which two gendarmes were killed.

Generations of musicians, writers and artists have patronized 12
the **Hôtel la Louisiane**, at the opposite corner (entrance at 60 rue de Seine). In 1943, Simone de Beauvoir and Jean-Paul Sartre lived here, though in separate rooms, to accommodate their complicated sex lives. Near the front entrance, a plaque commemorates Jacques Francesco of the 2nd Armored Division who died during the uprising of August 24, 1944. After the war, the hotel's low rates and proximity to the clubs of St. Germain made it popular with itinerant musicians, particularly American jazz performers, who made entire floors communal, cooking and sharing soul food and participating in late-night jam sessions.

Continue along rue de Buci to intersection with rue Dauphine, turn into Dauphine, follow until rue Christine, then take Christine to 7 rue des Grands-Augustins, the **Hôtel de Savoie.** A plaque identifies the loft in this 15th-century *hôtel particulier* or private mansion as
13 **Pablo Picasso's studio** and Paris home from 1936 to 1955. Spain, though nominally neutral, collaborated with the Nazis, so Picasso and other Spanish citizens were generally left alone. His anti-Nazi sympa-

thies, however, were no secret. A Gestapo man searching his apartment noticed a photograph of *Guernica,* painted in his loft, and inspired by a bombing raid on that Catalan town. "Did you do that?" he asked. "No," Picasso replied tersely. "*You* did."

(**JB**: It was hoped this building could be preserved as a national monument but it is now being converted into a hotel, though the proprietors promise that the studio will remain available for cultural events. Many years ago, I attended a concert there by the jazz violinist Didier Lockwood. That his music reverberated from the walls where *Guernica* had hung gave it a special resonance. I hope that, in the conversion, that quality isn't lost.)

14

Continue down rue des Grands-Augustins, turn right on Quai des Grands-Augustins and follow the river to ⓮ **Place St. Michel**. Francisque Duret's figure of St. Michael slaying a demon dominates this intersection. Below him, two winged chimeras spout water. Eight other sculptors contributed to the fountain. The rock on which he stands is by Félix Saupin, the ornaments and foliage by Claude Vignon. *Power and Moderation,* supporting the arms of Paris on the upper pediment, is by Auguste-Hyacinthe Debay. Four additional sculptures represent the cardinal virtues: *Prudence,* holding a mirror and a snake, by Jean-Auguste Barre; *Justice,* holding a sword, by Elias Robert; *Temperance,* by Charles Gumery, and *Strength,* also by Debay, which shows Hercules dressed in the skin of the Nemean lion, which he slew as the first of his 12 labors.

In 1944, an additional inscription was added to the fountain. On one side, it reads "In memory of the soldiers of the French Forces of the Interior and the inhabitants of the 5th and 6th arrondissements who, on these places, died while fighting." It continues on the verso "The year MCMXLIV. From August 19 to 25, after 50 months of German occupation, the people of Paris, at the approach of the liberating armies, rose up against oppression."

American strategy called for Paris to remain in German hands until the entire country was subdued, then to place all France under military control, as would happen in Austria and Germany. Accordingly, the Allied armies held back until de Gaulle forced their hand by exhorting Parisans to attack the already dispirited occupying troops. On August 19, 1944, Gaullist sympathizers within the *gendarmerie* seized the *Préfecture* (police headquarters) just across the river. Defense of Pont St. Michel and the route into or out of Paris was in the hands of the **Maquis de St. Severin**, a group headquartered in the church of that name a few blocks away. They were armed with stolen German rifles and grenades, and homemade "Molotov Cocktails." Simply bottles

Members of the French resistance, Paris, 1944

Crowds of Parisians celebrating the entry of Allied troops into Paris scatter for cover as a sniper fires from a building on the Place de la Concorde. August 26, 1944

filled with petrol emulsified with soap powder and the neck stuffed with a cloth wick, these were effective against tanks, as the burning petrol trickled through cracks in the armor. (Their name was a gibe at Vyacheslav Molotov, Soviet foreign minister. When Finland, at the beginning of the war, accused Russia of dropping incendiary bombs, Molotov insisted they were "humanitarian food deliveries"—at which the Finns sarcastically proposed the "Molotov cocktail" to wash them down.)

None of the defenders knew that the Swedish consul-general, Raoul Nordling, had already persuaded the German military governor, General Dietrich von Choltitz, to surrender and avoid further bloodshed. The offer created dissent among the already divided fighters. Most of the arguments against a ceasefire came from the Communists. Best organized of the resistance groups, they hoped to turn their wartime exploits into peacetime power—an idea de Gaulle derided; what hope for a one-party system, he joked, in a country with many hundred kinds of cheese?

General de Gaulle and his entourage set off from the Arc de Triomphe down the Champs Elysees to Notre Dame for Thanksgiving service following the city's liberation in August 1944

The survival of Paris rested in a knife edge. While negotiations dragged on, German engineers continued to plant explosives all over the city. Should they be forced to retreat, the Fuhrer had ordered "Paris must not pass into the enemy's hands, except as a field of ruins." Meanwhile, German *Panzers* arrived at Place St. Michel, backed by armored cars, but after assaulting the barricades for an hour, withdrew. Officially they were short of ammunition, but it's more likely they had heard of the imminent armistice.

American troops under General George S. Patton advanced to the suburbs but paused while de Gaulle flew from London to lead the triumphant French, which Generals Eisenhower and Omar Bradley had agreed, reluctantly, should enter the city first. On August 24, the pealing of church bells signalled the arrival of French tanks under General

Leclerc. The next day, von Choltitz formally surrendered the garrison. However, as part of a compromise, he didn't capitulate only to the Allies but to a hurriedly created interim city government which the Communists dominated. For Paris, the Occupation was over.

De Gaulle, still relatively unknown to the French, succeeded in turning public adulation into political muscle. American author John dos Passos, an old Paris hand, watched him skillfully alternating between stern Father of the Nation and avuncular *ami de famille*, and decided "There's more to him than we've been led to believe." Once the smoke cleared, it was de Gaulle and not the Communists who headed the provisional government. After the more prominent traitors had been executed or jailed and others had suffered the rough justice meted out by vengeful victims, he declined to prosecute the remaining collaborators. When Marcel Ophuls' 1969 four-hour documentary film *Le Chagrin et la Pitié* (The Sorrow and the Pity) exposed the full extent of collaboration, he blocked its broadcast on French TV. He also hampered the production of such films as *Is Paris Burning?* which showed favorably the wartime work of the Communists, his political rivals.

At Notre Dame, August 1944

Robert Desnos

Paul Éluard

Antoine de Saint-Exupéry

Cross Pont St. Michel to Promenade Maurice-Careme and follow the river to ⓯ the **Mémorial des Martyrs de la Déportation**. Built on the site of the former Paris morgue and inaugurated by President de Gaulle is 1962, it testifies to the people deported from Vichy France during World War II.

To visit the memorial, descend the staircase past a metal portcullis into the hexagonal rotunda. The walls display excerpts from the writings of Louis Aragon, Robert Desnos, Paul Éluard, Antoine de Saint-Exupéry and Jean-Paul Sartre, although Desnos was the only one of them actually deported. Arrested in February 1944, he died of typhoid in Theresienstadt camp a month after liberation, nursed by a student who recognized him from references in André Breton's novel *Nadja.* The wall bears part of his poem *The Heart That Hated War.* It includes the lines "All that remains to me is to be the shadow among shadows/ To be a hundred times more of a shadow than the shadow."

A circular plaque on the floor is inscribed "They descended into the mouth of the earth and they did not return." An eternal flame burns

The promenade passes Notre-Dame Cathedral and leads to the Mémorial

and the tomb of the Unknown Deportee bears the inscription "Dedicated to the living memory of the 200,000 French deportees sleeping in the night and the fog, exterminated in the Nazi concentration camps." Along both walls, lighted crystals symbolize those deported. At the end of the tunnel is a single bright light. Urns at both ends contain bones and ashes from the camps. Small rooms resemble prison cells, as does a barred opening looking out on the Seine. At the exit to the chamber is the injunction "Forgive but never forget."

(**JB**: The phrase "night and fog" refers to Hitler's so-called "*Nacht und nebel*" directive of December 1941. It ordered that political activists and resistants in occupied territories, rather than being publicly tried or executed, at the risk of making them martyrs, were instead to be kidnapped, imprisoned, murdered, or otherwise made to disappear without trace, as into the night and fog. Alain Resnais resuscitated the phrase in 1969 in the title of *Nuit et Brouillard,* his pioneering documentary about the deportations.)

The memorial was generally acclaimed, but drew criticism for failing to differentiate between Jews and the less numerous victims of other racial minorities, as well as political activists and resistants. Historian Peter Carrier cites the phrase "200,000 French deportees" as misleading. "By identifying victims as French nationals, [it] distorts the historical record by suggesting that victims died willingly for a national cause rather than as victims of state persecution. [The memorial] therefore symbolically assimilates the specific Jewish memory of the Second World War into national memory." The corrected figures are believed to be 160,000 persons deported, 76,000 of them Jewish, of whom 74,000 died. Exit onto forecourt of Notre Dame, then cross Pont d'Arcole to rue de Rivoli and **Metro Hotel de Ville (Lines 1 and 11.)**

One of the worst crimes committed under the Occupation isn't specifically referenced in the memorial. In the early hours of July 16, 1942, *gendarmes*—ordinary policemen—began rounding up thousands of Jews. Rather than French citizens, they targeted foreign nationals, particularly those who had fled to France from other countries to escape Nazi invasion. (Something similar took place under the 1789 revolution. France started by welcoming citizens of other oppressed countries, then accused them of plotting to overthrow it.) The 2,573 men, 5,165 women and 3,625 children were taken from their homes, and about 6,000 immediately shipped to prison camps in Germany. The rest languished in the Vélodrome d'Hiver, an indoor arena on rue Nélaton in the 15th *arrondissement* dating back to 1909. There was

Crowds celebrating the liberation of the city, *Paris*. August 25, 1944

scarcely space to lie down. A glass ceiling made it stifling by day, as all ventilation had been blocked to prevent escape, and frigid at night. No provision had been made for food, water, or sanitation. Many of those imprisoned remained there for a week before being shipped to their deaths.

Why the Vel d'Hiver? At the outbreak of war, the French arrested all German nationals as possible enemy aliens, and confined them in this building—which is almost certainly why the Germans, connoisseurs of recrimination, chose to pen French deportees in the same place. Such staged demonstrations typified the early months of the

A memorial to the Vel d'Hiv Roundup, on Quai de Grenelle

Occupation. Justifying the invasion of France as payback for Germany's humiliation at the end of World War I, Hitler insisted that France sign its surrender at a site in the Compiègne forest, maintained as a monument, where Germany capitulated in 1918, and in the same railway car, which they took from the museum where it was preserved, demolishing a wall in the process. The surrender was filmed, and the world's press invited to watch. During the ceremony, a band played. Once the crowd left, the monument was dynamited.

After the war, neither the Vel d'Hiver's management nor the city of Paris acknowledged its unsavory history. It remained in use until 1959, hosting boxing matches, Far West shows, a high mass celebrated by the Archbishop of Paris, and the last French bullfight before they were declared illegal. A plaque now marks where it stood, and there is a small peace garden nearby. Successive presidents declined to take responsibility for the atrocity, insisting that the Republic ceased to exist once Vichy took over. In 1995, President Jacques Chirac reversed this position, acknowledging the role of the French State in the persecution of Jews and others during the War.

WALK 10

PILGRIMAGE: A PARIS OF BELIEF

START: Metro Saint-Michel (Line 4)
FINISH: Metro Censier-Daubenton (Line 7)

PILGRIMAGE: A PARIS OF BELIEF

1. Cathedral of Notre-Dame-de-Paris
2. Wallace Water Fountain: 37 rue de la Bûcherie
3. Square René Viviani
4. Saint Julien-le-Pauvre: 1 rue Saint-Julien le Pauvre
5. Salvador Dalì Sundial: 27 rue Saint-Jacques
6. Musée de Cluny-Musée National du Moyen Âge: 28 rue Du Sommerard
7. Square Samuel-Paty
8. Medieval Garden of Cluny
9. Sorbonne
10. Statue of Michel de Montaigne
11. Collège de France
12. Église Saint Éphrem-le-Syriaque: 17 rue des Carmes
13. Calvin's Tower: 21 rue Valette
14. Pantheon
15. Université Panthéon-Sorbonne
16. Town Hall of the 5th Arrondissement
17. Hôtel des Grands Hommes: 17 pl. du Panthéon
18. Church of Saint Etienne du Mont: Place Sainte-Geneviève
19. Apartments of Verlaine and Hemingway: 39 rue Descartes
20. Hemingway's First Paris Apartment: 74 rue du Cardinal Lemoine
21. Place de la Contrescarpe
22. George Orwell's Apartment: 6 rue du Pot de Fer
23. Mouffetard Market
24. Saint-Médard Church: 141 rue Mouffetard
25. Square Saint-Médard/Miss. Tic

Previous page: *The Rooftops of Notre Dame*, 1910, Georges Redon

Quai des Orfèvres
Ile de la Cité
Seine
St.Michel
Notre Dame
Ile St. Louis
déon
Cluny-
la Sorbone
Odéon
Rue Racine
Maubert
Mutualité
Rue des Carmes
Rue des Bièvre
Pont Marie
de Vaugirard
Sorbone
Rue des Écoles
Sorbonne
Université
UPMC
Rue Valette
Rue Soufflot
Cardinal Lemoine
Boulevard Saint Michel
Rue Saint-Jacques
Panthéon
Rue Descartes
Rue Monge
Rue Linné
Rue Lhomond
Rue Mouffetard
Rue Erasme
de l' Observatoire
Rue Claude- Bernard
Censier-Daubenton
Boulevard de Port-Royal
200 ft
50 m

The French, perceived as Christian, are in fact ruled by many beliefs, only some of them religious. In December 1804, Napoléon I took the crown of France from the hands of Pope Pius VII and placed it on his own head, signifying that he would rule not "by the grace of God" or the approval of Rome but at the will of his subjects. In doing so, he formally severed the Catholic church from the French state.

Today, 51 percent of French people say they have no religion. Of the rest, 10 percent follow Islam and 34 percent are Jews. Only 29 percent identify as Catholic and, of those, a mere 8 percent regularly attend mass. Yet churches are everywhere, such Catholic feasts as the Assumption, Ascension and the Epiphany are public holidays, and people celebrate christening, marriage and burial according to traditional Catholic rites: "theme" weddings are frowned on, likewise composing your own vows. Until recently, one Paris church defiantly continued to celebrate mass in Latin, long after other countries abandoned the practice. And if the piety of a nation is measurable by its patron saints, Paris has three.

The Revolution of 1789 killed or exiled more than 30,000 priests and nuns, and turned churches into factories. Yet many revolutionaries retained their belief in God: just not the one revered by the Catholic church. Maximilien Robespierre proposed an alternative religion, replacing a humanized deity with one who embodied Reason. Surviving houses of worship were reopened, with a sign over their entrances announcing that "The French people recognize the Supreme Being and the immortality of the soul." Generations of philosophers, many of them French, have grappled with this contradiction. "If God did not exist," mused Voltaire, "it would be necessary to invent Him," and Blaise Pascal (1623–1662) replaced faith with a persuasively logical argument for belief. Known as Pascal's Wager, it reasons that maybe there isn't a God—but why not live as if there is? You may miss out on some pleasures in this life, but you stand to win Paradise.

We start our walk at **Metro Saint Michel (Line 4)** Follow the river, turn right into rue de Petit Pont and turn left to **rue de la Bûcherie**, across from the Ile de la Cité and ❶ the **Cathedral of Notre-Dame-de-Paris**. In January 1924, a bronze star set in the cathedral's *parvis or forecourt* became the "Point Zero" from which all French highways were measured. (Incidentally, newcomers will find it easier to get around Paris if they remember that all streets are numbered with the lowest number closest to the river.)

Point Zero

This area is called the Latin Quarter because teachers in the religious schools that sprang up in the shadow of the cathedral communicated with their students from many countries in Latin, the common language of the church. In the 10th century, one of the best minds belonged to Peter Abélard, a young priest whose love for his student Héloise drove her jealous guardian to have him castrated. [1-1]

Abélard and Héloise, 1882

With the Revolution of 1789, philanthropy ceased to be the responsibility of the church and passed into the hands of the charitable laity. One result was the appearance in the late 19th century of **Wallace water fountains (❷ 37 rue de la Bûcherie)**, an example of which stands on this square. More than fifty are scattered around the city, erected by British philanthropist Sir Richard Wallace following the Prussian siege of 1871. A lover of Paris, he wanted nobody in the city to ever again go thirsty. Cast from iron and painted dark green, they stand seven feet tall and weigh more than 1400 pounds. The four female figures, each slightly different, represent Kindness, Simplicity, Charity and Sobriety. The water, which runs constantly, comes direct from the city's supply and in summer is cooled to 44 degrees. Carbon dioxide is also added for sparkle, and some fountains are topped with *brumiseurs* that spray a cooling mist. Originally, two cups were attached by a chain and kept submerged between uses, but the city removed them in 1952 "for hygiene reasons," frustrating Wallace's generous impulse.

Continue along the front and turn into rue St.-Julien-le-Pauvre. The park, ❸ **Square René Viviani**, honors the Prime Minister who led France at the outbreak of the 1914–1918 war. It occupies the former grounds of the church of St. Julien-le-Pauvre, and boasts the oldest living tree in Paris—which, unusual for a city where most trees are either *platane* (plane trees) or *marrons* (chestnuts), is a Locust or *Robinia pseudoacacia*, brought from North America by royal botanist Jean Robin in 1601. A concrete buttress keeps it upright and, hopefully, alive for another century at least.

Next to the park, ❹ the **Church of Saint Julien-le-Pauvre** (Julien the Poor) is one of the city's oldest religious buildings, its ambitious design whittled down between the 12th and 19th centuries. In 1889 it was reconsecrated to the Melkite or Greek Orthodox faith. Portions of the earlier church on this site stand on the forecourt, to the left of the modern building, the façade of which incorporates a slab of stone said to be a fragment of the road that once connected Rome to this distant outpost of its empire.

The Dada group in the garden of the Saint-Julien-Le-Pauvre church, April 14, 1921

On April 14, 1921, church and park saw an event staged by the Dada group. Founded in Zurich during World War I by Tristan Tzara, Dada hoped, by behaving absurdly, to draw attention to war's irrationality. Accosting pedestrians, Dadaists urged them to "Be dirty!," told a man with a big nose to "trim it as you trim your hair!" and women to "wash their breasts as they wash their faces." Tzara expected shock and uproar, but blasé Parisians mostly shrugged and walked on. Furious, he blamed his former followers, led by André Breton and calling themselves Surrealists, who were less interested in creating disorder than in using Dada techniques to probe the unconscious. By 1924, Dada was almost forgotten. But Surrealism too went out of fashion, and Breton would complain, as Tzara had once done, "You just can't shock people anymore." [10-2]

At the end of rue de St. Julien-le-Pauvre, turn into rue Saint-Jacques. Both the Dadaists and Surrealists despised religion, one member of the latter, Benjamin Péret, even physically attacking nuns and priests in the street. Breton habitually referred to the crucifix as *cet-objet-la* (that thing) and Salvador Dalì attended mass specifically to sit in the back pews and masturbate.

Dalì makes an unexpected appearance at ❺ **27 rue Saint-Jacques**. In 1966, friends who owned this shop asked him to install a **sundial** on their wall. Shamelessly exhibitionist, he decorated the dial with burning blue eyes suggesting his own intense gaze and hired a brass band to play as a crane carried him and a pet ocelot ten feet from the sidewalk to make some final adjustments. The dial's shape, re-

sembling a scallop shell, refers to the route of the pilgrimage to the church of St. James/Jacques at Compostela, of which rue Saint-Jacques is a part. Pilgrims picked up a shell from the beach where they came ashore. As a timekeeper, incidentally, the sundial is a flop, since the wall receives no direct sun. But perhaps, for a Surrealist, that was part of the effect. Another plaque on the street side of the same building marks where René Vinchon, a *Gardien de la Paix* (policeman) died fighting the occupying Germans in August 1944.

Despite hotels and other advertisers indiscriminately co-opting the "*Quartier Latin*" label, the Latin Quarter ends officially at Boulevard St. Germain. Once you cross, you are climbing Mont Sainte-Geneviève. Diagonally opposite the intersection of rue Saint-Jacques and Boulevard St. Germain is the Hôtel de Cluny, former residence of the abbot of the 15th century Cluny abbey, now 6 the **Musée de Cluny-Musée National du Moyen Âge**. In 1832, archaeologist and art collector Alexandre du Sommerard bought the building to house his collection of medieval and Renaissance objects, which became the basis of the museum. The abbey rests on the foundations of Roman baths, parts of which the new building incorporates. A valued amenity in this chilly northern outpost of the empire, the baths included steam rooms, a plunge pool, exercise and sports areas, a library, and a lofty vaulted *tepidarium* or cooling-off chamber. A walkway allows modern visitors to appreciate their scale. Excavating this space in 1977, archaeologists found the heads of 28 statues torn from the façade of Notre Dame in 1793. The figures ac-

MUSÉE DE CLUNY

tually represented the biblical kings of Judah but revolutionaries took them for kings of France. A pious builder secretly bought the fragments and buried them in the abbey's consecrated ground.

A narrow lane, rue de Cluny, runs along the side of the abbey and leads to leafy 7 **Square Samuel-Paty**. Originally the Square de la Sorbonne, the park was renamed for mathematician Paul Painlevé, and subsequently for Samuel Paty, a French schoolteacher murdered in 2020 as an act of racial terror. Also in the park, a monument celebrates painter Pierre Puvis de Chavannes (1824–1898), fashionable in his day for historic and mythological murals, some of which decorate the interior of the Panthéon.

To visit the museum from Square Samuel Paty, continue to rue du Sommerard and the entrance. To visit 8 the abbey gardens (**Medieval Garden of Cluny**) only, enter by the gate at the northern, *i.e.*, lower edge of the square. Since medieval monarchs had no interest in the health of their subjects, it was left to the church to treat illness. The museum has recreated the abbey's medicinal herb garden. Another plot includes vegetables that made up most of the medieval diet. Flowers and plants in the Middle Ages often had a symbolic or romantic meaning. A *jardin celeste* (Celestial Garden) includes the rose, lily, violet and iris that surround the Virgin in paintings of the time, and *a Jardin de l'amour Courtois* (Garden of Courtly Love) shows how lovers communicated covertly in a language of flowers. Elsewhere in the garden, monks starved of sensual stimulation planted aromatic herbs between the stones of the paths so that their sandaled feet, crushing them, released their aroma.

Return to Square Samuel Paty and exit onto rue des Écoles, literally a "street of schools," since whole blocks are occupied by the city's oldest university, 9 the **Sorbonne**, and one of its most distinguished centers of learning, the Collège de France. Just outside the fence surrounding Square Samuel Paty and facing the Sorbonne entrance is 10 a bronze **statue of philosopher Michel Montaigne** (1533–1592). Students believe it is good luck before an exam to greet him by name and rub his right foot, which is polished to a gleam.

The Sorbonne began in 1257 when Robert de Sorbon (1201–1274), chaplain to King Louis IX (Saint Louis), started a free school for students too poor to afford private education. Over the centuries, it expanded, adding faculties of Science, Law, Medicine, Pharmacy, Literature, Theology, even Astronomy. (You can glimpse the dome of its rooftop observatory, built in 1895.) As the Sorbonne's reputation grew, however, so did its bureaucracy, symptomatic of the stagnant education system. A general frustration culminated in what the French now call les *évenéments de '68* (the '68 events). They actually began on the campus of the city's newest university, Paris Nanterre, but it was the decision by Sorbonne students in May to occupy their building that lit the fuse. When the rector locked them out three weeks before final exams, they surged into the streets, felling trees, tearing up cobblestones for use as missiles, and plastering walls with posters. One of these, part protest, part threat, showed a shocked, bloodstained face, with the message *Bourgeois, You Have Understood Nothing.* [10-3]

Next to the Sorbonne, ⓫ the **Collège de France**, established by François I in 1530, offers courses that are free and open to all, without conditions or registration. Each October, distinguished scholars deliver a series of lectures. As these are free, with no need to register or reserve a seat, and often take place in cold or wet weather, the hall quickly fills with people less interested in semiology or theoretical physics than staying warm and dry. The speaker sometimes faces an audience of which only those seated in the front rows understand what he is talking about. The rest are eating, sleeping, or, in extreme cases, trimming their toenails.

Continue along rue des Écoles and turn into rue des Carmes. ⓬ The **Église Saint Éphrem-le-Syriaque** is an 18th-century church with an imposing colonnaded entrance, built

rue des Carmes

on much older foundations, and currently dedicated to the Syrian Catholic rite. Services still take place but its superior acoustics mean that the church is used more often for performances of classical music. In the 1920s, **No. 30**, opposite, was occupied by **Paris's first Asian restaurant**. The author of a 1927 guidebook found its food less impressive than the clientele. "See dozens of Chinese men with white girls," he wrote. "A great novelty." The restaurant was probably Vietnamese rather than Chinese. In 1927, when Cochin, Tonkin and Annam—today's Vietnam—were French colonies, about 3,000 Vietnamese lived in Paris, augmented by French nationals and citizens of mixed race who had served as administrators there.

Calvin's Tower, 1909, G-H Manesse

At the intersection with rue Lanneau, rue des Carmes becomes rue Valette. At ⓭ **No. 21,** the hexagonal **Calvin's Tower** is all that remains of Collège Fortet, associated with the theologian John Calvin (1509–1564) who gave his name to Calvinism, one of the more rigorous creeds to emerge from the Protestant Reformation. King François I of France offered asylum to Calvin and his followers, whom the Catholic church had excommunicated, but in October 1534, in what became known as the Affair of the Placards, the rebels,

François I

John Calvin

Martin Luther

inspired by German theologian Martin Luther, who, in 1517, nailed a summary of his beliefs to a church door in Wittenberg, plastered anti-Catholic declarations all over Paris and four provincial cities. One such manifesto even appeared on the bedchamber door of the king, who promptly rescinded his former welcome. Rewards were offered for the capture of Calvin and his friends, and some were burned at the stake. Calvin, however, had explored escape routes from his tower through neighboring houses, and made it to more free-thinking Switzerland, where he became an important voice in the growth of the Protestant faith.

At the top of rue Valette, exit onto ⓮ **Place de la Panthéon**. Louis XV began this building as a church to house the remains of Saint Geneviève, but the revolution of 1789 halted construction. The mob publicly burned her body and threw her ashes into the Seine. Believers rescued just the bones of one finger, which, with a few other relics, were preserved in the nearby church of St. Etienne du Mont.

In 1791, the Convention, France's ruling body, voted to repurpose the building as a shrine to individuals who distinguished themselves

by achievement rather than piety. As church and state wrangled over ownership, Napoléon I allowed 41 men to be buried in its crypt. Most were military officers and officials of the Empire, but they also included explorer Louis-Antoine de Bougainville and the Revolution's official painter, Jacques-Louis David. Even though, during the period of church occupancy, Pierre Puvis de Chavanne had added murals inspired by incidents in the life of Saint Geneviève, in 1881 the clergy admitted defeat. An inscription was added above the entrance reading "A grateful nation honors its great men."

Victor Hugo, novelist and political activist (but certainly no saint), became the first person buried there in half a century. A million people lined the streets to watch his body pass after it lay in state under the Arc de Triomphe. Such elaborate ceremonial became integral to "Panthéonizing." The next person to be honored, author Émile Zola, had already been buried, but his body was exhumed for reinterment in the crypt. This would become standard practice but it hasn't always been possible. Nobody knows where World War II resistance leader Jean Moulin died, so the coffin installed in 1964 was empty, while that of entertainer Joséphine Baker, honored in 2021, contained only soil from three places related to her life; St. Louis, Paris, and Monaco, where her body remains.

In 1851, at the Observatory in Montparnasse, physicist Léon Foucault staged a graphic demonstration of the rotation of the earth. As a pendulum swung, always in the same arc, spectators could track the earth's slow turning on a compass disc on the floor. A few weeks later, Foucault persuaded the Panthéon, the tallest secular building in Paris, to host a more ambitious version of the experiment, suspending a 62-pound brass-coated lead weight on a 220-foot wire from the highest point of its dome. The pendulum continues to oscillate today.

It's customary for the newly elected President of France to visit the Panthéon on the day of his inauguration, paying respects to the great dead. Valéry Giscard d'Estaing displayed characteristic modesty in 1974, breaking with tradition by alighting from the official limou-

Pantheon interior

Chavanne's mural

Foucault's pendulum

sine and walking through the crowds before ascending the steps. In 1981, by contrast but true to type, François Mitterand recruited a movie star, a TV producer and a historian to plan his appearance. Carrying a single red rose, the symbol of his Socialist party, he descended to the crypt and laid roses on the tombs of Jean Moulin and others, while hidden helpers handed him additional blooms and filmed the event, and an orchestra outside played Beethoven's Ninth Symphony.

Among the buildings on Place du Panthéon facing the main façade are ⓯ the offices of the **Université Panthéon-Sorbonne** and the ⓰ ***mairie*** or **town hall of the 5th *arrondissement*.** At ⓱ **No. 17**, a former private mansion that became a rooming house after the Revolution is now the **Hôtel des Grands Hommes**. A plaque records that here, in 1919, André Breton pioneered automatic writing with his friend Philippe Soupault. Surrendering creativity purely to chance, the two men agreed that each, spontaneously, would say the first thing that came into his head—which, if the other concurred, was added to the text. A typical passage read "The neighbors of solitude leaned forward, and through the night was heard the whistling of streetlamps. The capricious house loses blood. Everybody loves a fire; when the color of the sky changes it's somebody dying." Published in 1920 as *Les Champs Magnétiques* (The Magnetic Fields), the text is regarded as the first true creative act of Surrealism.

Continue along the side of the Panthéon to ⓲ the **Church of Saint Etienne du Mont**. The building, both inside and out, is a riot of clashing styles, a clue to its repeated reconstruction. As well as its convo-

Interior of St. Etienne du Mont, 1864, Émile-Antoine-François Herson

luted marble rood screen and carved pulpit, a shrine to Saint Geneviève contains a gilded copper reliquary enclosing the few surviving fragments of her body. A side cloister displays twelve 17th-century stained glass windows, brought here from other Paris churches for safety during World War I. Revolutionary leader Jean-Paul Marat is buried in the churchyard and the church itself contains the tombs of authors Blaise Pascal and Jean Racine, but a greater claim to celebrity is made by a flight of steps on the northern or downhill side of the building. It's here, in Woody Allen's 2011 film *Midnight in Paris*, that footsore writer Owen Wilson accepts a lift from Scott and Zelda Fitzgerald in a 1928 Peugeot Landaulet.

Midnight in Paris (2011)

39 rue Descartes, 1934

Paul Verlaine

Take rue Clovis, opposite the church, and turn into rue Descartes. ⓳ **No. 39**, now a restaurant, has a double literary significance, signaled by two plaques beside the door and another higher on the façade. In this house, in 1896, the poet **Paul Verlaine** died. And for a time in 1922 and 1923, **Ernest Hemingway** rented a room on the top floor. Verlaine never recovered from his disastrous affair with the teenaged Arthur Rimbaud, for whom he gave up his wife, child, reputation, and even his freedom, when a bigoted judge imprisoned him for supposedly seducing his sociopathic lover. Addicted to absinthe and suffering from diabetes and syphilis, Verlaine stumbled back to this house each night from the cafés of Montparnasse. In June 1944, the British used lines from his poems in coded broadcasts to Occupied France. German radio operators struggled to translate "The long sobs of the violins of autumn wound my heart with a monotonous languor," unaware that the words signaled the imminence of D-Day.

Notwithstanding the plaque by the front door, this was never Ernest Hemingway's home. During 1922 and 1923, he did, however, rent a top-floor room as a place to work when life in a small apartment with wife Hadley and infant son John became too distracting. For 60 francs a month, he got an uncarpeted room with a table and chair, and a grate where he lit fires and sometimes roasted chestnuts in the embers. (Hemingway, incidentally, was not notably religious. He did convert to Catholicism for his marriage to Pauline Pfeiffer but it was a faith he wore lightly. He resorted to prayer once, during a bout of erectile dysfunction. Medical treatments failed. "Then one day Pauline said, 'Listen, Ernest, why don't you go pray?'" He went to a nearby church and offered up a short appeal to the Almighty. The therapy worked, since, when he returned home, "we made love like we invented it. We never had any trouble again.")

Continue along rue Descartes, turn left into rue Thouin, then, almost immediately, right into rue de Cardinal Lemoine, where **Ernest and Hadley Hemingway had their first Paris apartment** on the 4th floor at ⓴ **No. 74.** Realizing he had been naïve in thinking they could live for a year in a hotel on a thousand dollars, Ernest, in January 1922, moved with Hadley into a two-room apartment on the fourth floor of this building. There was no hot water, and the only lavatory, shared with the rest of the building, was what Hadley called "a step-on-two-pedals toilet"; i.e., a closet with a hole in the floor which required the user to straddle and squat. "The apartment wasn't ghastly," she said. "In fact, it was kind of fun." She was less enthusiastic about the drunks and derelicts sleeping in doorways, and the beggars looking for hand-outs. "I suppose they were the salt of the earth," she said dubiously, "except that some dirt had got into the salt."

Ernest Hemingway and Elizabeth Hadley with friends at a cafe, summer 1925

The street-level café next door doubled as *a bal musette, the Bal du Printemps* (Dance Hall of Spring.) Ernest called it a "noisy, rough music hall and hangout for sailors, whores, *apaches* (street gang members) and American expatriates, who nicknamed it 'Bucket of Blood,'" but is kinder in *The Sun Also Rises,* describing how the owner provided music, playing an accordion and pounding the beat with a ring of bells around one ankle. It was part of the etiquette of such places that one never spoke to one's partner, so the Hemingways, neither yet fluent in French, spent many evenings there. "I got lots of dances," Hadley recalled. And Ernest? "Well, he did his best."

Continue along rue du Cardinal Lemoine to 21 **Place Contrescarpe**, described by Hemingway in *A Moveable Feast.* Today it's well tended but in 1928 there was nothing here but a few trees, with the district's cesspool underneath. He called its Café des Amateurs "a sad, evilly run café where the drunkards of the quarter crowded together and I kept away from

it because of the smell of dirty bodies and the sour smell of drunkenness. The men and women who frequented the Amateurs stayed drunk all of the time, or all of the time they could afford it, mostly on wine which they bought by the half-liter or liter." Many worked in what he called "that wonderful narrow crowded market street" of rue Mouffetard. He describes how flower-sellers sat in the gutter, dunking white carnations in blue or purple dye to make them more exotic and saleable.

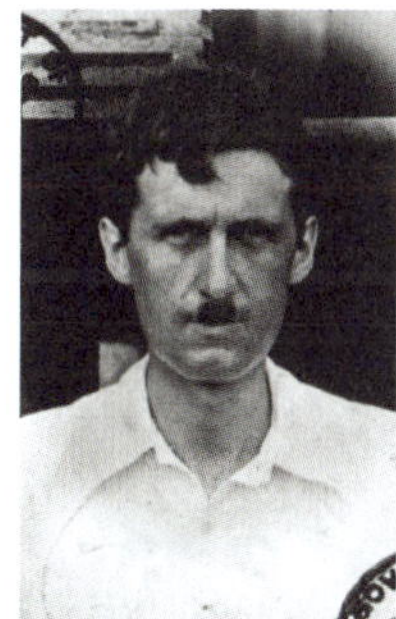

George Orwell, c.1922

Continue down rue Mouffetard to **rue du Pot de Fer**. In 1928, British author **George Orwell** worked as *a plongeur* or dishwasher in a Right Bank hotel but returned each night to a rooming house at ㉒ **No. 6.** "The walls were as thin as matchwood," he wrote, "and to hide the cracks they had been covered with layer after layer of pink paper. Long lines of bugs marched all day long like columns of soldiers and at night came down ravenously hungry so that one had to get up every few hours and kill them." Another lodger suggested burning some sulfur. The bugs, disliking the smell, retreated into the surrounding rooms—until their occupants burned sulfur also, and drove them back.

The Bièvre near Saint-Médard

Street Merchant, 1896

Rue Mouffetard, 1930

Continue into ㉓ the **Mouffetard market.** Rather than a street market, where sellers arrive once or twice a week, set up their stalls, and leave at the end of the day, Mouffetard is lined with permanent shops. It's at its best on winter mornings, when the harsh white lights of the open-fronted fish shops and butchers cut through the gloom.

Rue Mouffetard used to have one of the worst reputations in Paris. The name derives from *mouffle*—old French for "stink." Tanneries once lined the River Bièvre, which ran at the bottom of the hill. The stench of the urine and dog excrement used to remove hair from the hides became so stifling that the river was paved over. When the tanners moved on, the smell disappeared but the name stuck.

To both Honoré de Balzac and Victor Hugo, Mouffetard signified misery. Balzac's novel *Le Pére Goriot* takes place mostly in one of the residential tenements, "in a vale of crumbling stucco, watered by streams of black mud." In Hugo's *Les Miserables*, the fugitive Jean Valjean is so moved by the poverty of the pan-handlers that he gives them money. Hearing of a beggar who presses coins on others, his nemesis, the detective Javert, tracks him down, sending him once again on the run.

Place Saint-Médard, 1898-1900, Eugène Atget

The Church of St.-Médard on the rue Mouffetard, 1871, Johan Jongkind

Continue to the foot of the market. In the 1730s, ㉔ **Saint-Médard Church** became famous as the home of a sect, the convulsionists. People praying at the grave of François de Pâris, a pious deacon, claimed miraculous cures. But some were seized by fits. They sang, danced, spoke in tongues, stamped on bibles, barked like dogs, and swallowed glass or hot coals. Alarmed, Louis XV ordered the church closed, inspiring a protester to post this notice: "By order of the King/It is forbidden to the Divinity/To perform any more miracles/In this vicinity."

Our walk ends in ㉕ the park (**Square Saint-Médard/Miss. Tic**) at the foot of rue Mouffetard. The convulsionists are no more, but a hint of the sect survives. On Sunday mornings in good weather, people still gather here to dance to a small band. Others sing in the street. Centuries roll away, and we are once more in a world of belief. As the French say, "*Plus ça change, plus c'est la même chose*"—The more things change, the more they stay the same. Walk ends at **Metro Censier-Daubenton (Line 7.)**

WALK 11

PARIS IN REVOLT: ST. GERMAIN-DES-PRÉS AND ITS ABBEY

START: Metro Odéon (Line 4, 10)

FINISH: Metro Saint-Germain-des-Prés (Line 4)

PARIS IN REVOLT: ST. GERMAIN AND ITS ABBEY

1. **Statue of Georges Danton**
2. **Bronze Head of Charles Aznavour**
3. **Le Maison des Amis des Livres:**
   7 rue de l'Odéon
4. **Site of Shakespeare and Company:**
   12 rue de l'Odéon
5. **Site of Contact Press:**
   8 rue de l'Odéon
6. **Thomas Paine's Apartment:**
   10 rue de l'Odéon
7. **Camille Desmoulins' Apartment:**
   22 rue de l'Odéon
8. **La Mediterranée**
9. **Odéon Theater**
10. **Comédie Française:**
    14 rue de l'Ançienne Comédie
11. **Café Procope:**
    13 rue de l'Ançienne Comédie
12. **Cour du Commerce Saint-André:**
    19-21 rue de l'Ançienne Comédie
13. **Site of Marat's *L'Ami du peuple:***
    8 Cour du Commerce Saint-André
14. **Site of Tobias Schmidt's Workshop:**
    9 Cour du Commerce Saint-André
15. **Cour de Rohan**
16. **La Jacobine restaurant**
17. **Hôtel La Louisiane:**
    60 rue de Saine
18. **Café Chai:**
    26 rue de Buci
19. **James McNeill Whistler's studio:**
    1 rue Bourbon le Chateau
20. **Site of Black Sun Press:**
    2 rue Cardinale
21. **Place de Fürstenberg**
22. **Natalie Clifford Barney's Temple:**
    20 rue Jacob
23. **Musée National Eugène-Delacroix:**
    6 rue de Fürstenberg
24. **Abbot's Palace**
    3 rue de l'Abbaye
25. **6 rue de l'Abbaye**
26. **Place Juliette Gréco**
27. **Square Laurent Praché**
28. **Church of St. Germain-des-Prés**

- (!) **Site of Club Saint-Germain-des-Prés**
  13 rue Saint-Benoit
- (!) **Site of Prison de l'Abbaye**
  133 boulevard Saint-Germain

(!) indicates a place mentioned in the text, but not included in the tours.

Previous page: *The Death of Marat* (detail), 1793, Jacques-Louis David

Rue Jacob
Rue St. Benoit
Club St. Germain
Café de Flore
Les Deux Magots
Rue de Fürstemberg
Rue de l' Abbaye
Église St. Germain des Prés
Rue Cardinale
Rue de l' Echaudé
Rue de Seine
Rue de Mazarine
Rue Dauphine
Bd. Saint-Germain
Rue Gozlin
Prison de l' Abbaye
Rue de Buci
Mabillon
Rue du Four
Rue de l'Ancienne Comédie
Rue de Grégoire Tours
Rue Clément
Rue Mabillon
Rue Félibien
Le Marché de Saint-German
Rue Guisarde
Rue Lobineau
Rue Bonaparte
Rue des Canettes
Rue de Tournon
Odéon
Rue Monsieur le Prince
Rue Saint-Sulpice
St.-Sulpice
Église Saint-Sulpice
Place de Saint-Sulpice
Rue Palatine
Rue Servandori
Rue Garancière
Rue Férou
Rue de Condé
Rue de l' Odéon
Rue Casimir Delavigne
Rue Racine
Place de l' Odéon
Rue de Vaugirard
Jardin du Luxembourg
400 ft
100 m

This walk covers the area formerly occupied by the Abbey of St. Germain-des-Prés (Saint Germain in the Fields), most of which was destroyed in the Revolution of 1789. When people referred to the Left Bank during the 1890s, it was this area that they meant. Except for driving two avenues, Boulevard St. Germain and Boulevard St. Michel, along its edges, Georges-Eugène Haussmann left most of its narrow twisting streets and courtyards alone, preserving a village character which survives to this day.

We begin at ❶ Auguste Paris's massive **statue of Georges Danton** (1759-1794). It stands directly above **Metro Odéon (Lines 4 and 10.)** One of the two leaders of the 1789 Revolution, Danton helped bring down the monarchy, break the power of the church and set France on the road to becoming a modern state—acts for which he died on the guillotine, a fate engineered by his rival Maximilien Robespierre, who also became its victim. Erected near the site of his former home, the statue shows Danton flanked by a drummer boy and a citizen soldier with a musket. The drummer waves a leafy twig. This recalls one of his followers, Camille Desmoulins, who, after urging fellow revolutionaries to "adopt cockades by which we may know each other," improvised such a badge from leaves snatched from a tree.

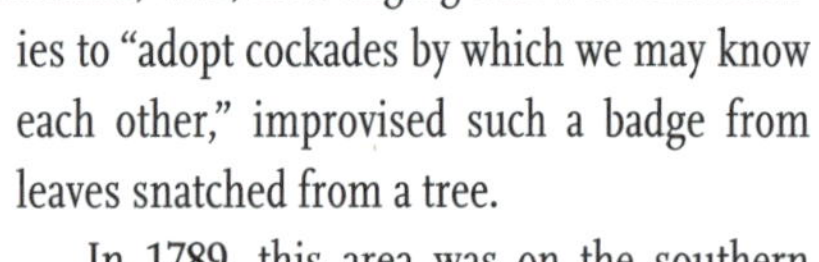

In 1789, this area was on the southern edge of Paris; not technically in the city at all, in fact, since Danton lived just outside the walls built by Philippe-Auguste in 1200 to protect the city while he was away at the Crusades. This suited the revolutionaries; plotting

Saint-Germain-des-Prés, 1615

to overthrow the government was best done as far as possible from the centers of power. Contrary to his statue's heroic pose, Danton was more orator than fighter. One of his famous phrases is carved into its massive plinth: "Audacity, more audacity, always more audacity!" His brusqueness and lack of manners polarized people. One called him "repulsive and atrocious," but to another he was "a colossus whose deep and spontaneous concern was to enjoy existence."

Three factions, the left-wing Jacobins or Montagnards, the centrist Plain, and the right-wing Girondins, dominated the revolutionary council, known as the Convention, but it was to Danton and Robespierre that most looked for leadership. Ascetic and formal, Robespierre could not have been less like the rough, loud Danton. While Danton grew up around pigs and cattle, the other attended Paris's best schools. At 12, he even composed an ode of welcome to Marie-Antoinette, Austrian wife-to-be of Louis XVI, and recited it to her in person. (This didn't prevent him from later voting for her execution and that of the entire royal family.) Robespierre's scorn of pleasure earned him the name "The Incorruptible." A refusal to accept bribes or amass a per-

Imaginary meeting between Robespierre, Danton and Marat (illustrating Victor Hugo's novel *Ninety-Three*),1882, Alfred Loudet

sonal fortune contrasted with the activities of Danton and his followers, who became increasingly implicated in financial scandals over the liquidation of aristocratic fortunes. Each time Danton rose to speak in the Convention, cries of "The accounts! The accounts!" drowned him out. Both men would die on the guillotine, victims of the factionalism they helped create, though Danton did so with more style. Robespierre tried to escape public humiliation with a failed suicide attempt, but Danton urged the executioner to hold up his severed head for the crowd. "They'll expect it. Believe me, it'll be good."

Behind the statue, turn left into the Carrefour de l'Odéon. On the central island, ❷ a bronze portrait head and plinth commemorate Franco-Armenian singer/actor/songwriter **Charles Aznavour** (1924–2018), born on rue Monsieur-le-Prince. Until 1760, this area was the

Paris estate of the Prince de Condé. He's recalled in two of three streets branching out of the carrefour or crossroads: to the right rue Condé and to the left rue Monsieur le Prince: as a cousin of Louis XIV, Condé—known as Le Grand Condé—was properly addressed not just as "Prince" but "Mr. Prince."

The central street, rue de l'Odéon, a single block long, is one of the oldest on the Left Bank, and the first in Paris to have a sidewalk. It takes its name from the theater at its end. (Odéon derives from the Greek *Oideion*, literally "singing place.") Because of its proximity to the Sorbonne, the street has numerous literary associations. A plaque at ❸ **No. 7** identifies the site of **Le Maison des Amis des Livres** (House of Friends of the Book), the bookshop of Adrienne Monnier, companion of Sylvia Beach, whose **Shakespeare and Company** was diagonally opposite at ❹ **No. 12.** At ❺ **No. 8**, Robert McAlmon edited **Contact Press**, which published Ernest Hemingway's first book, *Three Stories and Ten Poems*, in 1923. Contact was financed by McAlmon's wife, Winifred Ellerman, aka Bryher, who contracted a "white" marriage with gay McAlmon in order to live freely with her lover, the poet Hilda Doolitte aka "H.D." Locals duly mocked McAlmon as "Robber McAlimony."

Le Grand Condé, 1654-1658

Hemingway and McAlmon

Carrefour de l'Odéon, 1867-1868, Charles Marville

At ❻ **No. 10**, English-born political theorist Thomas Paine (1737–1809), author of *The Rights of Man*, lived from 1797 to 1802. Imprisoned during the Revolution as a supporter of the disgraced Danton, Paine escaped execution when the guard who identified those to be guillotined that day accidentally chalked the open door of Paine's cell. Closing the door hid the mark, and Paine survived.

(**JB**: **No. 18** also happens to be the building where I live, and have done so from shortly after I came to France in 1989. It was pure chance that the apartment two floors above the one occupied by Beach and Monnier happened to belong to the family of my wife-to-be. Or perhaps there's something to the theories of Carl-Gustav Jung, that what appear to be coincidences are in fact "synchronicities"—evidence of some cosmic order we can't comprehend.)

A plaque at 7 **No. 22** identifies the former home of **Camille Desmoulins** (1760–1794), a supporter of Danton who was executed with him. He was also a close friend of Robespierre, godfather of his son Horace. Desmoulins' last letter to his wife is famous. "I sense the shores of life fleeing before me. Still I see Lucile! I see my best beloved, my Lucile! My bound hands embrace you, and my head, separated, still turns its dying eyes upon you."

Thomas Paine

At the corner with Place de l'Odéon, 8 the restaurant **La Mediterranée** was a popular meeting place for literary and showbusiness figures after World War II. Jean Cocteau supplied the design for its plates and the signature on its marquee, and theater designer Christian Bérard painted a mural. 9 The **Odéon theater** from which the district takes its name dates from 1782, although it has burned twice and gone through extensive restoration. It was opened as a permanent home for the national theater, the Comedie Française, of which it remains a part. In 1968 it became the headquarters of the student revolution known as *les événements de '68.*

Arrest of Camille Desmoulins

In May of that year, students at the Sorbonne, furious that the administration had closed the university three weeks before final

Barrault addressing students

Rue de l'Odéon from Place de l'Odéon, between 1880 and 1945

exams, burst into the theater and demanded that its director, Jean-Louis Barrault, allow them to hold meetings there. To avoid a confrontation, Barrault admitted them, and even made a brief speech of welcome—a tactical error, since over the next six weeks the mob trashed the interior and looted the wardrobe department, treating priceless costumes as fancy dress. Minister for Cultural Affairs André Malraux let the occupation continue, gambling that the students would be satisfied, and not attack more important targets, such as the Elysée Palace. When the uprising petered out, Malraux used the pretext of his welcome speech to fire Barrault, who complained that the other had "thrown him to the mob, like a bone to a savage dog."

Georges-Eugène Haussmann

Exit Place de l'Odéon via rue Casimir-Delavigne, turn left into rue Monsieur le Prince and rejoin Boulevard St. Germain. The boulevard is one of many driven through the old slums of the city by Georges-Eugène

Haussmann who, as Préfet of the Seine from 1853 to 1870, modernized Paris on orders from Louis-Napoléon III. The emperor demanded streets so wide that, in the event of a revolution, they would discourage the building of barricades, and also permit him to imitate his distinguished predecessor, Napoléon I, in employing artillery to disperse insurgents with "a whiff of grapeshot." Haussmann obliged, but for the first time in the history of Paris left space for sidewalks, which brought Parisians out onto the street and encouraged the growth of cafes, shops and restaurants. The military revolution feared by Louis-Napoléon never took place, but the social revolution of Haussmann's boulevards created modern Paris.

Un Café du Boulevard (*A Parisian Café*), 1875, Ilya Repin (1844–1930)
Haussmann's boulevards transformed Parisian social life. During his time in Paris (1873–76), young Ukrainian realist painter Ilya Repin captured the city's festive café culture in *A Parisian Café*. The seated man reading a newspaper is writer Ferdinand Brunetière, while the central figure in black is thought to be either painter Jean-Léon Gérôme or writer Guy de Maupassant. Poet Catulle Mendès wears a top hat, and the tall man exiting is identified as Mackenzie Graves. The imposing woman in black is modeled after actress Anna Judic.

Louis XIV invites Molière to share his supper, 1813, Jean-Léon Gérôme

Cross Boulevard St. Germain to rue de l'Ançienne Comédie, formerly rue des Fossées-St. Germain. (*Fossées* [ditches] refers to the wall and moat that once enclosed the abbey, part of which ran down this street.) In 1680, Louis XIV, an accomplished dancer who loved performance and costume, formed ⑩ the **Comédie Française**, the world's oldest theater company still performing. A plaque at **No. 14** identifies the company's second home (1689–1770), a former *jeu de paume* or indoor tennis court.

Since 1680, the Comédie-Française had been performing at its first theater, the Hôtel Guénégaud. However, due to its close proximity to the newly constructed Collège des Quatre-Nations, the school's leaders requested that the company relocate to reduce the actors' perceived negative influence on the students.

Louis created the company to preserve and perform the work of France's most gifted playwright, Jean-Baptiste Poquelin, aka Molière. At the time, the idea of a theater troupe that didn't tour was radical. Few people wanted actors in their community. Poquelin took a stage name partly to save his family from the disgrace of his entering what was regarded as the most disreputable of professions. 'Actress" and "prostitute" were synonymous, and most theater companies, grumbled one magistrate, were "little better than traveling brothels." The typical actor was a vagabond who strutted in ragged costumes, clowning and declaiming as he debated whether to pick your pocket or ravish your wife. ("*Comédie*," by the way, has a different meaning in French. A play of any kind, even a tragedy such as *Macbeth* or *Hamlet*, is a "*comédie*," and "*comédien*"—"*comédienne*" for a woman—simply means "actor." A comic play is a *farce* and a performer specializing in comic roles a *farceur*.)

Cross rue de l'Ancienne Comedie to 11 **Café Procope**. Until Haussmann's modernization, this street, like most of Paris's thoroughfares, was unpaved dirt, dusty in summer and muddy in winter. There were no sidewalks; just a narrow ledge from which people could climb into a coach or onto a horse. In wet weather, some husky locals loitered at the intersection, ready, for a few coins, to piggy-back people across.

In 1696, Sicilian chef Francesco Procopio dei Coltelli, alias François Procope, furnished

Façade of the theater, 1752

The high-relief sculpture

Molière

Café Procope: rue de l'Ancienne Comédie, 1917, Charles Joseph Antoine Lansiaux

this former bathhouse with marble tables, paintings and wood paneling to attract clients from the theater opposite. It welcomed the greats of politics and the arts, including Napoléon I, Benjamin Franklin, Thomas Jefferson, Robespierre and Marat, and such poets as Paul Verlaine, proclaimed in 1894 by a gathering of 200 literary men in the Procope as "Prince of Poets." Addicted to absinthe and dying of syphilis, Verlaine managed a wan smile. He died two years later, at age 51. The café still owns his marble-topped table.

Café Procope, c.1779

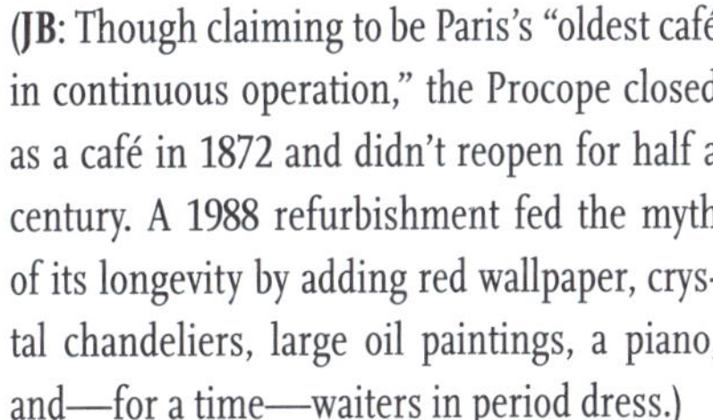

(**JB**: Though claiming to be Paris's "oldest café in continuous operation," the Procope closed as a café in 1872 and didn't reopen for half a century. A 1988 refurbishment fed the myth of its longevity by adding red wallpaper, crystal chandeliers, large oil paintings, a piano, and—for a time—waiters in period dress.)

A narrow alley at **No 19-21** leads to 12 **Cour du Commerce Saint-André**. Polish artist Balthus (Balthasar Klossowski de Rola), whose studio was nearby, painted this lane and part of the Passage between 1952 and 1954. Connecting Boulevard St. Germain to rue St. André-des-Arts, the Passage itself dates from 1776. Rear

Marat published *L'Ami du peuple* (Left: No.8)

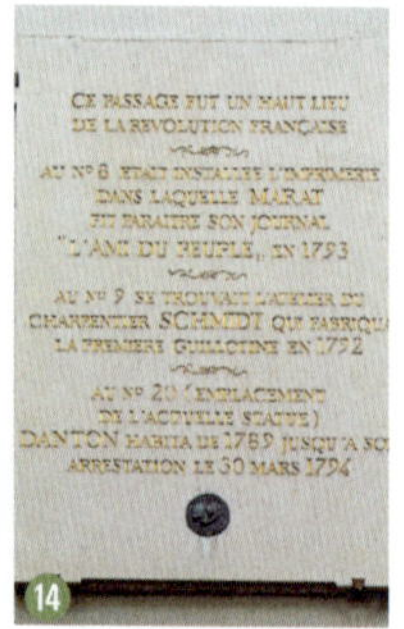

Danton's building (No.20) was demolished

entrances to restaurants, including Café Procope, line one side. On the other, former workshops have also become restaurants.

At ⑬ **No. 8**, the Provençal grocery **Maison Brémond**, part of a small chain started in 1830 in Aix-en-Provençe, is a reminder that people once came here to shop, not eat. A millstone in the window attests to its authenticity. Brémond stocks olive oil, spices and herbs, including "*le vrai Herbes de Provençe.*" (**JB**: I once questioned the owner about this. Surely *Herbes de Provençe* was just a mixture of whatever happened to be on hand; rosemary, oregano, thyme, savory, mint, dill, even dried orange rind. "Not at all!" he said, and gave me what he insisted was the true recipe—rosemary, oregano, thyme and sage in precise proportions, all sun-dried in southern France. "Don't be fooled by the stuff they sell in supermarkets. You know where they get their herbs?" He looked around conspiratorially and lowered his voice. "*Poland!*")

A plaque on the first floor façade of **No. 9** identifies this building as ⑭ the **workshop where Tobias Schmidt manufactured the first guillotine** in 1792. In the late 18th century, prison sentences for crimes

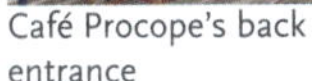

Café Procope's back entrance

Remains of Philippe-Auguste's Wall (No.4)

were uncommon. Most infractions were punished by whippings or brandings, and more serious crimes by exile, mutilation or death, often protracted and agonizing. Graft was wide-spread. You could bribe the executioner to drug you, or knock you unconscious before execution. It was even known for someone to substitute for the prisoner in return for a payment to his family. Once the guillotine became the official method of execution, it was usual to display the severed head to the crowd, proof that the right person had died. The tradition of preferential treatment for the privileged survived longest in Great Britain, where an aristocrat convicted of a capital crime could choose to be hanged with a rope of silk rather than hemp.

In 1789, physician Joseph-Ignace Guillotin, disgusted by the cruelty of capital punishment, urged the Convention to adopt a more humane system, based on a machine called the Mannaia, used in Italy since Roman times. With physiologist Antoine Louis, who had seen one in operation, Guillotin approached German harpsichord maker Schmidt. He built some prototypes and tested them on sheep and

corpses before executing the first living subject on April 25, 1792. [11-1]

On the right, a short alley leads to ⓯ the gated **Cour de Rohan**, former Paris residence of the Bishop of Rouen, now a complex of private apartments. Part of the 1958 musical *Gigi* was filmed here. The apartment to the left and above the gate was the home of Gigi's aunt Alicia, who urges her to follow family tradition and become a rich man's mistress.

Continue along the Passage and through the gate into the glazed lower portion. We can thank Napoléon I for the granite flagstones underfoot and Greco-Roman plasterwork overhead. Once he seized power in 1804 and made himself emperor, he urged *couturiers,* designers and architects to use classical motifs, reflecting his belief that Paris would be the capital of a new world empire, a modern Athens or Rome.

Pause to look through the window of ⓰ **La Jacobine restaurant.** An inner wall shows how most buildings of this era were constructed. Chestnut beams, called *poutres,* were laid out in a grid and the gaps

packed with rubble, which was covered with plaster, reinforced with horsehair. The result was surprisingly resilient. Chestnut resisted woodworm and dry rot, and absorbed changes in temperature and humidity. For exteriors, builders added a decorative façade of plaster. A few used stone, though, unlike the underlying structure, this could crack if the building subsided.

Cour du Commerce, de la rue Saint André des Arts, c.1866, Charles Marville

At the foot of the Passage, exit onto rue St. Andre des Arts. Just to the left of the exit, a patch of granite pavers shows how Haussmann created the streets of a rebuilt Paris. The former large slabs or *setts,* known as Belgian Blocks, helped horses' hooves to grip but cracked under heavy loads. Haussmann replaced them with smaller cubes of granite and, instead of cementing them, loosely bedded them in a layer of sand, which absorbed the pressure of heavy vehicles. Generations of protestors found the cobbles useful as missiles. During the events of May 1968, the sand beneath them inspired the *graffito "Sous la pavé, la plage!"* (Under the paving, a beach!), and a student poster captured a girl in the moment of hurling a cobble with the ecstatic motto "Beauty is in the Streets!"

Rue de Buci

Continue on left to the *Carrefour* or intersection and cross rue de l'Ancienne-Comédie into rue de Buci. In crossing, you are passing through the old walls of the former Abbey of St. Germain-des-Prés, demolished in 1789. Most of the surviving buildings are workers' housing circa 1800, with a scattering of earlier *hôtels particuliers* or private mansions, identified by their double *portes cochères* or coach entrances. Café-lined rue de Buci, formerly a market street, once exuded smells other than coffee and croissants. A resident of the time described how "one was knocked over by the stench of rotten cabbage leaves, fresh turnips, raw tripe, steers' red blood. Early morning and the fire hydrants spurting, turned on by the city's cleaners; below, the murky waters rolling over the ancient cobblestones, up-wafting the odor of stale wine, *Gauloises* butts. spermatozoa, Lysol." At No. 14, be-

Miles Davis

Dizzy Gillespie

Bud Powell

cause of subsidence, the stone façade of the building bulges outwards. Signs of a repaired crack run down the entire right-hand side.

⑰ The **Hôtel La Louisiane**, at the intersection of Buci and rue de Seine, (entrance at **60** rue de Seine) was popular with musicians in the 1950s and 1960s, including jazz stars Miles Davis, Dizzy Gillespie, Billie Holiday, Lester Young, Charlie Parker, John Coltrane and Chet Baker, followed by Jim Morrison of The Doors and members of Pink Floyd. Barbet Schroeder used La Louisiane for his 1969 film *More* and Bertrand Tavernier recreated it in 1986 for *'Round Midnight*, based on American pianist Bud Powell who, with other jazz greats, played in the basement of the **Club Saint-Germain-des-Prés** at (!) **13 rue Saint-Benoit.** [11-2]

Hôtel La Louisiane, c.1946

Follow rue de Buci to the corner with rue du Bourbon le Chateau. ⑱ The café **Chai** occupies the site of the former abbey wine store. Its discreet location made the café popular with pre-World War II political refugees,

Symphony in White, No. 1: The White Girl,1862, James McNeill Whistler

in particular Surrealists from the Balkans, forced to flee their royalist homes when the movement's founder André Breton insisted that all members join the Communist party. (Serbian film-maker Dusan Makavajev (*WR: Mysteries of the Organism*) told me that when, as a student, he visited Paris to interview these men, many suggested they meet at this café —where, he realized, they could sit in its rear booths, monitoring newcomers in the mirrors on the back wall. "I began to understand why the Surrealists liked *Alice Through the Looking Glass* so much.") **JB**: Note also the neon art in its (unisex) *toilettes.*

Enter rue Bourbon le Chateau. At ⓳ **No. 1**, American painter **James McNeill Whistler** (1834–1903) rented his first studio after arriving in 1855. Many French artists became his friends, including sculptor Auguste Rodin, painter Henri de Toulouse-Lautrec and poet Stéphane Mallarmé. Whistler frequently revisited Paris during a busy career. Always attractive to women, he shared this small studio with a French dressmaker named Héloise. When he taught in the Montparnasse *atelier* of a former model, so many young American women took his classes that she doubled the rates.

Turn right into rue Cardinale. ⑳ **No. 2 rue Cardinale** was formerly the printery of Roger Lescaret, who, beginning in 1927, produced the luxurious literary editions of **The Black Sun Press**, financed by expatriates **Harry and Caresse Crosby**. Wealthy and dissolute, the Crosbys smoked opium, indulged in group sex, kept a pet whippet named Clitoris and owned a yacht called Aphrodisiac. Harry also founded his own religion, based on sun worship. Publishing their own poetry introduced the Crosbys to book design, and they began producing editions of Proust, Poe, Hart Crane and D.H. Lawrence. These inspired Robert McAlmon, Edward Titus, William Bird, Nancy Cunard, Sylvia Beach and other expatriates to launch the Black Manikin, Three Mountains, Shakespeare and Company, Plain Editions, Hours and Contact presses, which published such literary benchmarks as *Tropic of Cancer* and *Ulysses*. [11-3]

Title page of The Black Sun Press

Exit rue Cardinale onto ㉑ **Place de Fürstenberg.** Not technically a square but a *rond-point* or roundabout, this *place* with its distinctive five-lamp fixture at the center has been called "the most romantic spot in Paris." Named for Cardinal Guillaume Egon de Fürstenberg, abbot of Saint-Germain-des-Prés, the space constituted part of the palace stables. It's often used by fashion photographers and appears in many films, including Martin Scorsese's *The Age of Innocence*, Vincente Minnelli's *Gigi*, and the series *Emily in Paris*. It also provides the entrance to the Ministry of Magical Affairs in the 2018 film *Fantastic Beasts: The Crimes of Grindelwald* based on the work of J.K. Rowling.

The Abbot's Palace from Place de Fürstenberg

Many writers have commented on its four slim *paulowia* trees. "The other night, when I passed by," wrote Henry Miller in *Tropic of Cancer*, "it was deserted, bleak, spectral. In the middle of the square four black trees that have not begun to blossom. Intellectual trees, nourished by the paving stones. Like T.S. Eliot's verse. Here, by God, if Marie Laurencin ever brought her Lesbians out into the open, this would be the place for them to commune. *Tres lesbienne ici.* Sterile, hybrid, dry." Painter Marie Laurencin (1883–1956), an intimate of Picasso and Apollinaire, also belonged to the Sapphic circle of hostess Natalie Clifford Barney which convened at Barney's home just around the corner at 22 **20 rue Jacob**. Critic Alec Pilcher calls the wan women of her pastel-tinted portraits "balletic wraiths"

"Temple of Friendship" stands in the garden of 20 rue Jacob.

and "sidesaddle Amazons" who depict the "queer femme with a Gallic twist."

㉓ **Nos. 6 rue de Fürstenberg** house a small museum devoted to **Eugéne Delacroix**, who spent most of 1857 to 1861 painting three murals in the church of St. Sulpice. Rather than travel each day from his home on the city outskirts, he converted these former outbuildings of the bishop's palace into a *pied à terre*, living here until his death in 1863. Large double doors and an arch give access to the courtyard. An elegant wooden staircase, added by Delacroix, leads to his former apartment. A small garden separates the rear from an additional building, sometimes used for performances.

Exit rue de Fürstenberg onto rue de l'Abbaye. The imposing ㉔ **Abbot's Palace** is, with the church, the largest building to survive from the old abbey. Constructed in 1586 as a residence for the Cardinal de Bourbon, it was only the second building in Paris to be built of both brick

Marie Laurencin, 1910

Natalie Clifford Barney

Eugéne Delacroix, 1837

and stone. Shops selling luxury furnishings line most of rue de l'Abbaye. The apartment building at 25 **No. 6**, however, boasts a particularly striking façade. Dated 1913, it's decorated with garlands of stone roses. Italian masons in Montparnasse hand-sculpted the blocks, which were assembled with impressive precision on site. The delicate yet stylized carving shows the voluptuousness of *art nouveau* surrendering to the streamlined precision of *art moderne* aka *art deco.*

Further up rue de l'Abbaye, the showroom of a furnishing store preserves what remains of a chapel to the Virgin, begun in 1255. When the 1789 Revolution sold off consecrated buildings for secular use, an arms dealer bought it to store weapons. On August 19, 1794, twelve tons of saltpeter exploded, demolishing the chapel and part of the abbey church. Worship in the church recommenced in 1803 but the chapel was never rebuilt. Much of the main church remained derelict for decades. Successive restorations, modernizing some elements but also exposing medieval stonework and wall paintings, have left it a jumble of styles.

Enter 26 Place Juliette Gréco. The street in front of the church has recently been dedicated to singer and actress Gréco (1927–2020), an important figure in the post-World War II bohemian scene. Pass through gate into 27 **Square Laurent Praché**. The 13th century chapel on what is now rue de l'Abbaye once

Demolition of the Abbey of Saint-Germain des Prés, 1798

continued across this little park to connect with the church wall. After the 1794 explosion, the destruction was continued by a doctor who intended to build a house on the site. He never did so, leaving some elements from the chapel still attached to the walls.

After World War II, admirers of Guillaume Apollinaire (1880–1918), champion of Cubism and coiner of the word "Surrealism," proposed dedicating the vacant lot to his memory. Pablo Picasso agreed to contribute a bust, but local government hesitated to celebrate the man who also wrote such pornographic works as *The Debauched Hospodar* and had been briefly imprisoned in 1911 as a suspect in the theft of the *Mona Lisa* from the Louvre. Nor did they wish to encourage Picasso in his recent embrace of Communism. Instead, they named the park for civil servant Laurent-Désiré Praché, mainly known for having introduced domestic gas to Paris. In 1959, however, the project revived. Picasso reneged on his promise of a bust of Apollinaire, but of-

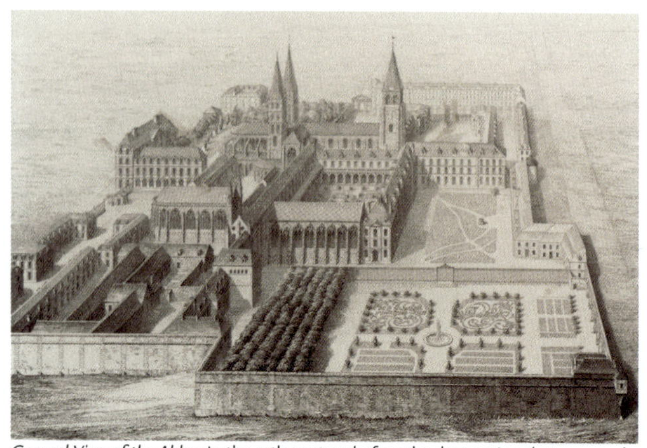

General View of the Abbey in the 17th century before the destruction that occurred during the Revolution

fered one of his mistress Dora Maar instead. Reasoning that a Picasso was a Picasso, they placed it on the plinth prepared for a likeness of Apollinaire, and left future generations to wonder why he had such an oddly feminine hairstyle. (Official directories call the bust, vaguely, *Tete d'une Femme.*) This is still, technically, Square Laurent Praché, though M. Praché is exiled to a tiny plaque attached to the church wall.

Enter rue Bonaparte and 28 **the church of St. Germain-des-Prés.** The first church on this site was consecrated in 558 but much of the present building dates from the 10th century. Some parts are Gothic, with flying buttresses and pointed windows, but most is in the rounded Romanesque style. When it was built, the city of Paris ended here, hence "*...des Prés*" (In the fields). Peasants on surrounding farms would have measured their day by its bells, pausing to pray at the Angelus at 11 a.m. and obeying their call to attend mass on Sunday.

During the Revolution, the surviving part of the abbey became ⓘ a prison for priests and other devout Catholics who refused to renounce their faith. In September 1792, as false rumors spread of a Prussian army headed for France, Georges Danton gave a speech declaring, "We ask that anyone refusing to give personal service or to furnish arms shall be punished with death." 160–220 people who declined to swear allegiance to the Revolution or take up arms in its defense were marched out of the abbey and hacked to death by a crowd with swords, pikes and axes. Those sentenced to death included priests, Swiss guards who had survived an earlier massacre at the Tuileries Palace, as well as a number of women, including the Princess de Lamballe.

Prison de l'Abbaye

Murder of Princess de Lamballe

René Descartes (1596–1650), 17th-century mathematician and philosopher ("I think, therefore I am") is buried here. He died in Sweden, where he was attempting to instruct a quarrelsome Queen Christina, and in the course of returning his remains to France a finger and skull were mislaid. The skull is preserved in the Musée de l'Homme. The whereabouts of his finger remain unknown. Another tomb celebrates Lord James—or Jacques Douglas (1617–1645), 12th Earl of

René Descartes, 1649

Angus, one of the Scots who followed Mary Queen of Scots to Catholic France rather than remain in Protestant England. When Douglas died in 1645, Louis XIV gave him this lavish monument. In effigy, he reclines on top, in full uniform, but unaccountably reading a book, an exotic pursuit for a man of action, few of whom had much education. His father, grandfather and uncle lie elsewhere in the church, as loyal to France in death as they were in life.

The church's most eccentric memorial is to John II Casimir Vasa, King of Poland and grand duke of Lithuania. In white marble, with gilded black marble curtains, this ostentatious creation, sculpted by Gaspard and Balthazard Marsy, shows him offering his crown and scepter to God. (It also contains his heart.) Hoping for a career in the church, the pious but ineffectual Casimir was educated as a Jesuit and created a cardinal by Pope Innocent X but, on the death of his half-brother in 1648, found himself king. Said to be "of a feeble and peaceful disposition," he was out of his depth in the snake pit of Russian, Swedish and Polish politics, and renounced the throne in 1668, fleeing to France, where Louis XIV took pity on him and made him abbot of St. Germain-des-Prés.

Exit onto rue Bonaparte. Walk ends at **Metro Saint-Germain-des-Prés (Line 4)**

WALK 12

SISTERS WHO DID IT FOR THEMSELVES: THE PARIS OF SINGLE WOMEN

START: Metro Pont Neuf (Line 7)
FINISH: Metro Vavin (Line 10)

SISTERS WHO DID IT FOR THEMSELVES: THE PARIS OF SINGLE WOMEN

1. **L'inconnue de la Seine**
2. **Site of Nancy Cunard's Hours Press**
   15 rue Guénégaud
3. **Hôtel d'Aubusson:**
   33 rue Dauphine
4. **Site of Le Tabou**
5. **Gertrude Stein and Alice B. Toklas's Apartment:**
   5 rue Christie
6. **Passage Commerce St. Andre**
7. **Site of Marat's House:**
   22 rue de l'Ecole-de-Médecine
8. **Shakespeare and Company:**
   12 rue de l'Odéon
9. **Medici Palace**
10. **La Rotonde:**
    105 Boulevard du Montparnasse
11. **Le Dôme**
    108 Boulevard du Montparnasse
12. **Le Select:**
    99 Boulevard du Montparnasse
13. **La Coupole:**
    102 Boulevard du Montparnasse
14. **Isadora Duncan's Apartment:**
    9 rue Delambre
15. **Place Joséphine Baker**
16. **Site of Le Sphinx:**
    31 Boulevard Edgar-Quinet
17. **Site of Le Monocle :**
    14 Boulevard Edgar-Quinet
18. **Man Ray and Kiki's Studio:**
    31 bis rue Campagne-Premiere
19. **Site of Chez Rosalie**
    3 bis rue Campagne-Premiere
20. **Site of Le Jockey**
    146 Boulevard du Montparnasse

(!) **Bobino music hall**
20 rue de la Gaité

(!) indicates a place mentioned in the text, but not included in the tours.

Previous page: *Autoportrait (Self-Portrait in a Green Bugatti)*, 1929, Tamala de Lempicka

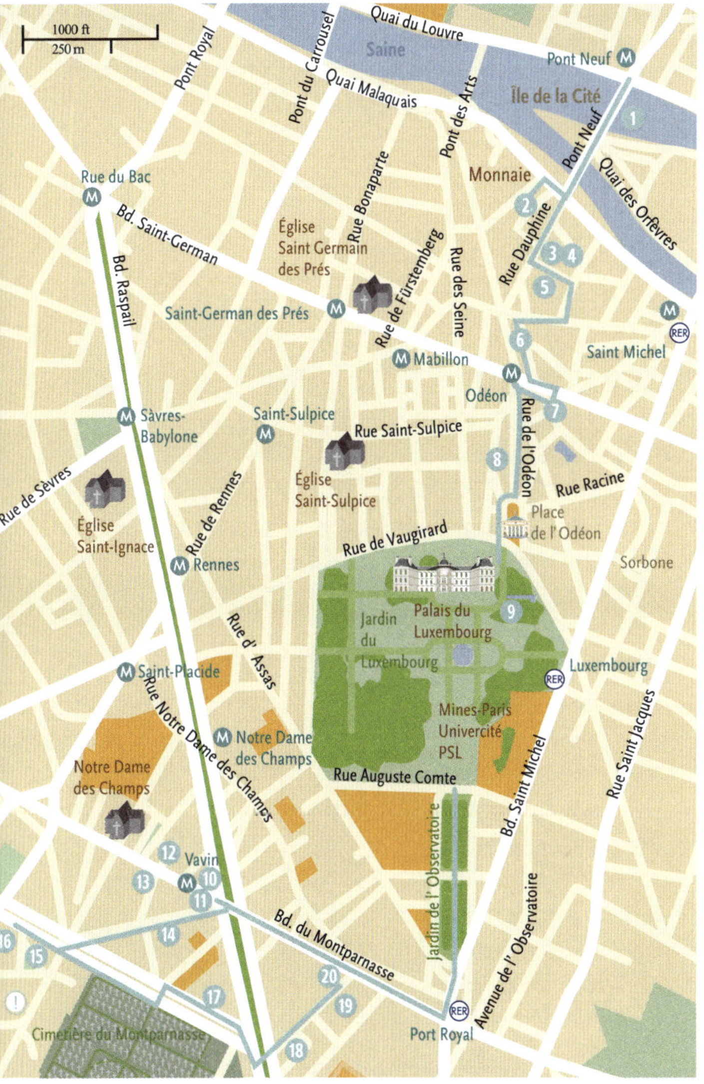

1000 ft
250 m
Quai du Louvre
Saine
Pont Neuf
Île de la Cité
Pont Royal
Pont du Carrousel
Quai Malaquais
Pont des Arts
Pont Neuf
Quai des Orfèvres
Monnaie
Rue du Bac
Bd. Saint-German
Bd. Raspail
Église Saint Germain des Prés
Rue Bonaparte
Rue de Fürstemberg
Rue des Seine
Rue Dauphine
Saint-German des Prés
Mabillon
Saint Michel
Odéon
Rue de l'Odéon
Sàvres-Babylone
Saint-Sulpice
Rue Saint-Sulpice
Église Saint-Sulpice
Rue Racine
Rue de Sèvres
Église Saint-Ignace
Rue de Rennes
Rennes
Rue de Vaugirard
Place de l'Odéon
Sorbone
Rue d' Assas
Jardin du Luxembourg
Palais du Luxembourg
Luxembourg
Saint-Placide
Rue Notre Dame des Champs
Notre Dame des Champs
Mines-Paris Univercité PSL
Rue Saint Jacques
Notre Dame des Champs
Rue Auguste Comte
Bd. Saint Michel
Jardin de l' Observatoire
Vavin
Bd. du Montparnasse
Avenue de l' Observatoire
Cimetière du Montparnasse
Port Royal
1
2
3
4
5
6
7
8
9
10
11
12
13
14
15
16
17
18
19
20

"France," it's been said—not entirely kindly—"is the woman of Europe." It can't be an accident that the nation is always referred to as feminine—*La France*—and that, where the national symbols of Great Britain and the United States, John Bull and Uncle Sam, are male, a woman represents France—and, moreover, a woman with no male partner.

The role is shared by Saint Joan of Arc, often referred to as *la Pucelle* (the virgin), and revolutionary symbol Marianne, a bust of whom, based on a figure in Eugéne Delacroix's 1830 painting *La Liberté guidant le peuple* (Liberty Leading the People), has pride of place in every town hall. Aggression characterizes both personae but while France pays lip service to this militant archetype, the modern nation seldom settles problems by force. "Going to war without France," sneered an American general, "is like going hunting without an accordion." Instead, she prevails by the more feminine traits of intelligence, charm and cunning.

The history of France can be seen as a narrative of single women. One walk can't hope to do justice to them all, but the fact that our stroll across the left bank of the Seine intersects with the lives of so many is evidence of their numbers. We begin at **Metro Pont Neuf (Line 7.)** situated on Quai du Louvre, the point at which Pont Neuf meets the Right Bank of the Seine.

Paradoxically, the first woman of note, known as ❶ L'**Inconnue de la Seine** (Unknown Woman of the Seine), has no name, and achieved fame only at her death. Around 1900, plaster casts appeared on the art market of a young woman's face, eyes closed and downcast, lips slightly upturned in a smile as enigmatic as that of the Mona Lisa. Buyers

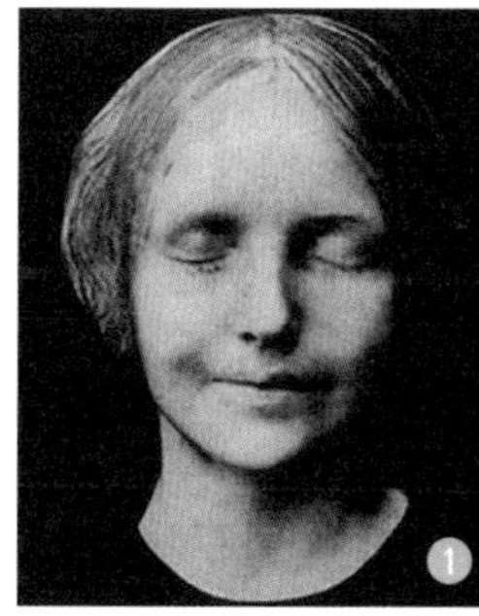

were told it was the death mask of a drowning victim, perhaps a suicide. Her body had been taken from the Seine and displayed with the other unidentified dead on a marble slab at the morgue, behind Notre-Dame, where an artist, moved by her peaceful expression, made a wax impression of her face. The *Inconnue* was soon famous. She inspired stories and poems. Poet Richard LeGallienne thought she looked "not ancient, not modern; but of yesterday, today, and forever." Soon, however, doubts arose. Anatomists now think the musculature is too firm to have come from a corpse. In an ironic postscript, Norwegian toymaker Asmund Laerdal chose her as the face of Resusci Anne, the plastic figure he designed in the 1950s for use in demonstrating mouth-to-mouth resuscitation. Since then, more than 300 million people have kissed those dead lips. [12-1]

Continue across Pont Neuf to the Quai de Conti to enter rue Guenegaud. 2 **No. 15** was the home and workplace of British poet, publisher and political activist **Nancy Cunard** (1896–1965). Daughter of shipping millionaire Sir Bache Cunard and his American wife Maud (who preferred to be called "Emerald"), she grew up privileged but rebellious. In 1920 she moved to Paris. An early hysterectomy allowed her to pursue her sexual agenda without fear of pregnancy, and she had affairs with Aldous Huxley, Michael Arlen and Louis Aragon, inspiring characters in all their books. Attracted

Nancy Cunard,1928

to African culture, she took up with jazz musician Henry Crowder—"Is it true," demanded Emerald, appalled, "that my daughter knows a Negro?"—and developed a personal style with African elements. Constantin Brâncusi sculpted her and Man Ray photographed her, big-eyed and rail-thin, arms encircled by bulky ivory bangles from wrist to elbow.

Emerald agreed to ignore Nancy's lovers, provided she remained in Paris, where, with Crowder, she set up the Hours Press, producing elegantly designed books of poetry. Active in American civil rights and anti-Fascist activities during the Spanish Civil War, she returned to France after living in London from 1940 to 1945, working for the resistance as a translator, to find that collaborators had maliciously destroyed her library and printing press. Plagued by mental illness and alcohol—she called gin "my white king"—she alternated spells in mental hospitals with freeloading on friends. Found wandering the streets of Paris, she died emaciated and alone, but survived by the art she inspired.

Return to Quai de Conti and turn right into rue Dauphine and continue to the intersection with rue Christine. During the Occupation, **Simone de Beauvoir** (1908–1996), future author of the pioneering feminist text *The Second Sex,* lost her teaching license for seducing a (female) student, and was reduced to living at what was then the rundown

In the tiny Tabou Tomb, 1947

3 **Hôtel d'Aubusson**: "a filthy shack," she wrote, "with an icy stone staircase that smelt of mold and other unnameable odors. My room was a shambles; an iron bedstead, a wardrobe, a table, two wooden chairs; peeling walls and a miserable yellow light from a single bulb. The kitchen doubled as a toilet." Shortly after, she moved into the nearby Hôtel de Louisiane, joining sometime lover Jean-Paul Sartre, although they occupied separate rooms, to accommodate Sartre's serial seductions and Beauvoir's lesbian affairs. Elsewhere in the hotel, their protegée Juliette Gréco (1927–2020) shared her bed with lovers of both sexes, including trumpeter Miles Davis (1926–1991).

Gréco, long-haired, big-eyed, often barefoot, but dressed always in black, was the poster girl for a generation which, while understanding little of Sartre's philosophy, nevertheless styled itself "existentialist." Sartre denounced her followers but nevertheless let her set his poems to music in songs that exploited her breathy and insinuating voice.

Miles Davis and Juliette Greco

Among her biggest hits was *Deshabillez-moi* (Undress Me.) In April 1947, at **No. 33 rue Dauphine**, in the Aubusson Hôtel crypt (now the spa of the modernized hotel) Gréco and author/musician Boris Vian launched the archetypal basement jazz club 4 **Le Tabou.** (See plaque high up on rue Christine side.) Without proper ventilation, sweating, smoking, jiving customers created a miasma suggestive of a railway tunnel through which a steam locomotive had recently passed. Neighbors, furious about the noise of departing clients when it closed at 4 a.m., emptied chamber pots on their heads. Even so, it was the most fashionable *boite* on the Left Bank.

Turn into rue Christine. At 5 **No. 5, Gertrude Stein** (1874–1946) and her companion **Alice B. Toklas** (1877–1967) shared an apartment from March 1938 until Stein's death in July 1946. Toklas remained until 1964, custodian of the art collection Stein entrusted to her care—until members of the Stein family broke in during a brief absence and, on the pretext that her security was inadequate, seized the paintings.

In 1941, when Gertrude and Alice risked being interned and possibly deported to Germany, Anglophile writer and collaborator Bernard Faÿ helped them relocate in a remote village, under Vichy protection, and suggested, as a further guarantee of their safety, that Stein translate some of Marshal Petain's speeches for US publication. (Fortunately for her reputation, the project was never com-

pleted.) After the war, Faÿ, a devout Catholic and particular enemy of the Freemasons, was sentenced to life in prison. In 1951, Alice paid the bribes that permitted him to break jail and flee to Switzerland.

Continue, turn right into rue des Grands Augustins, and turn right again into rue Saint-André des Arts. At Nos. 59-61 turn left into a narrow lane into 6 **Passage Commerce St. Andre**. This *allée*, lined on one side by the back doors of restaurants, on the other by former workshops (mostly now also restaurants), hasn't changed substantially since the middle 1700s. A stone tower in the restaurant (No. 4) on the left-hand or eastern side is one of 34 remaining from the 33-foot-high wall that once surrounded the city. During the Revolution, its cellar (No. 8) housed the printery where Jean-Paul Marat (1743–1793), leader of the radical Jacobins, published his newspaper *L'Ami du Peuple* (The Peoples' Friend.) Marat urged his followers to "put under arrest all the enemies of our Revolution and all suspicious people. Let us mercilessly exterminate all the conspirators if we do not want to be exterminated ourselves."

Plagued by a skin disease, he seldom left home 7 (30 rue des Cordeliers/now **22 rue de l'Ecole-de-Médecine**), but worked in a bath of water laced with oatmeal and vinegar to relieve itching. Despite this, he respected the etiquette of the Revolution—that no person was superior to another, and even the most eminent should be available to all. In July 1793, his servant admitted 24-year-old **Charlotte Corday** (1768–1793) who claimed to have a list of secret royalist sympathizers in her hometown of Caen. As Marat read the names, gloating "They will be on the guillotine before noon tomorrow," Corday, who secretly supported a faction hostile to the Jacobins, produced a knife and stabbed Marat to the heart, then waited quietly to be arrested. (The scene inspired the famous painting by Jacques-Louis David: p.317, who removed all signs of Marat's skin problem and posed his body to recall heroic Roman statuary.)

Marat's House, rue de l'Ecole de Médecine

Charlotte Corday, 1793 painted at her request, a few hours before her execution

Four days later, following a speedy trial, Corday went, unrepentant, to the guillotine. At the time, it was rumored that people could survive for several minutes after beheading, and life continued even in a severed limb. As Corday's head tumbled into the basket, a carpenter repairing the guillotine platform grabbed it by the hair, held it up and, to test the theory, slapped its cheeks. People gasped. A woman swore her face "exhibited this last impression of offended modesty." Murderess or not, Corday was a citizen of the

James Joyce, Sylvia Beach and Adrienne Monnier, 1938

ULYSSES

by

JAMES JOYCE

IS NOW READY

~~will be published in the Autumn of 1921~~

by

"SHAKESPEARE AND COMPANY"

— SYLVIA BEACH —

12, RUE DE L'ODÉON, PARIS — VIe

new France, and deserved, even in death, to be treated with respect. The carpenter barely escaped with his life.

Cross Boulevard St. Germain and enter rue de l'Odéon. In 1919, the hat of an American woman blew off as she walked up this street. The proprietor of a bookshop called *La Maison des Amis des Livres* (The House of Friends of Books, No.7) stepped out and rescued it. This meeting changed not only the lives of both women but literature also, since the American, **Sylvia Beach** (1887–1962), would remain in Paris, open her own bookshop and publish *Ulysses*, a novel that overturned traditional concepts of narrative. There were three loves in her life, she wrote: her shop, 8 **Shakespeare and Company**, James Joyce, author of *Ulysses*, and the woman who rescued her hat, **Adrienne Monnier** (1892–1955). An official plaque marks the site of Adrienne's shop but the only sign at **No.12** is a modest tribute erected by the James Joyce Society of Sweden and Finland.

From 1921 to 1941, Beach provided expatriates with a place to borrow books, receive mail, and meet. It was a precarious living, made even more so when she volunteered to publish *Ulysses*, since the author seized almost every penny it earned. "I understood that, working with or for James Joyce," she wrote wearily, "the pleasure was mine, the profits were his." At No.18, Beach and Monnier shared an apartment from 1921 until 1936. When Monnier, during Beach's absence in America, started an affair with young German photographer Giselle Freund, Sylvia moved out, although the three continued to have lunch together each day until Monnier committed suicide in 1955. Beach moved into the tiny apartment above her shop, where she died in 1962. [12-2]

Continue to the theater at the end of rue de l'Odéon and cross rue de Vaugirard to the Luxembourg Gardens, dominated by 9 the **Medici Palace**, today the home of the French Senate. Though not technically single, **Marie de Médici** (1575–1642), who built the palace, was wid-

Day of the Dupes (1630): Cardinal de Richelie, Marie de Médici and Louis XIII at the Medici Palace

owed early in her marriage. Thereafter, she ruled France as regent for her son, the future Louis XIII, helped by the nation's wily first minister, Armand Jean du Plessis, Cardinal Richelieu.

Marie came from Italy to marry Henry IV as part of a complex dynastic alliance. Traditionally, the royal family lived in the ancient palace of the Louvre, but she found it drafty and damp, and, choosing a commanding site on the Left Bank, ordered a new residence to remind her of her Florentine childhood. Architects suggested copying the palace in which she was born, Palazzo Pitti (today a famous art gallery.) "Very well," she said—"but bigger." She also demanded formal gardens, like Florence's Boboli Gardens, where she played as a child. But Marie never saw the palace completed. In 1617, Louis came of age and demanded the throne. A three-year stand-off ended with him seizing power and imprisoning her. She escaped to Germany, where she died in 1642.

The hill on which thc Luxcmbourg palacc and gardcns stand is sacred to another single woman. Many assume the nation's patron saint is Joan of Arc (1412–1431) but, while she has her admirers, she's a relative newcomer, not canonized, i.e., elevated to sainthood, until 1920. The saint charged specifically with representing Paris and Parisians is **Geneviève** (422–512) Her history of activism on the city's behalf makes her the go-to saint of politicians. She was born in Nan-

Vision of Saint Geneviève, 1892, Alphonse Osbert, Musée d'Orsay

terre, a satellite town—where, significantly, almost 2,000 years later, events at the local university sparked the 1968 student revolution. In 451, she led a "prayer marathon" that many believed saved Paris from Attila the Hun. When Childeric besieged the city in 464, she acted as an intermediary, collecting food and convincing him to release his prisoners. She was also credited with ending an outbreak of ergot poisoning in 1129, caused by a fungus growing on improperly-stored grain. For centuries after her death, her mummified body was paraded through the city each year, and more often at times of crisis. For this reason, the hill on which the Luxembourg is situated is referred to as Mont St. Geneviève.

Exit the Gardens onto rue Guynemer and take rue Vavin to Boulevard du Montparnasse, where four famous cafés, the 10 **Rotonde**, 11 **Dôme**, 12 **Select** and 13 **Coupole**, dominate the intersection with Boulevard Raspail. All were patronized by a woman who typifies the Paris of *les années folles*.

The frank sexuality and raw humor of **Alice Prin**, aka **Kiki de Montparnasse** (1901–1953) made her coronation in 1929 as "Queen of Montparnasse" a foregone conclusion. Introducing her *Memoirs*,

La Rotonde, c.1925

Ernest Hemingway wrote that she "dominated the era of Montparnasse more than Queen Victoria ever dominated the Victorian era [and was] about as close as people get nowadays to being a queen—but that, of course, is very different from being a lady."

Kiki came to Paris at 12 years old, and adapted readily to the easy morality of the painting community. Despite a less than classical figure (she was wide-hipped, with small breasts), she flourished as a model, trading on her vulgar talk and frank sexuality. Among those whom she served as model and/or lover were Chaim Soutinc, Man Ray, Tsuguharu Foujita, Francis Picabia and Alexander Calder. Another lover, magazine publisher Louis Broca, persuaded her to write her memoirs. Little more than a succession of vague reminiscences, which she illustrated with drawings and photographs made of her

La Rotonde, 1933

Kiki de Montparnasse by Man Ray, 1923

by various artists, as well as her own naïve paintings, the book sold well. Kiki reveled in her notoriety, singing in cabaret, exhibiting her paintings, and making an abortive attempt at an American movie career. (She failed to turn up for a screen test, claiming she had to go back to the hotel for her comb.) Drugs and alcohol ruined her health. When she returned to Paris in 1945, having fled the German occupation, she haunted the cafés, amusing tourists, and panhandling for money to buy cocaine. She died a pauper, the café owners of Montparnasse paying for her funeral.

At the Café du Dôme, turn into rue Delambre. At ⓮ **No. 9**, in an *art deco* building dating from 1926, American dancer **Isadora Duncan** (1877–1927) lived briefly at the end of a life so outrageous that wit and poet Dorothy Parker christened her "Duncan Disorderly." Isadora encountered the sculptor Auguste Rodin shortly after her parents brought her to Paris in 1898. "He gazed at me with lowered lids, his eyes blazing," she recalled. "He ran his hands over my neck, breast, stroked my arms and ran his hands over my hips, my bare legs and feet. He began to knead my whole body as if it were clay." Having memorized her dimensions, he was anxious to explore further, but Isadora, to her later regret, fended him off.

Touring with her troupe, the Isadorables, Duncan led the emigré community in alcohol-fueled misbehavior, partying, as she danced, in a minimum of clothing. Novelist Michel Georges-Michel described how, reclining on a couch, Roman fashion, she "poured out champagne from an immense amphora of jade to all those who reached up with their cups. She let down her hair, loosened her clothing, and asked everybody to follow her example. 'It is as indecent to be dressed when the company is nude as to be sober when everybody is drunk.'" After her final Paris appearance, at the Mogador Theater in 1927, she returned to Nice, to die shortly after in a freak accident, her neck broken when her long scarf caught in the wheel of a sports car in which she was a passenger. [12-3]

Isadora Duncan

Rue Delambre ends at the Boulevard Edgar-Quinet. Cross and turn right to rue Poinsot, you will find the 15 **Place Joséphine Baker**. Though she did marry, twice, African-American Baker (1906–1975) abandoned both husbands, thereafter, moving from man to man as her career demanded. Among her numerous lovers were novelist Georges Simenon and graphic artist Paul Colin, who designed the posters for her first Paris appearance in *La Revue Négre* (1925). American journalist Janet Flanner left a vivid description of that debut. "She made her entry entirely nude except for a pink flamingo feather between her limbs. She was being carried upside down and doing the splits

on the shoulder of a black giant. Midstage he paused, and with his long fingers holding her basket-wise around the waist, swung her in a slow cartwheel to the stage floor, where she stood. She was an unforgettable female ebony statue. A scream of salutation spread through the theater. Whatever happened next was unimportant. The two specific elements had been established and were unforgettable—her magnificent dark body, a new model that to the French proved for the first time that black was beautiful, and the acute response of the white masculine public in the capital of hedonism of all Europe—Paris."

Baker enjoyed a glittering career in France, but by the 1960s was bankrupt and in poor health. Princess Grace of Monaco, the former actress Grace Kelly, gave her an apartment in Monaco and helped find her work. In April 1975, she opened at ⓘ the **Bobino music hall** at 20 rue de la Gaité in a retrospective revue, *Joséphine à Bobino*. The first-night

Josephine Baker with writer Georges Simenon and his wife Tigy and her fiancé and agent Guiseppe Abatino around 1928 at her restaurant Chez Josephine in Paris

audience included Sophia Loren, Mick Jagger, Shirley Bassey, Diana Ross and Liza Minnelli. Four days later, she died of a cerebral hemorrhage. In 2000, this square was renamed for her and in 2015 the Metro station nearest the Bobino, formerly Gaité, became Gaité-Joséphine Baker. She is also buried, symbolically, in the Panthéon, in a coffin containing earth from the three places with which she was associated, Monaco, Paris, and the city of her birth, St. Louis. [12-4]

Between the wars, Boulevard Edgar-Quinet was known as the "Red Light District" of the Left Bank. The premiere establishment in Montparnasse, 16 site of **Le Sphinx** at **No. 31**, attracted the cream of show business and politics. It closed in 1946, put out of business by another formidable single woman, **Marthe Richard** (1889–1982), politician, prostitute and sometime spy. After a youthful career on the streets of her native Bordeaux, she enjoyed a career as a pioneering aviatrix, claiming many records for solo flights—until it was discovered that she flew only until she was out of sight before landing, putting her plane onto a train, and traveling in comfort to within a few miles of her destination. During World War I, she spied for France, becoming the mis-

Marthe Richard

Illustration from *La Vie Parisienne* in 1917

Illustration from *La Vie Parisienne* in 1920

tress of Baron Hans von Krohn, Germany's intelligence chief in Spain. She flourished during the World War II Occupation, staging sex parties for the Nazi high command while claiming she did so as a cover for clandestine resistance activities. In 1945, she entered politics with the backing of the Catholic church and, at its urging, campaigned against prostitution. Thanks to her, brothels became illegal across France in April 1946, and 1,400 were closed, to disastrous effect. Weekly medical examinations of sex workers were no longer required, and pimps and petty criminals once again invaded the business. Until her death in 1982 at the age of 92, Richard insisted she had acted for the public good. Asked to what she attributed her long life, she replied, straight-faced, "Abstinence."

Continue along the boulevard to ⑰ **No. 14**, for site of **Le Monocle**. The presence of Natalie

Clifford Barney and Gertrude Stein, both of whom held famous salons, made Paris the Sapphic capital of Europe. From the 1920s to the end of World War II, Le Monocle was the premier club for cross-dressing females. Clients were asked to wear male evening clothes and, if possible, a monocle. Photographs of the club owner, Lucienne Franchi, aka Lulu de Montparnasse, suavely dressed in a tuxedo, hair cut short and slicked back, inspired Simone de Beauvoir to sneer at "crop-haired lesbians who wore ties and even monocles on occasion." Her scorn was misplaced. Many women who affected mannish clothes, bobbed hair and unusual eyeware were not lesbians at all but followers of the androgynous *garçonne* (boy-girl) style, inspired by Victor Margueritte's 1922 novel *La Garçonne*, about a woman who, finding her fiancé has a mistress, revenges herself by adopting male behavior, shortening her hair, wearing mannish clothes, enjoying promiscuous sex and experimenting with drugs. [12-5]

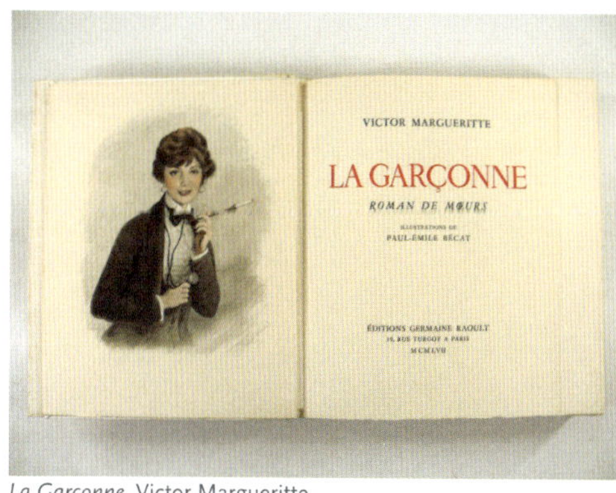

La Garçonne, Victor Margueritte

At the intersection with Boulevard St. Michel, cross the boulevard and enter rue Campagne-Premiere. 18 The building at **31 bis rue Campagne-Premiere**, dating from 1911, was designed by André Arfvidson, and contains 20 duplex artists studio apartments, one of which American photographer and artist **Man Ray** shared first with **Kiki of Montparnasse**, then **Lee Miller**. Kiki met Man Ray shortly after he arrived in Paris in 1921, and he asked her to pose for him. "Presently she undressed," he wrote, "while I sat on the bed with the camera before me. When she came out from behind the screen, I motioned for her to come and sit beside me. I put my arms around her, and she did the same, our lips met and we both lay down. No pictures were taken that afternoon."

Ray's photographs made Kiki famous. He encouraged her to shave her eyebrows, drawing them back in an exaggerated double curve, like the Spanish diacritical mark the tilde. According to Kay Boyle, he applied her makeup himself, "putting other eyebrows back, in any color

Noire et Blanche, 1926, Man Ray

he might have selected for her mask that day. Her heavy eyelids might be done in copper one day and in royal blue another, or else in silver or jade." When she left Ray in her abortive search for a movie career, she was replaced as his model and lover by young American Lee Miller, who in turn left him for British Surrealist Roland Penrose.

Lee Miller, 1929, Man Ray

(**JB**: Ray's last model Jacqueline Goddard told me of a key moment in the decline of Ray's relationship with Miller. "I met Man in Le Dôme," she confided. "I don't remember when. He was still with Lee, though it was ending. He was sure there were other men. [*I knew* there were, but I could not say that. None of us could.] He was angry, saying terrible things about Lee. . . . We had a drink. It was raining outside, and he wore a long *impermeable* . . . (raincoat). And as he moved, I heard something heavy bump against the leg of the chair. And I knew it was a gun. He was a passionate man. And he loved her. Perhaps he would not have shot her . . . one never knows . . ."

"But he didn't," I said.

Jacqueline smiled. "I like to think I am responsible for that. He got up to leave, and I said I would walk with him. We left the Dôme, and walked down Edgar-Quinet in the rain."

I imagined them strolling along the boulevard, with the wall of Montparnasse cemetery just across the street, and the soft, cold rain sifting down through the plane trees to bead on her magnificent head and the set, angry face of the little man with the pistol in his raincoat pocket.

"We walked past his studio on rue Campagne Premiere. The light was on. Lee was there. Alone . . . ? Who could tell? But I feared that, if he went in and found her with someone, he would use the gun. So I said, 'Man, walk with me. Walk with me in the rain.' And he walked away, and Lee Miller and Man Ray were saved."

"And Kiki. Did you ever see her again?"

Jacqueline shook her head. "Not until after the war. Poor Kiki. She came to the cafés, always asking for money. She said it was to pay for her gas, her electricity. . . . But it was a lie. It all went. . . ." She sniffed melodramatically. In the last years of her life that ended in 1953, Kiki became a slave to cocaine.)

Continue along the street. At ⑲ **No. 3, Rosalie Tobia**, a former model of Italian descent who worked for Odilon Redon and William Bouguereau, opened **Chez Rosalie** in 1907. The tiny restaurant extended credit to artists. They paid her with drawings. New to Paris in 1914, artist and writer Nina Hamnett, hailed as the queen of London's bohemia, ate her first French meal here. "I sat down alone and began my dinner," she wrote. "Suddenly the door opened and in came a man with a roll of newspaper under his arm. He wore a black hat and a corduroy suit. He had curly black hair

Dream on the Threshold, 1893, with Rosalie Tobia as model, by W. A. Bouguereau

Rosalie Tobia at Chez Rosalie

and brown eyes and was very good looking. He came straight up to me and said, pointing to his chest, '*Je suis Modigliani, Juif, Jew,*' unrolled his newspaper and produced some drawings. 'Cinq francs.'" Some of his "scribbles," as Rosalie called them, decorated her walls. Others were used as fire-lighters or toilet paper.

Hilaire Hiler's nightclub 20 **Le Jockey** was located in a building, now demolished, on the corner with the boulevard. Hiler, born Hiler Harzberg, opened the Jockey in 1923, when he was just 25 and newly arrived in Paris, and ran it until 1930. The name was a swipe at that bastion of privilege, the Jockey Club de Paris. In an attempt to imitate a western saloon, he decorated the outside with stylized images of cowboys and Indians. The interior, according to a 1927 guide, offered "low, cracked ceilings, tattered walls covered with posters, cartoons painted with shoe polish and a sign reading, 'The only client we ever lost, died.'" Robert McAlmon wrote

Le Jockey, 1929, Archibald J. Motley, Jr.

that "almost anybody of the writing, painting, musical, gigolo-ing, whoring, pimping or drinking world was apt to turn up at the Jockey." The club became an "after": somewhere to party once the Dôme and Coupole closed at 2 a.m. "Go at 11 o'clock," advised a guidebook. "See famous painters and the real Bon Vivants of Paris. An indescribable atmosphere." After midnight, the place roared. "People were drinking, singing, talking, laughing, in a cloud of smoke from all the tobacco in the world," wrote artist Jean Oberlé. "From time to time, we went out on the boulevard to take a good breath of fresh air, and then plunged in again."

Among other habituées were Joe Alex, the Martiniquaise actor and dancer who would carry Joséphine Baker on stage for her sensational

Artists at the Jockey in Paris (c.1921). Back row from left to right: Bill Bird, unknown, Holger Cahill, Miller, Les Copeland, Hilaire Hiler, Curtis Moffitt. Middle: Kiki de Montparnasse, Martha Dennison, Jane Heap, Margaret Anderson, Ezra Pound. Front: Man Ray, Mina Loy, Tristan Tzara, Jean Cocteau.

premiere appearance in *Revue Négre*, and teenage actress Lois Moran, who infatuated Scott Fitzgerald, and inspired the character of Rosemary Hoyt in his last completed novel, *Tender is the Night.* All appear briefly in the 1924 film *Le Lion des Mogols*, for which director Jean Epstein recreated the club, as "Le Jokey."

Kiki served as mistress of ceremonies for its weekly talent show. Her own performances made up in energy what they lacked in talent. "I can't sing when I'm not drunk," she said, "and not when I'm doing anything else. I'm astonished by these women who can sing and pee at the same time. My ear is good but not my memory." Her bawdy songs, not to mention some revealing glimpses under her skirt—she wore no underwear—made her one of the sights of Montparnasse. On weekends, automobiles jammed the narrow street and sidewalks. Patrons from film and theater included Russian actor Ivan Mosjoukine, with whom Kiki, ever hopeful of a movie career, carried on an affair at the nearby Hôtel Istria. Walk ends at **Metro Vavin (Line 10)**, at the corner of Boulevard du Montparnasse and Boulevard Raspail.

"So we beat on," writes Scott Fitzgerald at the end of *The Great Gatsby*, "boats against the current, borne back ceaselessly into the past." About what we hope to find there, opinion is divided. The French, however, are in no doubt. The past is a treasure, preserved by the miracle of memory. Reality may be, in Marcel Proust's words, "as fugitive, alas, as the years," but as he demonstrated in his account of his own life, *In Search of Lost Time*, the means of re-experiencing it lie within reach, to be found again in a few bars of a string quartet or the taste of some crumbs of cake in a spoonful of tea. That the past is always with us is not in doubt, and Paris is the proof. "He who contemplates the depths of Paris is seized with vertigo," wrote Victor Hugo. "Nowhere is more fantastic. Nowhere is more tragic. Nowhere is more sublime."

VINTAGE COVERS OF LA VIE PARISIENNE: A Glimpse into Parisian Elegance and Culture

Cover design by Chéri Hérouard, 1917 (left); George Barbier, 1918

La Vie Parisienne, the iconic magazine of the Belle Époque, captured the essence of Parisian life through its elegant covers. Reflecting the vibrant culture of the time, the illustrations showcased Paris' fashion, art, and the evolving role of women in society. From chic cyclists to lavish balls, these covers offer a glimpse into a Paris where luxury, modernity, and romance intertwined.

Zyg Brunner, 1927

George Barbier, 1927

Chéri Hérouard, 1923; Maurice Milliere, 1926; Rene Vincent, 1920s

Rene Vincent, 1920

René Vincent 1922

Georges Léonnec 1929

Tip for Travelers:
You can browse original vintage magazines like *Le Rire* and *La Vie Parisienne* at the flea markets (*marché aux puces*) around Paris, or visit the Musée Carnavalet and Musée des Arts Décoratifs to see some originals up close!

MORE STORIES TO READ

For further reading about the fascinating people, places, and history described in the walks in this book, please see the following Museyon titles about Paris, all by John Baxter.

Walk 1

[1-1] Fishing for Compliments: Francois Vatel's Suicide over the Disgrace of the Missing Fish in *Eating Eternity*

Walk 2

[2-1] Arise, You Wretched of the Earth: The Paris Commune in *Chronicles of Old Paris*

[2-2] A La Dame Aux Camélias: Marie Duplessis in *Chronicles of Old Paris*

Walk 3

[3-1] "Little Girl, Can You Do the Charleston?": Le Jazz Hot in *The Golden Moments of Paris*

[3-2] Unhealthy Relations: George Sand and Alfred de Musset in *Of Love and Paris*

[3-3] Passion's Playthings: George Sand and Frédéric Chopin in *Chronicles of Old Paris*

Walk 4

[4-1] In the White City: The Birth of Art Deco in *The Golden Moment of Paris*
Co Co Chanel: Little Black Dressmaker in *Chronicles of Old Paris*

[4-2] Beauty is in the Streets: The Student Revolution of 1968 in *Chronicles of Old Paris*

[4-3] The Black Pearl: She Proved Black Was Beautiful in *Chronicles of Old Paris*

[4-4] Villa Noailles: Cement, Celluloid and Surrealism in *French Riviera and Its Artists*

[4-5] Puttin' on the Ritz: Diana, Princess of Wales and Dodi Al Fayed in *Of Love and Paris*

Walk 5

[5-1] Unhealthy Relations: George Sand and Alfred de Musset in *Of Love and Paris*
Passion's Playthings: George Sand and Frédéric Chopin in *Chronicles of Old Paris*

[5-2] Drunk on Words: Arthur Rimbaud and Paul Verlaine in *Of Love and Paris*

[5-3] Four's a Crowd: Gala and Salvador Dalì, Paul Éluard, Max Ernst in *Of Love and Paris*

[5-4] Man and Women: Man Ray and Kiki de Montparnasse in *Of Love and Paris*

[5-5] The Importance of Being Ernest: Hemingway in Paris in *Chronicles of Old Paris*
The Heavyweight Champion of Montparnasse: Hemingway's Knockout in *The Golden Moments of Paris*

[5-6] Of Time and Light: The Rational Eye of Paul Cézanne in *The French Riviera and Its Artists*

Walk 6

[6-1] The Opera Garnier: One Man's Glittering Vision in *Chronicles of Old Paris*

Walk 7

[7-1] A Half-Crazed Cad: The Wild Ride of Harry and Caresse Crosby in *The Golden Moments of Paris*
Kicking the Gong Around: Harry and Caresse Crosby in *Of Love and Paris*

Walk 8

[8-1] The Lovers of Montparnasse: Amadeo Modigliani and Jeanne Hébuterne in *Of Love and Paris*

[8-2] To Dance and Die: Ballet on the Riviera in *French Riviera and Its Artists*

[8-3] The Black Pearl: She Proved Black Was Beautiful in *Chronicles of Old Paris*

"Little Girl, Can You Do the Charleston?": Le Jazz Hot in *The Golden Moments of Paris*

[8-4] Love for Sale: Maisons Closes and Pools De Luxe in *The Golden Moments of Paris*

[8-5] The Carousel of Sex: Catherine Millet and Jacques Henric in *Of Love and Paris*

[8-6] Man and Woman: Man Ray and Kiki de Montparnasse in *Of Love and Paris*

[8-7] A Cloud in Trousers: Louis Aragon and Elsa Triolet in *Of Love and Paris*

Walk 9

[9-1] General of the Armies of the Night: Jean Moulin and the World

War II Resistance in *Chronicles of Old Paris*

[9-2] The Sadness of St. Louis: Django Reinhardt and Le Jazz Hot in *Chronicles of Old Paris*

Walk 10

[10-1] Latin Lovers: Héloise and Abélard in *Chronicles of Old Paris*

[10-2] The Razor and the Eye: Luis Buñuel, Salvador Dalì and Surrealism in *The Golden Moments of Paris*
Shooting Into the Crowd: Surrealism in *Chronicles of Old Paris*

[10-3] Beauty is in the Streets: The Student Revolution of 1968 in *Chronicles of Old Paris*

Walk 11

[11-1] Like a Breath on the Back of Your Neck: The Useful Invention of Dr. Guillotin in *Chronicles of Old Paris*

[11-2] The Sadness of St. Louis: Django Reinhardt and le Jazz Hot in *Chronicles of Old Paris*

[11-3] A Half-Crazed Cad. The Wild Ride of Harry and Caresse Crosby in *The Golden Moments of Paris*
Kicking the Gong Around: Harry and Caresse Crosby in *Of Love and Paris*

Walk 12

[12-1] As Though It Knew: The Unknown Woman of the Seine in *The Golden Moments of Paris*

[12-2] Friends of the Book: Sylvia Beach and Adrienne Monnier in *Of Love and Paris*
The First Lady of Bohemia: Sylvia Beach and Shakespeare and Company in *The Golden Moments of Paris*

[12-3] To Dance and Die: Ballet on the Riviera in *French Riviera and Its Artists*

[12-4] The Black Pearl: She Proved Black Was Beautiful in *Chronicles of Old Paris*

[12-5] The Kindest Cut: The Bob Fad and The Garconne Scandal in *The Golden Moments of Paris*

Cafe Terrace, Champs-Elysees, 1935

CREDITS

John Baxter and MUSEYON Books would like to thank the many people and institutions that helped with the creation of this book including:

Alte Pinakothek, Munich
Ateneum Art Museum, Helsinki
Bibliothèque Historique de la Ville de Paris
Bibliothèque Municipale de Nancy
Bibliothèque Nationale de France
Buffalo AKG Art Museum
Centre Pompidou
Clark Art Institute
Foujita Foundation
Graves Art Gallery, Sheffield
Hamburger Kunsthalle
Imperial War Museum
John F. Kennedy Presidential Library and Museum
Library of Congress
Malden Public Library
Manchester Art Gallery
Musée Carnavalet, Histoire de Paris
Musée d'Art et d'Histoire
Musée d'Art et d'Industrie André Diligent
Musée de Grenoble
Musée de la Libération de Paris
Musée de la Monnaie
Musée d'Orsay
Musée du Général Leclerc
Musée du Louvre
Musée Gustave Moreau
Musée Jean Moulin
Musée national d'art moderne, Centre Pompidou
Musée Yves Saint Laurent Paris
Musei di Strada Nuova
Museo de Arte de Sao Paulo
National Archives at College Park
National Gallery of Art, London
National Gallery of Art, Washington D.C.
National Gallery of Australia
National Museum Cardiff
New York Public Library
Norton Simon Art Foundation
Ordrupgaard
Petit Palais, Geneva
Pixabay
Philadelphia Museum of Art
Rhode Island School of Design
Rijksmuseum
Royal Museums of Fine Arts of Belgium
Smithsonian American Art Museum
State Hermitage Museum
State Library Victoria
Terra Foundation for American Art
The Art Institute of Chicago
The Barnes Foundation
The British Library
The Cleveland Museum of Art
The Courtauld, London
The J. Paul Getty Museum
The Metropolitan Museum of Art
The Morgan Library & Museum
The University of Auckland
The Wallace Collection
Unsplash
Wikimedia Commons

19: Le Marche aux Legumes (The Vegetable Market), 1878, Victor Gabriel Gilbert (1847-1935), oil on canvass, 90.2 cm x 130.8 cm; 23: Les Halles, 1898-1924, Eugène Atget, (1857-1927), Bibliothèque nationale de France; 24: Les Halles centrales, Jules Arnout, 1848, Lithograph; Jonathan Ferreira; 25: Guilhem Vellut; 26: Morning soup at Les Halles, 1897, Jean-Jacques Rousseau, Le Petit Journal, Musée Carnavalet, Histoire de Paris; 27: Meizhi Lang; 29: Palais-Royal, 1815, Georg-Emmanuel Opiz (1775-1841), Bibliothèque nationale de France; 30: Speech made at the Palais Royal by Camille Desmoulins: July 12,

1789, Bibliothèque nationale de France; 31: French writer Colette (1873-1954) at her balcony, 1932, nce Mondial Photo-Presse, Bibliothèque nationale de France; 32: Patrick-Lang Wallner, 34: View of Paris and the Seine, taken from the middle of the Pont-Neuf. On the right, the Louvre Palace, 1665-1666, Hendrick Mommers, oil on canvas, 98 cm x 145 cm, Louvre Museum; 40: The chestnut merchant, 1933, Agence Meurisse (Paris); 42: Paris. Boulevard Richard Lenoir, No. 47. Restaurant Véron. Customers are starting to flock. Watch out for the pommes frites!, 1915, Charles Lansials (1855-1939), Bibliothèque historique de la Ville de Paris; 43: Sylvia Beach Standing in Front of Shakespeare and Company With Margaret Newitt, 1936, Gisèle Freund, Princeton University Library; 44: Café Voltaire, place de l'Odéon, 6ème arrondissement, Paris, Eugène Atget, (1857-1927), Musée Carnavalet, Histoire de Paris; 45: Portrait of Camille Desmoulins with family, 1792, David Jacques Louis (1748-1825), oil on canvas,100 cm x 123 cm, Versailles, castles of Versailles and Trianon; 47: Paolo Botio, Maria Orlova, Any Lane, 48: Paris Blues (1961), United Artists; 50: Albert Brasseur in "Le petit café" by Tristan Bernard / drawing by Yves Marevéry, 1912;

51: Bal du Moulin de la Galette, 1876, Pierre-Auguste Renoir (1841-1919), 131.5 cm x 176.5cm, Musée d'Orsay; 55: Giuseppe Mondi; 56: The Hill of Montmartre with Stone Quarry, June-July 1886 Vincent van Gogh (1853-1890), oil on canvas, 56.3 cm x 62.6 cm, Van Gogh Museum, Amsterdam (Vincent van Gogh Foundation); 58: Portrait de Louise Michel (1830-1905), pendant la Commune de Paris 1871, 1871, Appert, Ernest Charles (1831-1890), Musée Carnavalet, Histoire de Paris; 61: Rue du Chevalier de la Barre, 1923, Eugène Atget (1857-1927), Gelatin silver chloride print Image: 21.5 cm × 16.9 cm (8 7/16 × 6 5/8 in.), The J. Paul Getty Museum, Los Angeles; 63: The Swing, 1876, Pierre-Auguste Renoir, oil on canvas, 92 cm × 73 cm, Musée d'Orsay; La Maison Rose, Bastien-nvs; 64: La Rue des Saules à Montmartre, 1867, Paul Cézanne, oil on canvas, 31.5 cm × 39.5 cm, private collection; 65: Le Consulat, Alexandra Smielova; 66: Ambassadeurs Aristide Bruant, 1892, Henri de Toulouse-Lautrec (1864-1901), lithograph, 150 cm x 100 cm; 66: Portrait of Jehan Rictus by Félix Vallotton; Tournée du Chat Noir de Rodolphe Salis (Tour of Rodolphe Salis' Chat Noir), 1896, Théophile Steinlen (1859-1923), lithograph, 136cm x 96 cm; 67: Beatrice (Portrait de Béatrice Hastings), 1916, Amedeo Modigliani, oil on canvas with newsprint, The Barnes Foundation; 69: Nhi Dam, 71: Moulin de la Galette. Restaurant. Salons. Cabinets. Jardin des Jeux (Moulin de la Galette. Restaurant. Lounges. Cabinets. Games garden), 1880, J. Jonchère, Bibliothèque nationale de France; Moulin de la Galette, 1897, Jérôme Auguste Roedel; Moulin de la Galette le seul bal où l'on vient pour danser (Moulin de la Galette the only ball where you come to dance), 1898, René Péan (1875-1940), Bibliothèque nationale de France; Christopher Columbus discovers the Moulin de la Galette, June 23, 1926, at 10 a.m. big night party, 1926, Maurice Neumont (1868-1930), Bibliothèque nationale de France; 73: Les Demoiselles d'Avignon, 1907, Pablo Picasso, oil on canvas, 244 cm x 234 cm, Museum of Modern Art, New York; 74: Terrace of a Cafe on Montmartre (La Guinguette), 1886, Vincent van Gogh (1853–1890), oil on canvas, 49cm x 64 cm, Musée d'Orsay; In the Café: Agostina Segatori in Le Tambourin, 1887, Vincent van Gogh (1853 - 1890), oil on canvas, 55.5 cm x 47 cm, Van Gogh Museum, Amsterdam; View from Theo's Apartment, March-April 1887, Vincent van Gogh (1853 - 1890), oil on canvas, 45.9 cm; x 38.1 cm, Van Gogh Museum, Amsterdam; Le Moulin de la Galette, 1886, Vincent van Gogh (1853–1890), oil on canvas, 38 cm x 46.5 cm, Neue Nationalgalerie, Berlin; 75: Portrait de Juliette Récamier, née Bernard (1777-1849), 1800, Jacques-Louis David, Musée du Louvre; 79: La Place Clichy, 1912, Pierre Bonnard (1867-1947), oil on canvas, 145.7 x 209.5 cm, Musée national d'art moderne, Centre Pompidou; Ladies of Café Wepler, 1926, Albert André, oil on canvas, 63 cm x 60 cm, Saint-Denis, Musée d'Art et d'Histoire; Café Wepler, c. 1908–10, reworked in 1912. Edouard Vuillard (French, 1868–1940), oil on fabric, height: 91.8 x 132.7 cm, The Cleveland Museum of Art; 80: Un moment volé (A stolen moment), Albert Guillaume (1873-1942), oil on panel, 35 x 26.7 cm;

81: Moulin Rouge, La Goulue, Henri de Toulouse-Lautrec (1864–1901), 1891, Lithograph, height: 190 cm (74.8 in) ; width: 116.5 cm (45.9 in), The Metropolitan Museum of Art; 85: La Rue Pigalle Apres Minuit, Paris, book illustration, 1952; 86: Dans un café, 1875-1876, Edgar Degas (1834-1917), oil on canvas, 92.0 x 68.5 cm, Musée d'Orsay; In a Private Dining Room (At the Rat Mort), Henri de Toulouse-Lautrec (1864-1901), c.1899, oil on canvas, 55.1 x 46 cm, The Courtauld, London; 87: In the Café, 1882-1884, Fernando Lungren, oil on canvas, 79.7 × 104.8 cm, The Art Institute of Chicago; Dinner with Friends, 1903, Josef Engelhart (1864-1941); Coffee Conversation, 1877-78, Giovanni Boldini, oil on canvas; Three Women in a Café, 1916, Jules Pascin (1885–1930), Pen and black ink on red-brown paper, 7.5 x 7.4 cm, The Metropolitan Museum of Art; Cafe-Concert, 1878, Edouard Manet, oil on canvas, 47 x 39 cm, Walters Art Museum, Baltimore, MD; 88: French Cancan (1955); Divan Japonais, 1892-93, Henri de Toulouse-Lautrec, Lithograph printed in four colors, wove paper, 80.8 x 60.8 cm, The Metropolitan Museum of Art; Bal Tabarin, 1904, Jules-Alexandre Grün (1868–1938); Trianon Concert, 1897, Georges Meunier (1869-1942); 90: Cabaret du Néant, 1928, Agence Rol, Bibliothèque nationale de France; La Lune Rousse, cabaret artistique, 36 Boulevard de Clichy, 1904, Charles Léandre, Bibliothèque nationale de France; 91: La Lune Rousse, 36 boulevard de Clichy, Carte photo, CPArama; 92: Cabaret de L'Enfer : Bd de Clichy, 1910-1912, Eugène Atget (1857-1927), Bibliothèque nationale de France; 95: Moulin Rouge Posters by Jules Chéret, Henri de Toulouse-Lautrec and Charles Gesmar; 97: Alex Child; 98: Le Café de Paris (Can Can Dancers), 1880-1899, Jean Béraud; 33.8 x 55 cm, Private collection; 100: At the Moulin Rouge, 1892-1895, Henri de Toulouse-Lautrec (1864-1901), oil on canvas, 123 x141 cm, The Art Institute of Chicago; 104: Portrait of George Sand, 1838, Eugène Delacroix (1798-1863), oil on canvas, 78 x 56.5 cm, Ordrupgaard; Frédéric Chopin, 1838, Eugène Delacroix (1798-1863), oil on canvas, 46 x 38 cm, Musée du Louvre; 106: Dead Poet Carried by a Centaur, c. 1890, Gustave Moreau (1826-1898), water color, 33.5 cm x 24.5 cm, Musée Gustave Moreau; 108: Façade des cabarets Le Ciel et L'Enfer, 1909, Bibliothèque nationale de France; 109: Cabaret du Néant vault of the sad ghosts, c.1900; Cabaret de l'Enfer customers, 1904, Harry C. Ellis;

111: Marie-Antoinette, 1783, Vigeed Le Brun Louise-Elisabeth, 116.8 x 88.9 cm, Versailles, castles of Versailles and Trianon; La Parisienne ("The Blue Lady"), 1874, Pierre-Auguste Renoir, oil on canvas, 160 x 105.5 cm (41.5 in), National Museum Cardiff; Portrait de l'artiste, 1911, Clémentine-Hélène Dufau oil on canvas, height: 181 x 70 cm, Musée d'Orsay; La Musicienne, 1929, Tamara de Lempicka, oil on canvas, 115.8 x 73 cm, private collection; 114: Costume Study for Vaslav Nijinsky in the Role of Iksender in the Ballet La Péri (The Flower of Immortality), 1922, Léon Bakst (1866–1924), watercolor and gold and silver paints over graphite, height: 67.6 x 47.9 cm, The Metropolitan Museum of Art; 121: Ernest Hemingway in an American Red Cross ambulance during World War I in Italy, 1918, Ernest Hemingway Collection. John F. Kennedy Presidential Library and Museum, Boston; 124: Duchess of Galliera with her son Filippo, Maria Brignole-Sale, 1856, Léon Cogniet (1794–1880), Musei di Strada Nuova; Lace exhibition at the Musée Galliéra, Paris, 1904. From an article published in L'Illustration on 14 May 1904, José Roy, New York Public Library; 128: Musée Yves Saint Laurent Paris; 133: The Swing, c.1767-1768, Jean-Honoré Fragonard (1732-1806), oil on canvas, 81 x 64.2 cm, The Wallace Collection; Marie-Antoinette, Queen of France (1755-1793), 1778, Vigeed Le Brun Louise-Elisabeth, 223 x158 cm, Versailles, castles of Versailles and Trianon; Joséphine-Éléonore-Marie-Pauline de Galard de Brassac de Béarn (1825–1860), Princesse de Broglie, 1851-1853, Jean Auguste Dominique Ingres (1780–1867), oil on canvas, 121.3 x 90.8 cm, The Metropolitan Museum of New York; Portrait of the Marquise de Miramon, née, Thérèse Feuillant, 1866, James Tissot, oil on canvas, 128.3 x 77.2 cm, The J. Paul Getty Museum; The Holiday (Still on Top), 1874-1875, James Tissot (1836-1902), oil on canvas, 87.6 x 53.3 cm, Auckland Art Gallery; Madame X (Madame Pierre Gautreau), 1883-1884, John Singer Sargent (1856-1925), oil on canvas, 208.6 x 109.9 cm, The Metropolitan Museum of Art; Blanche Vesni□, née Ulman, 1913, Jean Béraud (1849–1935), oil on canvas, 81.2 x 40.8 cm, private collection; La cigarette, 1921, Henri Lebasque (1865-1937), 54 x 65 cm, Musée d'Art et d'Industrie André Diligent; Portrait de Mademoiselle Chanel, 1923, Marie Laurencin, oil on canvas,

92 x 73 cm, Foujita Foundation; 134: Symphony in Black, 1923, Etré, Gouache on Paper, private collection; A magazine cover from the June 28, 1896 issue of La Nouvelle Mode, a vintage French fashion publication; La Vie Parisienne, 1926; Léon Benigni, Femina, Léon Benigni produced a large number of covers and full-page plates for Femina magazine in the second half of the 1920's and the early 1930's. Another cover design for Femina, for the October 1930 issue of the magazine, is included in a recent survey of fashion illustration; 135: Eduardo Benito, Vogue Magazine Cover Featuring A Woman In A Gown, September 1st, 1926; Brigitte Bardot's first cover for ELLE, photo by Jean Chevalier, January 7, 1952; Jeanne Paquin Gown, 1914, George Barbier, Gazette du Bon Ton; Cigarette Couple, December 1919, Georges Lepape; 136: llustration by Paul Poiret from 1908. As appeared in Les Robes de Paul Poiret by Paul Iribe;

137: Luxembourg Gardens. Monument to Chopin, 1909, Henri Rousseau (1844–1910), oil on canvas, height: 38 cm; width: 47 cm, State Hermitage Museum; 140: View of the Luxembourg Palace from the Garden Side, print, 1750, Bibliothèque nationale de France; 141: La Bohême, 1912, Adrien Barrère (1874-1931), engraving, Bibliothèque nationale de France; 145: November 14, 1926, Luxembourg Garden, crowd around the large pond, Agence Rol, 1926, Bibliothèque nationale de France; 147: The Apotheosis of Henry IV and the Proclamation of the Regency of Marie de Médicis on May 14, 1610 (detail), part of Marie de Médici cycle, 1623-25, Peter Paul Rubens (1577-1640), oil on canvas, 394 x 727 cm, Musée du Louvre; 148: Children's games in the Luxembourg Garden: donkey rides, Agence Mondial, 1932, Bibliothèque nationale de France; Children in the Luxembourg Garden, playing with sailboats on the large pond in the garden, Agence Rol, 1913, Bibliothèque nationale de France; February 16, 1933, laying of the first stone of the puppet theater, outdoor puppet show, Luxembourg Garden, Agence Rol, Bibliothèque nationale de France; 150: Peter Paul Rubens (1577–1640), The Drunken Silenus, 1616-1617, oil on panel, 212 x 214.5 cm, Alte Pinakothek, Munich; 152: In the Luxembourg (Garden), 1889, Charles Courtney Curran (1861–1942), oil on canvas, 23.3 x 31.1 cm, Terra Foundation for American Art; 159: The Execution of Marshal Ney (1868), Jean-Léon Gérôme (1824–1904), oil on canvas, 65.2 x104.2 cm, Graves Art Gallery, Sheffield; 160: In the Luxembourg Gardens, 1879, John Singer Sargent (1856–1925), oil on canvas, 65.7 x 92.4 cm, Philadelphia Museum of Art; At the Luxembourg Gardens, 1883, Pierre-Auguste Renoir (1841-1919), oil on canvas, 64 x 53 cm, private collection; The Luxembourg Gardens, 1901, Henri Matisse (1869-1954), oil on canvas, 59.5 x 81.5 cm, State Hermitage Museum; Terrace in the Luxembourg Gardens, 1886, Vincent van Gogh (1853–1890), oil on panel, 27 x 46 cm, Clark Art Institute; 161: Luxembourg Gardens, 1906, William James Glackens (1870–1938), oil on canvas, 60.6 x 81.6 cm, National Gallery of Art; A Nanny in the Luxembourg Gardens, c.1872, Edgar Degas (1834–1917), oil on canvas, 65 x 92 cm, National Gallery of Australia; The Luxembourg Gardens, Paris, 1887, Albert Edelfelt (1854–1905), oil on canvas, 141.5 x 186 cm, Ateneum Art Museum, Helsinki; Jardin du Luxembourg, c.1948, Lois Mailou Jones (1905-1998), oil on canvas, 60.5 x 73 cm, Smithsonian American Art Museum; 163: Portrait of Ernest Hemingway and Pauline Pfeiffer, Paris, c.1927, Ernest Hemingway Collection. John F. Kennedy Presidential Library and Museum, Boston; Gertrude Stein with Jack "Bumby" Hemingway in the Luxembourg Gardens, 1924, Ernest Hemingway Collection. John F. Kennedy Presidential Library and Museum, Boston; 164: Jardin du Luxembourg, 1928, Agence; Meurisse, Bibliothèque nationale de France; 167: Jardin du Luxembourg. no. 27, 1878, Charles Marville, photo, 35.5 x 26.5 cm, State Library Victoria;

169: Boulevard des Capucines, Jean Béraud (1849-1935), oil on canvas, 50.8 x 73 cm, private collection; 173: The Opera Garnier Staircase, 1877, Louis Béroud (1852-1930), oil on canvas, height: 84 x 73.5 cm, Musée Carnavalet; 174: Nana, 1877, Édouard Manet, oil on canvas, 154 × 115 cm, Hamburger Kunsthalle; 175: The Store Front Of Couturier Doucet (detail), Jean Beraud; An Elegant Evening (detail), c1890, Victor Gabriel Gilbert (1847-1933), oil on canvas, private collection; Café de Paris, Albert Guillaume (1873-1942), oil on canvas, 68.5 x 126 cm, private collection; 176: The Lady of the Camellias, 1896, Alphonse Mucha (1860-1939), lithograph, 207.3 × 72.2 cm, Library of Congress; Dreamer, 1897, Alphonse Mucha, lithograph, 72.7 × 55.2 cm, poster for the publishing house Champenois, private collection; Chocolat Idéal, 1897, Alphonse Mucha, lithograph, 117 x 78 cm; 178: The poster advertising the Lumière brothers cinematographe, showing a famous comedy (L'Arroseur Arrosé, 1895), 1896, Marcellin Auzolle; 182: Olympia, 1893, Jules Chéret, poster; 185: Workers leaving the Maison Paquin, in the rue de la Paix, c.1900, Jean Beraud, oil on canvas, 55 x 42 cm, Musée Carnavalet; 186: Studio Paquin, Paris, c.1905, Isaac Israels (1865-1934), oil on canvas, 49 x 60 cm, private collection; Five Hours at Paquin, 1906, Henri Gervex (1852–1929), oil on canvas, 111.7 x 172.7 cm, private collection; 189: The Belle Époque, The Bar at Maxim's, c.1890, Pierre-Victor Galland (1822-1892); 190: The Merry Widow (1934); 191: Bonjour Tristesse (1958); 194: The Inauguration of the Statue of Louis XV (detail), 1766, Augustin de Saint-Aubin (French, Paris 1736-1807 Paris), Etching and engraving, The Metropolitan Museum of Art; 195: Execution of Louis XVI on 21 January 1793, in what is now the Place de la Concorde, facing the empty pedestal where the statue of his grandfather, Louis XV, had stood, 1794, Bibliothèque nationale de France; 196: Statue of a personification of the city of Nantes at Place de la Concorde in Paris, c.1850-1880, Rijksmuseum; 197: Place de la concorde, c.1872, Joaquín Pallarés Allustante (1853-1935), oil on canvas, 27.6 x 40 cm, private collection; 201: The Garden of the Tuileries on a Winter Afternoon, 1899, Camille Pisarro (1830-1903), oil on canvas, 73.7 x 92.1 cm, The Metropolitan Museum of Art; La Place des Pyramides, 1875, Giuseppe De Nittis (1846-1884), oil on canvas, 92.3 x 75.0 cm, Musée d'Orsay; 204: Emilie-Louise Delabigne (1848–1910), Called Valtesse de la Bigne, 1879, Edouard Manet (1832–1883), pastel on canvas, 55.2 x 35.6 cm, The Metropolitan Museum of Art; 205: Édouard Lièvre (1829–1886): State Bed of Valtesse de la Bigne, Paris, circa 1875, constructed of wood, gilded bronze, green silk velvet, bequeathed by Émilie Louise de la Bigne, known as Valtesse de la Bigne, 1911, Musée des Arts Décoratifs, Paris; Mrs Valtesse de la Bigne, 1879, Henri Gervex, oil on canvas, 205.0 x 120.2 cm, Musée d'Orsay; 206: L'Arrivée des midinettes, 1901, Jean Béraud (1849-1935), oil on panel, 52.5 x 66 cm, private collection; 207: One of the five watercolors illustrating the first American edition of the Phantom of the Opera by Gaston Leroux, 1911, André Castaigne (1861-1921);

209: Paris Le Quai Malaquais, c.1874, Auguste Renoir (1841–1919), oil on canvas, 38 x 46 cm, private collection; 213: Bastien-NVS; 214: Gabrielle d'Estrées and one of her sisters, 1575-1600, unknown artist, oil on wood (oak), 96 x 125 cm, Musée du Louvre; 215: View of the Seine below Pont-Neuf, on the left the Hôtel des Monnaies, on the right the Louvre, 1782, Pierre-Antoine Demachy, oil on canvas, Musée de la Monnaie; 217: View of the Pont Neuf and Tour de Nesle, Jacques Callot(1592–1635), etching, Buffalo AKG Art Museum; 219: Windy Day on the Pont des Arts, c.1880-1881, Jean Béraud (1849–1936), oil on canvas, 39.7 x 56.5 cm, The Metropolitan Museum of Art; 220: Hernán Piñera, 222: Le Quai Malaquais, c.1890, Hippolyte Blancard, Musée Carnavalet, Histoire de Paris; 223: Les Quat'z'arts, Adolphe Willette(1857-1926); 227: Le 28 juillet 1830. La Liberté guidant le peuple, 1830, Eugène Delacroix (1798 -1863), oil on canvas, 260 x 297 cm, Musée du Louvre; 228: Florencia Potter; 233: Piscine Deligny, bain de soleil, 1934, Agence de presse Meurisse, Bibliothèque nationale de France;

235: Le Bal Bullier, 1931, Jules Flandrin (1871-1947), oil on canvas, 222 x 206.2 cm, Musée de Grenoble; 242: Illustrations of Paris, 1927, the café La Rotonde, a popular meeting place for artists in the Montparnasse district of Paris in the early 20th century. Engraving by Foujita; 245: Jeanne Hébuterne, 1919, Amedeo Modigliani (1884-1920), oil on canvas, 91.4 x 73 cm, The Metropolitan Museum of Art; Self Portrait, 1919, Amedeo Modigliani (1884-1920), oil on canvas, 100 x 64.5 cm, Museo de Arte de Sao Paulo; 249: The American Dingobar in Paris, 1925, George Grosz (1893-1959), watercolor and pen and brown ink on paper, 63.5 x 46.4 cm, Private Collection; 252: Maison Close, c.1916, Atget; 253: Le Sphinx, James Boswell (1906-71), print, 31.5 x 50.5 cm, The University of Auckland; 259: Kiki de Montparnasse, 1924, Moise Kisling (1891-1953), oil on canvas, 55 x

38.1 cm, private collection; Portrait de Kiki de Montparnasse, 1925, Tsuguharu Foujita, oil and pen and ink on canvas, 41.5 x 33.3 cm; Kiki de Montparnasse, 1920, Gustaw Gwozdecki; Kiki de Montparnasse, 1921, Maurice Mendjizky; Portrait de Kiki, 1923, MAN RAY (1890-1976), oil on canvas, 61.3 x 45.6 cm, private collection; Kiki de Montparnasse, c1921, Jacqueline Marval; Kiki de Montparnasse, c1922-1924, Kees van Dongen; Kiki de Montparnasse in a Red Jumper and a Blue Scarf, Moise Kisling, 1925, Petit Palais, Geneva; Le Violon d'Ingres, 1924, Man Ray; 261: A famous cabaret in Paris, early 20th century. Engraving by J. Oberlé. At the "Jockey"; 263: Le Bal Bullier, 1860-69, A. Provost, New York Public Library;

265: The Astronomer (detail), 1668, Johannes Vermeer (1632-1675), oil on canvas, 51 x 45 cm, Musée du Louvre; 271: Bon Marché ad, Winter 1933-34, print, 27.1 x 20.9 cm, Bibliothèque municipale de Nancy; 272: Oh-la-la, between 1940-1944, Gefreiter G. Schmitz, printed on paper, 20.9 x 15 cm, Musée de la Libération de Paris - Musée du Général Leclerc - Musée Jean Moulin; 274: Memorial to Mme Boucicaut and Baroness Clara de Hirsh, honoring their charitable work, in the Square Boucicaut, Paris, France. Sculptor Paul Moreau-Vauthier (1871-1936); dedicated in 1914; 275: Rue du Four, off rue Bonaparte, c.1867, Charles Marville (1813-1879), GDC Collection; 282: Members of the French resistance, Paris, 1944; 283: Crowds of Parisians celebrating the entry of Allied troops into Paris scatter for cover as a sniper fires from a building on the Place de la Concorde. Although the Germans surrendered the city, small bands of snipers still remained. August 26, 1944, National Archives at College Park; 284: General Charles de Gaulle and his entourage set off from the Arc de Triumphe down the Champs Elysees to Notre Dame for Thanksgiving service following the city's liberation in August 1944, Imperial War Museum; 285: A tank of the French 2nd Armored Division in front of the Cathedral of Notre-Dame, 26 August 1944; 289: Crowds celebrating the liberation of the city. Paris., France. August 25th, 1944, Robert Capa; 290: A memorial to the Vel' d'Hiv Roundup, on Quai de Grenelle in Paris;

291: The Rooftops of Notre Dame, 1910, Georges Redon (1869 -1943), oil on canvas, 55.9 x 73.7 cm, 1910 painting by French artist Georges Redon showing the gallery of chimeras at Notre-Dame de Paris; 295: Abelard and his Pupil Heloise, 1882, Edmund Blair Leighton (1852–1922); 297: The Dada group in the garden of the Saint-Julien-Le-Pauvre church in Paris, April 14, 1921, D. R. Centre Pompidou; 304: Calvin's Tower: view of the Place du Panthéon, August 1909, Georges-Henri Manesse (1854–1942), Black stone, Watercolour, Paper, Carnavalet Museum, History of Paris; 306: Kreshen; 309: Interior of St. Etienne du Mont, 1864, Émile-Antoine-François Herson, watercolor and gum heightening, 18.1 x 25.5 cm, Walters Art Museum; 319: Midnight in Paris (2011); Facade of the building where Paul Verlaine lived, 39 rue Descartes, Paris, 1934, Jean Roubier, Centre Pompidou; 312: Ernest Hemingway and Elizabeth Hadley Richardson with friends at a cafe, Pamplona, Spain, summer 1925, Ernest Hemingway Collection. John F. Kennedy Presidential Library and Museum, Boston; 314: The Bièvre near Saint-Médard, between rue Mouffetard and rue Pascal, Auguste Péquégnot (1819-1878), Musée Carnavalet, Histoire de Paris; 315: Place Saint-Médard, 1898-1900, Eugène Atget (1857-1927), albumen silver print, J. Paul Getty Museum; 316: The Church of St.-Médard on the Rue Mouffetard, 1871, Johan Barthold Jongkind (1819-1891), oil on canvas, 43.2 x 56 cm, Norton Simon Art Foundation;

317: The Death of Marat (detail), 1793, Jacques-Louis David (1748-1825), oil on canvas, 165 x 128 cm, Royal Museums of Fine Arts of Belgium; 322: Marat having a lively conversation with Danton and Robespierre, 1882, Alfred Loudet (1836-1898), oil on canvas, 302 x 400 cm, Musée de la Révolution française, imaginary meeting between Robespierre, Danton and Marat (illustrating Victor Hugo's novel Ninety-Three); 324: Carrefour de l'Odéon, 1867-1868, Charles Marville, Photographie, Bibliothèque Historique de la Ville de Paris; 326: Rue de l'Odéon, 1880-1945, postcards, Bibliothèque Historique de la Ville de Paris; 327: Un Café du Boulevard, A Parisian Café, 1875, Ilya Repin (1844-1930), oil on canvas, 120.6 x 191.8 cm; 328: Louis XIV and Molière, 1862, Jean-Léon Gérôme (1824 –1904), 42 x 75 cm, Louis XIV invites Molière to share his supper—an unfounded Romantic anecdote, Malden Public Library; 329: Portrait of Molière (1622-1673), c.1730, Charles-Antoine Coypel (1694 –1752), oil on canvas, Bibliotheque; 330: Café Procope, rue de l'ancienne Comédie, 6ème arrondissement, Paris, 1917, Charles Joseph Antoine Lansiaux, Musée Carnavalet, Histoire de Paris; 334: Vue de la Cour du Rohan, 1897, Herminie Waternau (1862 -1913), Musée Carnavalet, Histoire de Paris; 335: Cour du Commerce, de la rue Saint André des Arts, c.1866, Charles Marville (1813-1879), Bibliothèque Historique de la Ville de Paris; 338: Symphony in White, No. 1: The White Girl,1862, James Abbott McNeill Whistler(1834 –1903), oil on canvas, 213 x 107.9 cm, National Gallery of Art, Washington D.C.: 343: Demolition of the Abbey of Saint-Germain des Prés, 1798, Pierre-Antoine Demachy, drawing, Carnavalet Museum, History of Paris; 344: St. Abbey German des Prés. / General view of the abbey, Emile Ollivier (graveur: 1800 – 1864) and Albert Lenoir (dessinateur: 1801-1891), print, 44.1 x 59.3 cm, Carnavalet Museum, History of Paris; 345: The History of the French Revolution: Murder of the Princess de Lambelle, 1881, Louis Adolphe, Translated by F. Shoberl, The British Library; Portrait of te French philosopher and mathematician René Descartes (1596-1650), 1649, After Frans Hals (1582/1583–1666), oil on canvas, 77.5 x 68.5 cm, Musée du Louvre;

347: Autoportrait (Self-Portrait in a Green Bugatti), 1929, Tamala de Lempicka, oil on panel, 35 cm x 27 cm, private collection; 353: In the tiny Tabou Tomb, in 1947, Juliette Gréco (in the second plane, on the left) dances the be-bop to the sound of the orchestra of Boris Vian (to the "chrompinette"). GON-AgUE DREU/GRAMMA RAPIIO; 355: "Gertrude Stein and Alice B. Toklas in wallpapered room, 5 Rue Christine". 1938. Cecil Beaton. Paris, France. (Gertrude Stein & Alice B. Toklas). 356: Marat's House, Rue de l'Ecole de Médecine in 1866, Albert Maignan (1845-1908), draughtsman, Marat's House, Rue de l'Ecole de Médecine in 1866, Paris, Musée Carnavalet-Histoire de Paris; Charlotte Corday, painted at her request by Jean-Jacques Hauer, a few hours before her execution, 17 July 1793, Jean-Jacques Hauer (1751-1829); 357: James Joyce, Silvia Beach and Adrienne Monnier at Shakespeare and Company, 1938, photo by Gisèle Freund Le Centre Pompidou; Subscribers' bulletin for Ulysses by James Joyce, Paris: Shakespeare and Company, 1921, The Morgan Library & Museum; 358: Day of the Dupes (1630), King Louis XIII, his mother Marie de Médicis and Cardinal de Richelieu during the Journée des Dupes. Maurice Leloir (1853 –1940) Composition by Maurice Leloir for Théodore Cahu's illustrated book, Richelieu, originally published in Paris, Librairie ancienne Furne, Combet & Cie, 1901; 360: Vision of Saint Geneviève, 1892, Alphonse Osbert (1857 – 1939), oil on canvas, 235 x 138 cm, Musée d'Orsay; 361: French painter and models in 1920s Paris in Montparnasse café 'La Rotonde'. Walls covered with artists' paintings. Bohemian literary and social life in Paris Sisley Huddleston 1928; 366: La Vie Parisienne: elegant manners, things of the day, fantasies, travel, theater, music, fashion by Marcelin, Émile (1825-1887), publisher, Bibliothèque nationale de France; 368: Noire et Blanche, 1926, Man Ray (1890-1976), Gelatin silver print. 20.6 x 27.5 cm; 372: Noire et Blanche, 1926, Man Ray (1890-1976), Gelatin silver print. 20.6 x 27.5 cm; 375: Cover of La Vie Parisienne designed by the illustrator Chéri Hérouard (1881-1961), June 1917; the magazine plate by George Barber, 1918; 376: The magazine plate by Zyg Brunner, 1927; The magazine cover by George Barbier, 1927; 377: Clockwise from top: the magazine plate by Chéri Hérouard, 1923; the magazine cover by Maurice Milliere, 1926; the magazine plate by Rene Vincent, 1920s; the magazine cover by Rene Vincent, 1922; the magazine cover by Rene Vincent, 1920; 378: the magazine cover by Georges Léonnec, 1929.

INDEX

ABOUT MUSEYON

Named after the Mouseion, the ancient library of Alexandria, Museyon is a New York City-based independent publisher that explores cultural obsessions such as art, history and travel. Expertly curated and carefully researched, Museyon books offer rich entertainment, with fascinating anecdotes, beautiful images and quality information.

Next page: Paris by Night, a dance club in Montmartre from *'L'Amour et l'Esprit Gaulois'* by Edmond Haraucourt, c.1925, Manuel Orazi